This Splendid Game

This Splendid Game

Maine Campaigns and Elections, 1940–2002

Christian P. Potholm

LEXINGTON BOOKS
Lanham • Boulder • New York • Oxford

LEXINGTON BOOKS

Published in the United States of America
by Lexington Books
A Member of the Rowman & Littlefield Publishing Group
4501 Forbes Boulevard, Suite 200, Lanham, Maryland 20706
www.rowmanlittlefield.com

PO Box 317
Oxford
OX2 9RU, UK

Cover photo courtesy of Christian P. Potholm. Photo of political campaign
buttons taken from the private collection of George Smith in Mt. Vernon, Maine.

British Library Cataloguing in Publication Information Available

Library of Congress Cataloging-in-Publication Data

Potholm, Christian P., 1940–
   This splendid game : Maine campaigns and elections, 1940–2002 /
Christian P. Potholm.
      p. cm.
Includes bibliographical references and index.
   ISBN 0-7391-0603-1 (hardcover : alk. paper) — ISBN 0-7391-0604-X (pbk. :
alk. paper)
   1. Elections—Maine—History. 2. Political
campaigns—Maine—History. I. Title: Maine campaigns and elections,
1940–2002. II. Title.
   JK2890.P68 2003
   324.9741'043—dc21

                                                          2002155189

Printed in the United States of America

To all those who have played this splendid game, whether knowing victory or defeat.

Contents

Foreword

I have been so blessed in many ways. Politics has been such a treat for me over the years. Beginning with Gene McCarthy's run for president in 1968 when I was teaching at Dartmouth College, I have enjoyed participating in the great game of politics as well as teaching about it. It is truly "A Splendid Game."

It has been my good fortune to participate in Maine politics for the last thirty years. Given a chance by such terrific people as Bill Cohen, Skip Thurlow, Dave Emery, Dana Connors, Mark Mutty, Rhette Stearns, Rob Gardiner, Steve Clarkin, Gus Garcelon, Kent Womack, Jay Espy, and Angus King as well as many others, I have had the opportunity of a lifetime to see politics up close and personal and even to have a chance to influence the outcome of some key races.

During the last thirty years, I have been on the inside of most major campaigns in Maine—on one side or the other. It's been an invaluable opportunity to see how campaigns really work and how the dynamics of campaign specifics affect the outcome of different races. To see campaigns from beginning to end is to see the race unfold not as it must but as it could.

I have been so lucky and blessed to be able to have played so long on the political playing fields of the Pine Tree State. I feel I have had an unprecedented opportunity to see politics "up close and personal" and to gain knowledge that would be impossible to duplicate if one were not on the inside of a variety of campaigns over a long period of time.

At the same time, I am cognizant of the dangers of writing about elections in which I've been a participant. There is, of course, a natural tendency to overestimate one's role or to disregard some important aspects of the opposing campaigns by not examining them as closely as your own efforts.

In order to get a lot of this predilection out of the way, I tried to cover most of the insider's aspects—the fun and the foolishness, the "inside baseball" aspects—in my earlier, *An Insider's Guide to Maine Politics, 1946–1996* (Lanham, Md.: Madison Books, 1998).

Following its publication, I was extremely pleased and gratified at the number of Maine political players of all persuasions who told me the book was "fair" and that I had resisted making hay and political capital at the expense of others. I've tried to bend over backwards to make sure that characteristic carries over to *This Splendid Game.*

When it comes to writing about politics, especially campaigns of which one has been a part, it is important to try to put one's experience into perspective. As Jason, the son of Alexicles, puts it in *The Tides of War*, "Memory is a queer goddess, whose gifts metamorphose with the passage of years. One cannot call to mind that which occurred an hour past yet summons events 70 years gone, as if they were unfolding here and now."

This is as true for me as for many of those whom I contacted about their role in Maine's political history. Yet I have been greatly aided by the contributions of the many people I contacted about the book. I needed to ground my experience in both the reality as presented in the press and the memories of others who were in the trenches both with me and against me.

Toward that end, I enlisted some of the most knowledgeable people on the subject of Maine political history and especially those who were important participants in their own right, to read the chapters about which they knew so much as well as to comment on the hypotheses found in this work:

Maria Fuentes, whose knowledge of politics and people in Maine is unsurpassed, copyedited the entire manuscript. With a dozen previous books, I've never had a better copyeditor and she improved tremendously the entire manuscript. I don't know what I would do without her.

Paul Mills, Maine's unofficial but incredibly knowledgeable political historian, read most of the manuscript at various stages and added greatly to its depth and feel with his perspicacious insights. Even after having his help on two previous books, Paul Mills continues to astound me with his prodigious memory of all things political. His monthly column in the *Sun Journal* is always interesting and very informative.

Peter Burr was, as always, a delight to work with and I am particularly grateful to him for his polling statistics and for having found the Teddy Roosevelt quote (at the end of chapter 1), which so poignantly captures my sense of the political realm in Maine. Peter's grasp of Maine politics is extraordinary.

Congressman Dave Emery, who continues to make a major contribution to his native state and whose assistance to me has been monumental, also allowed me to tap his wealth of knowledge about the process of Maine politics. I appreciate his many contributions to my activities and

my writings. Bowdoin students always find him among the most interesting and perspicacious of the guest lecturers and research resources I
bring to the class.

I would also like to thank John Cole for his insightful reading of the entire manuscript. There is no one writing about Maine who better captures
its glories and its ambiguities and I am very grateful for his input into this
project.

On the research side, I would like to give special thanks to Christopher
M. Beam and Andrea L'Hommedieu of the Edmund S. Muskie Archives
and Oral History Project who provided me with such important docu-
mentation on the 1954 election. I'm also very grateful to Greg Gallant of
the Margaret Chase Smith Library for his research assistance and careful
reading of and suggestions for chapter 1.

Year after year, my Maine politics students take advantage of the
tremendous archival material available in both the Ed Muskie and Margaret Chase Smith facilities as well as the George Mitchell papers at Bowdoin College and the William S. Cohen papers at the University of Maine.
Scholars and students are truly fortunate to have such marvelous docu-
ments available to them and such marvelous guides to assist them as well.

Others who read particular chapters and helped me appreciate various
situations include Doug Hodgkin, Don Nicoll, Sandy Maisel, Kay Rand,
George Smith, Jim Erwin, Bob Leason, Tom Daffron, Stan Tupper, Mert
Henry, Mike Healy, Governor Ken Curtis, Barry Hobbins, Neil Rolde,
Paul Violette, and Lance Tapley.

They read one or more chapters of the work and offered important suggestions and information to flesh out my portraits and to correct my er-
rors of fact and interpretation. I really value their insights and knowledge
of the Maine political scene.

Scholarship is such a collective enterprise.

I would also like to thank all those who helped me with political analysis in general and this work in particular with thoughts, comments, information, student papers and oral presentations, and the like. Over the
years, I've had political interactions that have helped me enormously to
understand the true nature of politics in Maine. Many people have contributed to my political growth over the years; among those are many past
and present participants in the process itself as well as a number of the reporters who cover politics in the Pine Tree State.

This large group includes Robert "Bob" Fuller, Ted O'Meara, Alan
Caron, Dora Mills, Julie L'Heureux, Dennis Bailey, Kay Rand, Amanda
Boothby, Roger Putnam, Lil Caron, Bennett Katz, Wakine Tanous, Harry
Richardson, Georgette Berube, Dick Hewes, Craig McEwen, Congress-
man John Baldacci, Jack Linnell, Jason Fortin, Mal Leary, Jim McGregor,
Linda Hornbeck, Ted Cohen, Daryn Demeritt, Steve Joyce, David Ott,

Rick Mullins, Patty O'Brien Ames, John Day, Skip and Susanne Magee, Joe Sewall, Phil Merrill, A. J. Higgins, Jock McKernan, Paul Carrier, Kristine St. Peter, Congressman James Longley, and Dick Morgan.

Also, Peter Cianchette, Suzie Dana, Congressman Tom Allen, Mike Carosi, Senator Susan Collins, Papri Bhattacharya, Dan Levine, Fred Nutter, Bart Jansen, Tinder Jit, Collette Cushing, Senator George Mitchell, Dick Barringer, Kathy Gilliland, Dennis Bailey, Steve Abbott, Abby Holman, Joel Moser, Peter Webster, Allen Springer, Brian Levy, Jean Yarborough, Jamie Baird, Dave "Ed" Butler, Jenna Goldman, Susan Longley, Paul Nyhus, Al Diamond, Congressman Tom Andrews, Carol Emery, Liz Chapman, Paul Franco, Mike O'Leary, Emily Reycroft, Jeff Milliken, Craig Brown, Mark Gartley, Chuck Cianchette, Tony Buxton, Roger Mallar, and Beryll-Ann Johnson.

Also, Jeff Nevins, Joyce Brown, Howard Dana, Chris Lockewood, Dana Connors, Frank O'Hara, Craig McEwen, David Rush, Senator Bill Hathaway, Sharon Miller, Craig Cleaves, Sarah Manz, Marty Hill, Senator Ed Muskie, Chris Williams, John Rensenbrink, Kati Duglin, Fred Hill, Bonnie Washuk, Allen Springer, Dick Wiley, Tony Small, Dan Watham, Governor Angus King, Nick Miller, Kevin Bougie, Jim Chalmers, Marcia Weigle, Richard "Dick" Mullins, and Mark Mogensen.

Also of note are Rosemary Baldacci, Charlie Micholeau, Travis Cummings, Erin Lehane, Tom Tureen, Chuck Winner, Bob Deis, Paul Mandebach, Jamie Suzor, Steve Cerf, Bob Monks, Felicia Knight, Ed Gilfillen, Taylor Washburn, Wes Ridlon, James Bass, Connie LaPointe, Bob Tyrer, Anna Mullins, Ezra Smith, Marty Hill, Seth Ritter, Ted Nutter, Pam Green, Steve Campbell, Paul Franco, Cynthia Bergman, Josh Ney, Marc Hetherington, Mike Michaud, Susan Price, Congressman Peter Kyros, Dick Ames, Edi Smith, Richard Morgan, Denise Gitsham, Alex Ray, Tommy Black, Jerry Plante, John Turner, John Nutting, Secretary of Defense Bill Cohen, Allen Titus, John DeWitt, Kent Chabotar, John Clifford, Governor Joe Brennan, Joy O'Brien, Jim Hodge, Anna Mullins, Bernie Lacroix, Keith Brown, Shep Lee, Heather Potholm Mullins, Lance Guo, Senator Olympia Snowe, Henry Laurence, Chris Duval, Pat Eltman, Jeff Mills, Jeff Toorish, Rick Hornbeck, Governor Ken Curtis, and Gil Barndollar.

And I wouldn't want to forget Mike Morris, Janet Martin, Dan Lieberfeld, Bill Nimitz, Shawn Faircloth, Lori Handrahan, Jonathan Weiler, Neila Smith, Kevin Raye, Jim Erwin Sr., Gordon Smith, Grace Fellows, Severin Beliveau, Harry Richardson, Sean Scott, Maribeth Toorish, Chris Burke, David Flanagan, Duke Dutremble, Tom LaPointe, Hoolai Paoa, Dan Paradee, Chris Lockwood, Donald Soctomah, Pat Donahue, Senator Susan Collins, Paula Valente, George Campbell, Susan Castonguay, Sharon Miller, Chuck Beitz, Chris Williams, Josh Weinstein, John Gould, Roy Lenardson, Jason Fortin, and James Sterns. I thank them all.

Special kudos also go to my very able research assistants, Lawrence Delasotta, Leah Bressack, Susan Price, and my capable and always patient executive assistant Pat Leask. I appreciate all their extra effort on this project.

Finally, I'm very grateful to Jed Lyons who not only participated in some early political activity with me, but also over the years has sent some of my best books out to the public for their perusal!

Christian P. Potholm
Harpswell, Maine

1

This Splendid Game

One of the great joys of my life has been politics. Winning or losing, in candidate and ballot measure campaigns, I have always found it to be "This Splendid Game." I hope this book gives a little something back to the political system either in terms of new knowledge or new ways of looking at the political realities of the Pine Tree State. I hope it also inspires future political actors to become involved in the process. Politics in Maine can be a wonderful occupation or avocation and sometimes, a combination of both. I hope this book encourages more people to join in "This Splendid Game."

The people of Maine have been blessed with their open, honest, responsive political system and the hundreds of participants who have made it work over the years.

Politics in Maine is the way politics should be.

In teaching Maine politics over the past decade, though, I have been frustrated to discover that no book or even series of articles covers the course of politics in the Pine Tree State since World War II. Lecturing on the important figures and campaigns over the years, I wished I had a single book to assign, one that would put the past fifty years of accomplishments and failures in some common perspective.

This is particularly the case since the malleability of history has long been a theme of my courses and my political activity. Many followers of politics seem to assume that y had to happen because x did happen. I wanted to show the ebb and flow of campaigns, how they did not have to turn out the way they actually did. In many cases, it was the campaign itself, the campaign qua campaign, that determined the outcome. It was the campaign activity from both sides that determined the outcome, an outcome that could have gone either way.

Although this point of view is often questioned, I believe there was nothing preordained about Margaret Chase Smith winning in 1948. Ed

1

Muskie was not guaranteed an upset victory in 1954. Ken Curtis beat Jim Erwin in 1970 in the contest for the governor's mansion because he ran a much better campaign. When that contest began, he was trailing Erwin by 28 percent. He looked doomed—and he would have been doomed if he had not done the things he did and Erwin the things he did. Even then, Curtis barely won.

If Bill Cohen hadn't walked across the state, he wouldn't have won in 1972. The Maine Yankee atomic plant was kept open in 1980 because it ran an enormously expensive *and* effective campaign against skillful, determined, and nearly successful opponents. In both cases, the campaign for Elmer Violette and that to shut down the nuclear plant undertook actions, focused on themes, and used certain techniques that turned out to be not as effective as their opponents'.

Both Angus King (1994) and James B. Longley (1974) had less than 10 percent of the vote when they started their races and they needed high quality campaigns (each different in nature but drawing on the same spectrum of voters) in order to win.

So the first theme of this work is the theme of malleability, that political events were—and are—not preordained and the outcome of the key elections we study not guaranteed, no matter what people believe today.

I'll also try to build "the case for campaigns." I focus on the campaign itself, what I call the campaign qua campaign, to give the reader a sense of what might have been as well as what was. I seek to capture the ebb and flow of political fortunes, of the parties, of the movements, of the individuals. In short, I try to capture the essence of modern Maine politics.

In this regard, I am interested in the campaign, not the governing that follows the campaign. I'm simply not interested in what political figures do after they are elected. I'm only interested in what got them elected or what failed to get them elected. Therefore this work pays a lot of attention to the dynamics of a particular campaign and focuses on the methods, strategies, and participants, all of which came together to put one candidate over the top and had another candidate come up short.

My second major theme, therefore, is the primacy of campaigns qua campaigns. I believe that campaigns, in and of themselves, often determine the outcomes of elections, that the dynamics of the electoral process affect the outcomes, regardless of the candidates involved.

Of course, some could—and would—argue that it is the candidates themselves who should get credit for their own achievements. This is true and they have. But I would argue that it is more than possible to see campaigns as extensions of the candidates themselves. After all, they put together the teams that supported or, in some cases, hindered them. And I would certainly not seek to take credit away from the successful candidates studied in this book.

But I honestly believe that any realistic analysis of the campaigns qua campaigns of 1948, 1954, 1970, 1972, 1974, 1980, and 1994 must yield a firm understanding of the role played by members of the candidates' campaign teams and of the independent variable nature of that participation.

Finally, this work provides an overview of the last fifty years of Maine politics—who succeeded and who failed in the major, seminal elections. In this regard, I try to point out what was the true significance of various elections: What were the sea changes in Maine political processes? What changed over time in terms of how to run and win a campaign? What are the enduring patterns and trends? Why did some candidates succeed and others fail? What techniques were introduced when and what impact did they have?

One of the interesting things I learned doing interviews for this book was that until very recently both major political parties adopted different political techniques at different times. Only recently have the Republicans and Democrats had the same array of techniques in their repertoire. One reason the Greens and the anti-nuclear activists and such groups as the activist Gays and activist Christian Right have sometimes done so poorly in major elections is that they have not seen the most effective techniques as being efficacious!

People tend to assume that both—or all—major parties have the same tools and the same appreciation of those tools. Nothing could be further from the truth! In Maine political history, the Democrats discovered the power of television and used it effectively in the Muskie revolution and in the Curtis "miracle" of 1970. Republicans were very slow to grasp the power of television and Jim Erwin lost in 1970 in large part because he did not make use of it.

Democrats also made more efficacious use of polling in the 1950s and 1960s. But with the Cohen revolution of 1972, Republicans moved ahead with polling techniques and strategic uses. For the next thirty years, Republicans used tracking polling much more effectively than did Democrats. This is due in part to Democratic fascination with "get out the vote" efforts, often called GOTV.

While Republicans became obsessed with knowing exactly where they were in relation to their opponents so they could adjust messages and TV buys, Democrats continued to call voters in a different way, identifying those who were going to vote for their candidates so they could call them again on election day and send direct mail to those undecided. In the crucial election of 1994, Angus King adopted the Republican approach and his campaign had nightly tracking calls the entire time his commercials were on TV. Without such close monitoring, it is extremely unlikely that King would have prevailed over Joe Brennan.

Which elections did I choose to illustrate the above points? For the decade of the 1940s, I chose as the seminal election the senatorial contest of 1948. In it, the three-term congresswoman from Maine's 2nd Congressional District (CD), Margaret Chase Smith, challenged popular sitting governor Sumner Sewall and former governor Horace Hildreth as well as a Protestant minister, Albion Beverage, for the Republican U.S. Senate nomination. She was opposed in the general election by Democrat Adrian Scolten.

This was a most significant election. It was the first time in the twentieth century that an insurgent, nonbusiness female candidate prevailed over the party establishment. Margaret Chase Smith, of course, went on to be the first woman ever elected to both the U.S. House of Representatives and the Senate in her own right, not appointed to fill the position of her husband as others had been. In addition, the independent organization that Margaret Chase Smith used to propel her to victory was to have a huge impact on subsequent successful Republican candidates such as William S. Cohen and Olympia Snowe.

For the decade of the 1950s, there was only one choice, the crucial gubernatorial contest of 1954, which saw Edmund S. Muskie defeat incumbent Burton Cross and become the first Democrat in the postwar era to win the governorship. This victory set the stage for a huge Democratic revival that, by 1972, resulted in the Democrats controlling the governorship, both congressional offices, and one of the two U.S. Senate seats. The election of Muskie in 1954 led to a true political revolution in Maine politics.

That revolution saw its apogee in the 1970 contest between sitting governor Ken Curtis and his Republican challenger, Jim Erwin. Behind by 28 percentage points and bedeviled by a strong challenger, Plato Truman, in the Democratic primary, Curtis pulled off a major political miracle and signaled the high point of Democratic fortunes with only Margaret Chase Smith still standing as a Republican officeholder at the end of the 1970 election cycle. The Muskie tide was at its zenith.

However, the emergence of William S. Cohen in 1972, with his defeat of Abbott O. Greene in the Republican primary and Democrat Elmer Violette in the general election, began a Republican counterrevolution. Cohen was the only Republican elected in the 1972 cycle and his methods and strategies became the model for an entire subsequent generation of Republicans: Dave Emery, Jock McKernan, Olympia Snowe, and Susan Collins.

The next critical election that I have chosen to cover is the 1974 gubernatorial contest that saw the victory of Maine's first independent governor, James B. Longley, who bested George Mitchell and Jim Erwin and influences Maine politics to this day. I have paired that election with the gubernatorial campaign of 1994 that saw Angus King defeat Joe Brennan and Susan Collins to ensure that the independent tradition continued in Maine.

Also, and this is often overlooked by even knowledgeable observers and insiders, the King coalition and the Longley coalition were identical. Both were elected with a strong electoral alliance of rural Republicans and urban Franco American Democrats.

Thus in terms of party politics, this book ends up tracing the progress of Republican dominance to Democratic ascendancy to Republican rebirth and eventual Independent triumph so that by century's end, the state stood with a rough balance of one-third Republicans, one-third Democrats, and one-third Independents in terms of most likely voters in most election situations with half of the Democrats and Republicans and 75 percent of the Independents capable of alternating their vote.

The final election I have chosen to present comes from the 1980s and is a ballot measure, not a candidate campaign. The antinuclear movement and its attempt to shut down the Maine Yankee Nuclear power plant was to prove seminal. After that election, the number of ballot measures in Maine increased dramatically and the state became a battleground for national political interests of many different persuasions. The No side in that 1980 campaign also set the standard and provided the techniques and strategies that would ultimately dominate the next three decades of ballot measures.

I learned a lot researching and writing this work.

For one thing, I've always been fascinated by the role of the press in political campaigns. To look at six different campaigns through the contemporary eyes of the reporters and editors who commanded the stage at the time of those elections was very illuminating.

Teaching Maine politics, I always try to get students to look at print coverage both in terms of efficacy (Does "print media really drive the electronic media"?) and fairness. I tell them that there are a number of dimensions of "print fairness," or how to judge a newspaper.

These include:

1. Editorial Patterns (one party or another, one candidate or another)
2. Editorial Slants (fairness of comment for opponents of their favorites)
3. Reporting Coverage (amount and quality)
4. Reporting Coverage (fairness/balance)
5. Reporting Coverage (how influenced by editorial position of paper?)
6. Reporting Coverage (placement of political news within the paper, comparison of one candidate's location versus another's)
7. Degree of "Self-Fulfilling Prophecy" about the paper's editorial position (does the reporting fit the editorial stance so much it impedes the opponents from gaining ground?)
8. Reporting Quality (going beyond the conventional wisdom)

Now I may seem to be setting up straw men or straw women here—most readers may already assume that certain newspapers play political favorites and/or most reporters write their stories with an eye toward their editor's choices. But most of my students do not assume either to be true so on our mutual voyage of discovery we've often been surprised as reality moves away from the model of reportorial neutrality. Most of my students come to Maine politics with the assumption that daily newspapers are "fair" and "impartial."

I've always had pretty good working relationships with the print press—both reporters and editors—but over a thirty year period it is possible to see the quality of particular press coverage rise and fall depending on the era, management, and ownership. This work therefore highlights the various roles played by the two largest and most important papers in the state, the *Portland Press Herald* and the *Bangor Daily News*. The role of the press in Maine politics remains one of its most understudied aspects.

In looking over the past six decades of Maine political journalism, I've also been made aware of the incredible power of something Gene McCarthy told me about the press when he was running for president in 1968 in the New Hampshire primary. The press, he said, were like a flock of crows. They would all be sitting on one wire and not one would go to another wire while they were all clustered on the first wire. Then one would go over to a new wire, and then the others would follow. Pretty soon they'd all be on the other wire! I've always wanted to put this hypothesis to the test, and to see six different elections and the role of the press in each gave me considerable insight into the perspicuity of that remark.

Taken in total, the last sixty years of elections in Maine show clearly that the working press more often than not bring their expectations to a particular race and it is hard, damned hard, to get them to change those expectations. There is a powerful herd mentality among the Maine press corps and few working reporters ever stick their necks out to pick winners unless they have lots of company.

They almost always go with the conventional wisdom—right up until election day when that wisdom too often turns out to be incorrect. Part of this reason may be the reporter subculture itself and part of it may be that reporters are, as Paul Carrier says in chapter 6, merely reflecting existing "conventional wisdom."

But as you will see in this work, at several key points in Maine's political history, Peter Damborg (1954), Jim Brunelle (1970), and John Day (1974) caught enough of the political change to alert their readers to important changes. In these instances, they went beyond the "expectations" of their peers and editors.

There are also some current reporters who, in my experience at least, are willing to think outside the box and process new information as it becomes available. Mal Leary is particularly good at reading polling information and he may be the only reporter in Maine who truly understands what polls can and should do and how to read the future in the near-past.

Liz Chapman remains the best investigative political reporter in the state. Dogged and determined, willing to let the chips fall where they may and with a canine appetite for breaking news, she would have done well in any era. Bonnie Washuk also writes balanced pieces and, whatever her personal views, tries to be objective and thorough day in and day out. She succeeds more than most other reporters. During the 2002 election cycle, she and Christopher Williams combined to make their "Maine: Election Briefs" section the best in the state.

Bart Jansen also takes information from a variety of sources and makes up his own mind about political phenomena. A. J. Higgins is a fine reporter when it comes to balance and fairness and in "reading" a political situation although he is not always allowed to be as aggressive as some in seeking out or following up on a story.

Perhaps all working reporters need "sabbaticals" to enable them to take time off, recharge their professional batteries, and have a chance to look anew at political campaigns without the pressure of deadlines and away from the group-think of their colleagues.

I have always been particularly fascinated by the dimension played by the press in terms of expectations. To give some famous national examples that will be familiar to most readers: the press expected President Lyndon Johnson to win the Democratic primary for president in 1968; after all, he had 56 percent of the vote in a December 1967 poll and his closest challenger, Eugene McCarthy, had 26 percent.

Johnson, in fact, won the New Hampshire primary in February with 49.6 percent and McCarthy was a clear second with 41 percent of the vote. Yet the press called it a McCarthy victory and Johnson withdrew from the race in March.

Likewise, in 1972, Ed Muskie won the New Hampshire presidential primary handily, 46 percent (up from 26 percent in a December 1971 poll) to 37 percent for George McGovern with 6 percent for Sam Yorty and 4 percent for Wilbur Mills. But he was regarded by the press as having "lost" that primary and his presidential campaign floundered thereafter. The expectations reporters and editors put on campaigns are simply part of the game.

As Ward Just has so eloquently put it, "Expectation is the enemy of prediction." How the press "reads" a situation can have considerable impact on the ongoing situation and right or wrong, these expectations, and the editorial opinions that go with them, play an ironic and often bizarre role in Maine politics. So many times, the press act as cheerleaders for incumbents and front-runners and almost always assume that whoever is ahead in a particular poll is likely to remain there.

During the King campaign in 1994, I couldn't get many reporters to make the assumption that King *could* win, let alone that he was going to win.

Overall, in looking over the last sixty years of press coverage in Maine, I have been struck by two different aspects. The first is the decline in the amount of daily political coverage out on the campaign trail; the second is a seeming rise in partisanship on the part of the major newspapers in the state. Partisanship may involve any or all of four variables: (1) the editorial support of one party's candidates versus another's, (2) the placement, where the political stories are located, (3) the amount of coverage and its subcategory, the amount of coverage of campaign activities versus press releases, and (4) the relationship between editorial positions and press coverage and "slant."

In terms of coverage, when you look at the press accounts of the 1948, 1954, 1970, 1972, and 1974 elections, you see that the print media did quite a good job in providing its readers with campaign information. In those election cycles, reporters actually got out and went on the campaign trail. Reporters followed Margaret Chase Smith and Ed Muskie around. They were with Ken Curtis at mill gates and Jim Erwin at Rotary Club speeches. Many—perhaps even as many as eight or nine—walked with Bill Cohen on his walk. Those who took a day out on the campaign trail invariably had a better understanding of the walk and the impact it was having on ordinary voters than did those reporters who sat back in offices and refused to come out and see for themselves. Reporters attended James B. Longley's speeches and were with him at CMP headquarters when he got the *Bangor Daily News* to support him.

Reporters then provided more day-to-day coverage than they do today and they definitely got out on the actual campaign trail much more. Today, except for one "field" trip in the primary and another in the general election, most working reporters stay in the newsroom (either in Augusta or at their newspaper) and let the news come to them. They rely on press releases and their coverage of various press conferences to get the "go" of a particular campaign, relying too often on phone calls to the same eight or ten insiders. They watch TV along with the rest of us.

The papers themselves seem to have become much more partisan in their coverage as well. In researching this work, I was particularly struck by the role of Maine's two largest papers, the *Portland Press Herald* and *Bangor Daily News*. Both have strong editorial points of view and exhibit them in most elections. Both have some good reporters and have had some truly exceptional ones. Many reporters are quite independent of their various editors. But both papers also have reporters who are aware of and often seem driven by their editors' interests.

The *Portland Press Herald*, for example, has become increasing liberal and pro-Democratic over the years as its ownership has changed, and its editorials have reflected this increasing partisanship. Such activity is certainly fair enough. After all, one doesn't buy a newspaper in order to hide one's political desires, goals, and preferences. But sometimes this assertion goes beyond the editorial pages with some bizarre repercussions.

For its part, the *Bangor Daily News* has been somewhat more catholic in its choices, although over time, it has generally supported somewhat more conservative candidates for major office than the *Press Herald*. In addition, some would say its editorial choices can border on the erratic. For example, the *Bangor Daily News* endorsed independents James B. Longley and Herman "Buddy" Frankland (this, of course, was the Reverend Buddy Frankland before the incident with the lady in the choir) but not Angus King.

Most often, however, the BDN supports Republicans or conservative Democrats (read Bill Cohen, Olympia Snowe, and John Baldacci). And as chapter 7 shows, the paper's machinations on behalf of gubernatorial candidate Susan Collins in 1994 are now legendary.

As this study reveals, both major newspapers have and do play favorites. Readers who are not partisans are often not aware of the patterns of support or opposition that exist on the editorial page and even in the work of various reporters. Every publisher and editor I have ever spoken to about this denies strenuously that the editorial slant of the paper in any way impinges on the reporting.

They may be right.

Yet I know of hardly anyone inside Maine politics who believes such claims. Political insiders believe that the two largest Maine newspapers consistently play favorites, often on the editorial pages and from time to time in their news sections.

As campaigns heat up, reporters certainly know whom their editors support. Some resist the subtle and not-so-subtle pressures coming from their editors better than others. I'm sure that most reporters try to do an objective job but between the conventional wisdom (in the newsroom and within the political class) and their paper's editorial bent, this may be harder to do than they assume. Or, the preferences of the editors are the same as their own, in which case there is a natural fit.

Readers will see some prominent examples of this subtle and not-so-subtle interplay in this book. I believe the editorial stances of the paper often can obscure the reality of the political process when reporters follow the "party" line. Sometimes it even helps if the editor or publisher drives the reporter beyond conventional wisdom.

For example, the *Portland Press Herald* wanted George Mitchell to be governor in 1974 and therefore missed the rise of James B. Longley. They editorialized for Mitchell and published a most dubious poll "composite" saying he would win, and the paper's reporting missed the Longley surge entirely. This pattern repeated itself in the governor's race in 1994 when the PPH again championed the cause of the Democratic nominee, ignoring the rise of the Independent challenger.

Conversely, the *Bangor Daily News* wanted Longley to win in 1974, endorsed him, and gave his candidacy a huge boost the final weekend by publishing a poll as well as several news stories suggesting he could win. I give them high marks for not following the conventional wisdom, for following an accurate tracking poll right up to the very end, and taking their shot. In my opinion, they elected James B. Longley, putting his insurgent campaign over the top.

In the governor's race in 1994, however, the BDN turned true objective reporting upside down in a desperate effort to find some reason why Susan Collins could and should win. Their tortured machinations the last two weeks of the campaign were only matched by the very one-sided presentation provided by the *Portland Press Herald*.

Democratic activists also see what they take as a similar pattern of BDN activity in the 1996 senatorial race with the paper again intervening on behalf of Collins on both its editorial page and in its reporting and analysis.[1] Certainly, the BDN's actions depicted in chapter 7 show an interventionist endorsement style and a rush to assist one candidate over a need to inform the public as to the actual state of affairs.

Cynics of all party affiliations could see a pattern in subsequent events. The managing editor for the BDN, Mark Woodward, went on after the election to become communications director for Senator Collins—although he soon returned to his old job.

As for the PPH, that paper was very active in the 1996 gubernatorial election, promoting Joe Brennan for governor in its editorials, publishing very strange polling results, and doing a campaign-long string of stories saying why Angus King couldn't or shouldn't win. I believe in that campaign, the *Press Herald* also did its readers something of a disservice.

Perhaps these "tilts" to one candidate or another may have always been in political coverage although they may have gotten more blatant in recent years. This may be due in part to the fact that political reporters simply do not get out on the campaign trail as much as their counterparts in the 1940s, 1950s, 1960s, and 1970s. Readers need to watch editorials, political reporting, and story placement with an eye toward overall fairness and a sense of healthy skepticism.

Beyond the element of tilt, I would argue that the sheer quality of the print coverage of political campaigns has diminished over the years. Since reporters get out on the stump considerably less at the end of the twentieth century and the beginning of the twenty-first century than they did previously, the shadow of editorial preference hangs over and influences the ways political reporters cover their beats. They have less contact with real voters and less of a chance to see how the various campaigns are doing.

This is not to say that all reporters on the *Bangor Daily News* or the *Portland Press Herald* follow or even care about what their editors think or prefer. But it is to say that those who practice and follow politics have the right, indeed the obligation, to assume a certain overlap among "conventional wisdom," "actual political trends," and the "desired" outcome of the paper's editorial position. This is especially true for those reporters who sit in their offices and receive press releases rather than get out in the field.

I should also note that the two largest papers seem to be the worst offenders. The *Sun Journal, Central Maine Sentinel,* and *Kennebec Journal* seem to routinely do a better job at keeping their editorial comment separate from their reporting arm and their endorsements seem to be more balanced than their larger rivals. It is as if the *Bangor Daily News* and the *Portland Press Herald* assume that they should determine who gets to be governor or senator. Both the BDN and PPH seem to take it more as a corporate civic duty to try to influence the outcome of elections, given their circulation status as numbers two and one in the state.

But there is no need to take my word for all of this.

Any interested reader can peruse the chapters in this book and then go and see the total actual coverage for the elections in question and make up his or her own mind. It may be due to the impact of television and its concomitant overhang over the political print media, but earlier political reporters seem to have provided their readers with a greater depth and first-hand flavor of their political stories. It would appear that while editorials may have been even stronger earlier, they were more properly confined to the editorial page and did not bleed over into the day-to-day reporting as much.

Finally, in doing this book, I again came to the conclusion that Maine, as a political arena, is very fortunate to have had so many candidates of such high personal quality run for office.

Whether they ran good campaigns or poor campaigns, for the most part, they were good people who gave of their lives and time and hope and dreams to serve, however briefly or unsuccessfully, the common civic good. The Maine political arena truly attracts high caliber candidates and we owe them all a debt of gratitude for their activities on our behalf. They did not sit at home and complain about the political system or its goals and values and activities. They went out and made their case to the voters in "This Splendid Game" and abided by the wishes of those voters.

As Teddy Roosevelt put it:

> The credit belongs to those who are actually in the arena, who strive
> valiantly; who know the great enthusiasms, the great devotions, and spend
> themselves in a worthy cause; who at the best, know the triumph of high
> achievement, and who, at the worst, if they fail, fail while daring greatly, so
> that their place shall never be with those cold and timid souls who know nei-
> ther victory nor defeat.

I couldn't agree more!

This book is a tribute to all those who cared enough for their state to
step into the arena and play "This Splendid Game." Before the analysis of
each decade's seminal election, I have provided a straightforward description of each primary and general election of that era.

I apologize to readers beforehand for the prosaic and perhaps even dull
accounting that provides the matrix in which the seminal election took
place. But it too is a tribute to all those who took time out of their lives to
participate directly in the politics of the Pine Tree State. Everyone who ran
for major political office during this period deserves to be mentioned and
her or his effort placed on a readable historical record.

We owe these men and women a great deal, for they have kept our political system open and vibrant.

2

The 1940s:

Margaret Chase Smith vs. Adrian Scolten

THE DECADE'S MATRIX

Maine campaigns and elections in the 1940s had rhythms and processes that would be foreign to our eyes and ears today. For the most part they were much shorter, with a far slower tempo, far less mass media—in fact often no paid media at all—and more grassroots efforts and more personal letter writing to supporters. Primaries were held in June and general elections were in September so general election campaigns were compressed and often somewhat muted by today's standards. Campaigns also cost far less, even allowing for inflation. Ten thousand dollars was considered a lot to spend on a federal election.

By contrast, in 1999 Mark Lawrence, president of the Maine Senate, announced in April that he was seeking the U.S. Senate seat of Olympia Snowe which was not up until the year 2000. Eighteen months ahead of time! But he and Olympia Snowe ended up spending over $3 million, much of it on mass media. We are so used to the long and expensive campaigns that we hardly notice them or think about their duration.

The 1940s were a wonderful time to be a Republican in Maine. For Republicans, it was a glorious time indeed. The party, enjoying a huge registration advantage and still riding the wave of strong patriotism, a strong domestic economy, and a sense of national unity, won all the races of the decade. Think of that: for ten years, the Republicans won every race for governor, the U.S. Senate, and Congress. Every single one!

They ran up a total of 25 wins and 0 losses (including Margaret Chase Smith's win in the special congressional election of 1940 for Maine's 2nd District seat to fill out the term of her dead husband, Clyde Smith). This string of Republican victories is a feat unmatched in Maine's post–World War II political history.

In fact, the most competitive races in Maine during the 1940s were between the various Republican and Democratic candidates during their primaries rather than in the general elections. Whoever won those Republican primary elections then went on to win the general election.

The 1940 elections set the standard and the tone for most of the decade. In the Republican primary for governor, Sumner Sewall (31 percent) narrowly defeated Fred Payne (29 percent), Blin Page (24 percent), and Roy Fernald (15 percent) for the Republican gubernatorial nomination while the Democratic nominee, Fulton Redman, was unopposed.

In the general election, the Republican Sewall easily defeated Redman 64 percent to 36 percent while a Communist party candidate, Helen E. Knudsen, received .1 percent of the vote, 325 Mainers having cast their ballots for her.

Likewise, Owen Brewster defeated sitting Governor Lewis Barrows 59 percent to 41 percent in the Republican primary for U.S. Senate while Louis J. Brann, the former Democratic governor, was unopposed in his primary. In the general election, Brewster handily defeated Brann 59 percent to 41 percent while a Communist candidate, Lewis Gordon, received 305 votes or .1 percent of the total.

That same year saw the appearance on the official Maine political scene of Margaret Chase Smith. Smith, the widow of the popular Clyde Smith and his long time political operative and confidant, handily defeated Frederick Bonney (89 percent to 7 percent) in a special primary election to serve out the remaining portion of Clyde's term when he suffered a fatal heart attack. Margaret Chase Smith also got 249 votes or 3.3 percent as a write-in Democratic candidate!

The regular congressional races of 1940 showed continued Republican domination. In Maine's 1st CD, James C. Oliver (52 percent) defeated Bob Hale (33 percent), George Coe (11 percent), and William Holland (3 percent) for the right to face Democrat Peter MacDonald who was unopposed. The general election in the 1st CD saw Maine voters choosing Oliver (63 percent) over MacDonald (37 percent).

The story was the same in the 2nd CD. Faced with significant opposition in the regular Republican primary for a full term, Margaret Chase Smith (64 percent) decisively defeated John Marshall (16 percent), Hodgdon Buzzell (10 percent), Fred Bonney (6 percent), and Arthur Lancaster (4 percent). Edward Beauchamp, the Democrat, was unopposed in his primary but Margaret Chase Smith prevailed in the general election, 65 percent to 35 percent.

In Maine's 3rd CD, which disappeared in time for the 1962 election due to reapportionment, a four-way Republican primary saw Frank Fellows (44 percent) defeat J. Fred Burns (30 percent), Walter Miner (15 percent), and Roscoe Emery (12 percent), while in the Democratic contest, Thomas

Curran decisively defeated OSG Nickerson 78 percent to 22 percent. Fellows completed the Republican sweep of that year, defeating Curran 66 percent to 34 percent in the general.

World War II came to Maine like the rest of America on Sunday morning, December 7, 1941, with the Japanese attack on Pearl Harbor and Mainers rushed to the colors to support the nation.

The elections of 1942 brought few surprises and few close elections as Maine voters stayed with incumbents.

Sumner Sewall and George Lane Jr. were unopposed in the Republican and Democratic primaries, and in the general election for governor, Sewall was reelected, handily defeating Lane 67 percent to 33 percent.

Wallace White was unopposed in the Republican primary for U.S. Senate as was Fulton Redman, the Democrat, with White winning the general election 67 percent to 33 percent.

In Maine's 1st CD, Republican Bob Hale defeated James Oliver in a primary and then went on to defeat Louis Brann in the general election 57 percent to 43 percent after Brann had beaten Ray Stetson 85 percent to 15 percent.

The 2nd CD saw Margaret Chase Smith unopposed for her party's nomination and she decisively defeated Bradford Redonnett 68 percent to 32 percent in the general.

The primary contest for the 3rd CD was even more lopsided with Frank Fellows, receiving only a write-in challenge from Democrat Katherine Hickson, winning 15,391 to 368. Fellows was unopposed in the general election.

Maine voters had chosen to stay with any and all incumbents as they faced the years of World War II.

However, 1944 saw more spirited contests both within the parties and between them. Horace Hildreth, the Republican, defeated Roy Fernald and Ardine Richardson for the gubernatorial nomination, getting 54 percent in a three-way contest. Hildreth then handily defeated the Democratic nominee, Paul Jullien, 70 percent to 30 percent.

There was no Senate contest in 1944 but in all three congressional races, Republicans were elected. In the 1st CD, Robert Hale defeated Andrew Pettis, William Holland, and Fred McFarland in the Republican contest while Andrew Pettis defeated John Fitzgerald and Scott Kittredge in the Democratic primary. Hale then defeated Pettis 69 percent to 31 percent.

In the 2nd CD, Margaret Chase Smith was unopposed in her primary as was her opponent David Staples, and Smith went on to defeat Staples 68 percent to 32 percent. At the same time, in the 3rd CD, Frank Fellows was unopposed in the Republican primary and Ralph Graham faced no opposition in the Democratic, with Fellows easily defeating Graham in the general 77 percent to 23 percent.

In 1946, the first postwar election, incumbent Horace A. Hildreth, the Republican, won his gubernatorial primary over Roy Fernald and then defeated the Democratic nominee, F. Davis Clark, 61 percent to 39 percent for governor. Clark had earlier defeated his Democratic opponent, Leland B. Currier.

That same year, both Owen Brewster the Republican and Peter M. McDonald the Democrat were unopposed in their respective primaries for the U.S. Senate. Brewster handily defeated McDonald in the general election 64 percent to 36 percent.

In the three races for Congress, Republicans easily won all three that year. Republican Robert Hale defeated his Democratic opponent, John C. Fitzgerald, 60 percent to 40 percent in Maine's First District while Frank Fellows the Republican crushed John M. Coghill 73 percent to 27 percent in the Third District.

In Maine's Second Congressional race, Margaret Chase Smith, the Republican incumbent, beat Edward J. Beauchamp 61 percent to 39 percent, thereby continuing her string of victories in Maine's second congressional races and setting the stage for her dramatic, groundbreaking race for the U.S. Senate in 1948.

Referenda questions in 1946 revolved around two major issues: the providing for bonuses to pay veterans of World War II by raising cigarette, liquor, and other miscellaneous taxes, and questions concerning the regulation of liquor licenses by towns and cities. All passed, except the veterans' bonuses.

1948 was a watershed year in Maine politics, one that began important trends that are with us today and established patterns of political activity that have endured.

The race for governor was made more interesting by the decision of the sitting Republican governor, Horace Hildreth, to run for the Senate seat vacated by fellow Republican Wallace White.

Hildreth's move touched off a vigorous five-way race for the Republican gubernatorial nomination with Fred Payne, with 36 percent of the vote, ending up the winner over George Varney, Robinson Verrill, Roy Fernald, and Neil Bishop.

The Democratic primary was less crowded with Louis Lausier defeating Leland Currier before losing the general election to Payne 66 percent to 34 percent.

Republicans continued their domination of the Congressional delegation in 1948. Robert Hale easily defeated Frank Dunton, Ray Stetson, and Gunder Rasmussen in the Republican primary for the First Congressional seat, getting 77 percent of the vote and defeating the Democratic nominee, James McVicar, 63 percent to 37 percent.

In the Second Congressional, Charles Nelson got 59 percent in the Republican primary, overshadowing James Perkins Jr., James Glover, and Edwin Wixson. Although the Democratic candidate for the Second District, Benjamin Arena, was unopposed in his primary, he lost 33 percent to 67 percent to Nelson in the general election.

The Third Congressional District likewise stayed Republican in 1948 with Frank Fellows the Republican defeating F. Davis Clark, the 1946 Democratic nominee for governor, 71 percent to 29 percent.

These four races thus looked a lot like all the other races in the 1940s, where most of the competition was for the Republican nomination and the winner of that triumphing in the fall.

HOW TO EXPLAIN THE REPUBLICAN
DOMINATION OF THE 1940S?

There were a number of factors that tended to reinforce Republican hegemony over the Maine political system:

The first was the weight of history. The Republican party in Maine, formed in 1854 by antislavery forces, held sway over the Maine political scene for the better part of 100 years so the inertia was very much on the side of the Republicans.

We are now so far removed from the American Civil War and the last fifty years of American politics has seen such an ongoing alliance of African Americans with the Democratic party that we forget that the Republicans were the staunchest antislavery proponents and that the Democrats in the 1860s were the proslavery party, even in the North.

When the North won the Civil War, the Republicans reaped the political rewards at the national level and in Maine, which sent a higher percentage of its population to fight in the Civil War than any other northern state. Republicans were identified as the party which had saved the Union. Even many Irish Americans from Maine, registered Democrats when they went to war, came back to vote Republican.

That's also why General Ulysses S. Grant's slogan "Vote the Way You Shot" was so powerful all across the county but resonated much longer and more profoundly in Maine.

The second aspect of Republican dominance had to do with the leadership class. The contrast from today's ethos is profound. The Republican party in Maine during the period 1854 to 1954 was dominated by successful businessmen. Much of the political culture saw a connection between business success and the right to lead politically.

The Republican probusiness values dovetailed with the very leadership who had lived those values and who controlled the banks, the newspapers, the utilities. So for much of the period under review, this ethos continued as it had for almost a hundred years (except for the Depression of the 1930s and some brief eras of intraparty GOP divisions such as 1878 and 1880 and 1910 and 1914).

Third, the nearly 100 years of domination by Republicans in Maine and the prevailing probusiness ethos thus continued a process of self-reinforcement. The Republican party was much stronger, won most of the elections, produced most of the leaders so it kept reinforcing itself by attracting new leaders and more adherents.

The Republicans ended up dominating the political system in the 1940s because there were so many more of them.

Interestingly enough, Maine's Republican domination for much of the hundred years from 1854 until 1954 led to the phrase "As Maine Goes, So Goes the Nation."

This seemed especially to be true when Maine had its general election (until 1960) in September, and if it voted for Republicans and the Republicans won the presidency, the saying sounded good.

In 1936, however, when Maine joined Vermont in being the only state to go Republican in the Presidential race of that year, the Democratic National Chairman James Farley is widely quoted as saying, "As Maine goes, so goes Vermont." Indeed in the presidential elections of 1940, 1944, and 1948, Maine did not predict the outcome of the presidential elections.

In fact, Maine has been wrong in the closest presidential elections since World War II: 1948, 1960, 1968, 1976, and 2000!

On the national scene, at least in terms of the presidency, Democrats were victorious. If this book does nothing else, perhaps it can help to retire that slogan—at least for political races.

In Maine politics, however, the 1940s were an era of complete Republican domination, a domination that would not be seriously threatened until the Muskie Revolution of 1954.

SEMINAL ELECTION:
THE SENATORIAL ELECTION OF 1948

While the senatorial election of 1948 continued the overall pattern of Republican domination, it changed the nature of that dominance and also brought to national prominence the political career of Margaret Chase Smith. During the elections of that year, Margaret Chase Smith defeated three men, one a former governor and popular war hero, another a sitting popular governor plus another candidate, to get to the U.S. Senate. Before she was done with her political career, she had served 24 years as U.S. senator from 1949 until 1973. Coupled with her previous eight years in the House, she served Maine for 32 years.

The 1948 race for the U.S. Senate was both different and seminal. It is the case study to which we now turn as the most important election of the decade of the 1940s.

How did she do it? In some sense, the rough outline of the story of Margaret Chase Smith is well known. A strong-willed, very determined young woman from an impoverished background and childhood, she made herself into a political figure of national reputation. In doing so, she became the first woman to be elected to the United States Senate totally in her own right, not being appointed to fill out the term of a dead husband as other women had been. She then went on to become a respected national figure and served in the Senate until her defeat in 1972. She was also the first woman in Maine political history elected to the U.S. House of Representatives.

But there is so much more to the story of Margaret Chase Smith. Her political campaigns deserve to be studied, not just as models for grassroots organizing techniques and skillful use of campaign dynamics, but for the establishment of campaign dimensions that still dominate the course of Maine politics.

While it is true that many aspects of politics have changed in the last 50 years, especially with the advent of television and the 30-second commercial, the image positioning which she pioneered remains at the very heart of the electoral process in the twenty-first century.

Maine's two women senators, Olympia Snowe and Susan Collins, owe Margaret a debt for being a pioneer and making of Maine a political arena where women are not only fully accepted, but fully expected, and for providing a model of the campaign qua campaign necessary to be successful over time in the Maine arena.

But they are not the only ones who owe her a debt of gratitude for her moderate ideology and consensus coalition building, especially with like-minded Democrats and Independents. She also became the positive model for such male candidates as Bill Cohen, Dave Emery, and Jock McKernan.

It all started simply enough.

The retirement announcement of Republican Senator Wallace White in 1947 produced a rush to enter the Republican primary. The sitting governor, Horace Hildreth, former governor and World War I hero Sumner Sewall, and prominent minister Albion Beverage ended up contesting Second Congressional District Congresswoman Margaret Chase Smith.[1]

Both Hildreth and Sewall were very popular across the state and wealthy to boot. Much of the early Republican political talk of the 1948 election was about which of them would replace Wallace White as senator.

Sewall had been an air ace in World War I and served in the Maine House and Senate, before becoming governor from 1942–1946. Hildreth, a graduate of Bowdoin and Harvard, had been elected governor following Sewall and was the first choice of the Republican State Committee Chair, Alan Bird. The third candidate, Albion Beverage, a graduate of Bates and Bangor Theological Seminar, was less well known but still formidable.

But Margaret Chase Smith had other ideas. On Sunday, June 1, 1947, she announced that she would seek White's senate seat. Margaret was determined to move up the political ladder and to disprove the notion that "the Senate is no place for a woman." Her previous statewide activities and appearances helped her in terms of name recognition. This early, even precipitous announcement caught many party leaders off balance and gave Margaret some initial momentum and advantage.

Her early announcement also caught her potential opponents off guard. This was just as well for her, because in 1948, Smith was not the choice of the Republican Party establishment in the state.[2]

In fact, Maine's other Republican Senator, Owen Brewster, actively opposed her as did much of the state party apparatus.

However, William "Bill" Lewis, her close confidant since 1953 who would become her administrative assistant in 1949, had become an excellent campaign manager and her alter ego in some of her previous Congressional campaigns. He was now about to extrapolate his campaign expertise onto the broader, statewide canvas. He would also support her financially in 1948.

Lewis and Smith had built on her husband's extensive list of supporters and had added to that list for the past seven years. Margaret had a de facto statewide organization devoted to her personally as opposed to the Republican Party per se. True to her congressional campaign style, Margaret announced early, sending out letters on January 1, 1948, to her supporters and asking for help getting petition signatures.

The 1948 campaign also saw the first truly statewide direct mail effort with the Smith campaign sending postcards to various groups and organizations at strategic points in the campaign. This began a trend of "direct mail" whereby a particular candidate would target specific interest groups and send them a specially tailored message.

The "penny postcard" over the years would turn into a regular first class letter and modern candidates would spend hundreds of thousands of dollars in each election cycle to mail to dozens of interest groups as well as activists in their own party and their personal supporters.

As she toured Maine, Smith constantly reminded people of her stature both in Washington and across the nation and was diligent in seeking relief for Maine's natural disaster of 1947, the extensive forest fires that ravaged the state.[3] She also ran a grueling campaign schedule with fierce determination.

When she fell on some ice on February 13, 1948, and fractured her right elbow, she continued campaigning that day and night with a cast, not even taking a day off to recuperate. She was the hardest working candidate on the Maine political scene until the first congressional run of Bill Cohen in 1972 and both of them stand at the apex of Republican candidate efforts "on the ground" for the postwar period.

Remember too that all this campaigning was done under her self-inflicted prohibition of never missing a vote in the U.S. House of Representatives. Imagine her state of exhaustion after coming to Maine for the weekend, campaigning through several 18-hour days and then falling exhausted onto the night train to Washington from Waterville so she would arrive back in Congress for the first roll call of the new week and doing this weekend after weekend, month in and month out.[4]

This hard work and fierce determination to get every last vote did not come to Margaret in 1948. It was formed eight years earlier in the critical year of 1940 when her husband, Congressman Clyde Smith, died of a heart attack in April. Immediately following the service for him in Washington, she headed back to Maine and began campaigning in earnest for his seat.

Clyde Smith had been a popular if somewhat reluctant Congressman. An excellent campaigner and very successful as a politician in Maine, he would have much preferred to become governor but the Republican leadership pushed him toward the 2nd CD nomination.

At that time, Maine's 2nd CD was not as large as it is now and was composed of the counties of Somerset, Franklin, Waldo, Knox, Lincoln, Kennebec, and Androscoggin. Elected in 1936 and again in 1938 by comfortable margins, Clyde never really enjoyed Washington and had to be persuaded to run again after he suffered his first heart attack.

For her part, Margaret loved his first campaigns and she loved Washington and insisted on going there to run his office even though he may have preferred her to stay in Maine. She thrived on the political, organizational side of politics and when Clyde suffered his fatal heart attack, Margaret jumped into the race.

What followed can only be described as a whirlwind of activity. Campaigning at a breakneck speed, Margaret often put in 12-, 15-, even 18-hour days, crisscrossing the district from one end to the other. Her persistence paid off and in the May 13, 1940 special primary election, she defeated Frederick P. Bonney with more than 90 percent of the vote.

The Democratic nominee, Edward Beauchamp, chose not to contest the special general election in order to concentrate his efforts on the regular general election which was less than four months away, so Margaret was elected to fill out the remainder of Clyde's term.

But in addition to her Washington duties, she now had to continue campaigning since the regular Republican primary was in June. Here she faced much tougher opposition, being challenged by Bonney, John Marshall, Hodgdon Buzzell, and Arthur Lancaster. Again she triumphed, this time with nearly 64 percent of the vote.

In the September general election, she handily defeated the formidable former Lewiston (the largest urban area of the district) mayor Beauchamp 65 percent to 35 percent.

This was one of the most incredible six-month periods in Maine political history. In the space of that short time span, Margaret Chase Smith entered and won four congressional elections! She won the Republican nomination for Congress in the special election of 1940 and she won the special general election for Congress to fill out the remainder of Clyde's term. Then she won the Republican nomination for the regular 1940 congressional term in June and finally won the general election for Congress in Maine's Second Congressional District in September 1940. This accomplishment is unparalleled and unequalled in the last 60 years of Maine politics.

But the Republican Party establishment never really warmed up to Margaret. Her feisty, independent mindset and her (often justified) suspicion of their motives did not make for cordiality and cooperation. Nevertheless, the Republican establishment couldn't do much about her in the 2nd District, but once she challenged for the statewide senate seat, she became fair game.

Margaret's approach to her gender is worth noting here (and in the next section) for she used it to her advantage in both her congressional and Senate races in what we would today call a reverse spin. Although never a feminist (in the late twentieth century use of that term), Smith was still smart enough to appeal to women who in 1948 made up the majority of voters. She made a point of saying she was not asking for special treatment (and seldom was), but in not asking for support on the basis of her sex, she shrewdly underscored its very nature. This was one smart lady!

Such prominent groups as the Women's Christian Temperance Union backed her. The Daughters of the Revolution (DAR), while technically nonpartisan, also gave her a prominent award. She was fond of emphasizing her sex but appealed to voters by both mentioning it and downplaying it at the same time.

Even to our jaded twenty-first century ears, the following rings powerful and true as a positive positioning statement:

"I am proud to be a woman but I want it distinctly understood that I am not soliciting support because I am a woman. I solicit your support wholly on the basis of my record of eight years in Congress."[5]

Of course the more she said she didn't want support just because she was a woman, the more support she got. Although we don't have polling to know whether she was ever very far behind the popular governor

Horace Hildreth, we assume she was because he had been elected on a statewide basis and she had had only 1/3 of the state vote for her, only one CD out of three.

Influenced heavily by organizational efforts, however, the Smith forces showed that they were a force to be reckoned with as they turned in 25,000 names to get her on the ballot, well above the 3,600 necessary.[6]

Margaret Chase Smith ran a highly effective campaign and used ill-conceived attacks on her as a woman to her advantage. She really was able to have things come together in terms of image. She was a woman who appealed to many women by who she was and to many men by what she said and she was very skillful and careful about maintaining her image.

She was not deterred by the opposition to her candidacy and Margaret actually turned out to be one of those political figures who thrived on opposition and conflict. They didn't rattle her; they simply made her work harder.[7]

And work hard she did.

Over the years, Maine voters have always distinguished the characteristics and images of those who were representatives and those who were senators, expecting broader, bolder images for the latter. Margaret Chase Smith and Bill Lewis were very good at creating and maintaining a positive, forceful, "national" image.

Smith had no polling or focus groups to tell her this. She and Lewis simply believed it. Her spring trip to wartorn Europe suggested that she was already a "world" figure. She had a very useful knack of projecting herself onto the national stage: she went out and did things and made sure the national press covered her. She was always good for a strong quote and she was very adroit at fitting herself into a story as both a thinking woman and an authority figure. Smith also had a true politician's gift of listening to people she met and paying attention to their observations and concerns. She was always careful to respond to voters by return mail.

She also was, by the standards of the day, more "liberal" than her Republican opponents (almost always getting the endorsement of the American Federation of Labor [AFL]) but by the same token, her Republican credentials were strong as evidenced by her strong endorsements from the tough Republican Speaker of the U.S. House, Joe Martin.

This blurring of images and their concomitant combinations of appeal were a very important aspect of her success, long before polling and focus groups and political consultants would speak of "triangulation" and other techniques of broadening support. Her statement, for example, on whether she was prolabor or promanagement was a classic:

"The Public comes first. My voting record on labor legislation has been 100 percent for the public, rather than exclusively for either Labor or Management."[8]

One needs to always remember that Margaret came from a working class background and retained her concern for the working men and women of her district and later the state. Also, her support in heavily Democratic Androscoggin County shows that blue collar, Franco American voters appreciated that concern. Christened in the Roman Catholic church in Skowhegan, Smith was raised as a Protestant; one of her grandfathers was a Protestant minister.

Also, she played on an important dimension, her national stature. This may have been her most enduring legacy. Major Maine senators, from 1948 to present, from Ed Muskie through Bill Cohen and George Mitchell, Olympia Snowe and Susan Collins, are expected to play national roles. They are expected to "stand out in Washington." Curiously, they are not expected—as are other senators from such states as West Virginia or Mississippi—to be always looking for political pork to bring back to their state. They are expected to look out for the national interest and actually put that interest above state parochial interests.

Of course, Maine people like the best of both worlds when Maine senators can be national figures for a strong defense while at the same time ensuring that such facilities as the Portsmouth/Kittery Naval Shipyard or the Bath Iron Works get lots of national contracts.

In Margaret's recollections, the key to the 1948 election was the speech she gave to the Somerset County Republican Women's Club on May 21, 1948. She called it "the most crucial political speech I have given."[9] A month before, she had been sent a copy of an anonymous sheet of charges purporting to be her voting record and charging her with being pro-communist and anti-Republican.

The distortion of her record was set in the broader context of many personal attacks and smears. Her early relationship with Clyde Smith, her morals, her trips with military personnel, her self-promotion, were all singled out in a concerted whispering—and later, overt—negative campaign against her.

To the political charges, Margaret had wanted to respond immediately, but her campaign manager and close confidant Bill Lewis urged her to wait, believing the charges were coming from the Hildreth camp and that the wider they were disseminated the greater would be the backlash when they were exposed. This is very different from the way campaigns respond now—by fax and immediately before the next news cycle. Lewis even put up a map and added pins wherever the charges surfaced.

The material got wide circulation. The political writer for the *Bangor Daily News*, Lorin Arnold, quoted from the sheet and suggested that a politician's voting record was fair game, implying this was an accurate summary of it. By contrast, the *Portland Press Herald* continued to give Margaret superb coverage. This is another difference from today's campaigns. Now newspaper coverage of visits and position papers is extremely limited and it is very hard for candidates to "make news" unless it is by mistakes and foul-ups.

Lewis then felt the time had come for a rebuttal saying: "A home county audience will love to hear their daughter defend herself and rip into the smearers."[10] Carefully, with almost excruciating detail, Margaret demonstrated that all the charges were false, pointing out that the sheet had used only 71 of her 1,500 votes and even then had the math wrong.

Margaret then went on to cite the strong backing she had from Washington establishment Republicans and how they had voted with her. "If he had tried any harder, I concluded, this smear writer could not have picked better instances to show how the Republican Leaders voted the same way I did. It is no wonder that he was too ashamed and afraid to put his name on the smear sheet."[11]

According to General Lewis, this was the turning point in the campaign with many outraged voters coming up and saying they were switching their vote to Margaret and for all intents and purposes, the election was over a month before it was held. Because she had refuted the charges so impressively, no future charges could gain traction. "Margaret Smith's Answer" became part of the organizational kit that Lewis sent her local committees.

Margaret also got a good deal of very positive national press attention as the campaign wound down. On the eve of the Republican primary, for example, *Parade* ran an extremely flattering portrait of her entitled "The Lady from Maine."[12]

The *Parade* article called Margaret "trim, vigorous" and told readers she had been a member of the important House Armed Services Committee and during the war as "the only woman member of the naval committee" had toured the Pacific battle area and was "the first woman ever to sail on a U.S. destroyer in wartime." No candidate could ever ask for a more flattering portrait in the national media.

She also had her "last minute" radio address on June 20, 1948. She reframed the debate. She answered all criticisms, real and imaginary; she dominated the end of the campaign. Now from modern polling, we know that most elections are decided much earlier than the last night or the last weekend.

Nevertheless, her finishing on a strong note prevented any slippage and again focused people's attention on the *centrality of her candidacy*.

She ended up winning a majority of the votes (52 percent) in the Republican primary. On June 21, she received 63,786 voters, more than all her opponents combined. She won outright 13 of Maine's 16 counties, losing only Aroostook and Hancock to Hildreth and Sagadahoc to Sewall: The final tallies

Smith	63,786
Hildreth	30,949
Sewall	21,768
Beverage	6,399

And of great relevance for her general election chances, Smith ran up impressive margins among Republican voters in the working class Franco American areas. This showing presaged her very strong showing (for a Republican) in such Democratic bastions as Lewiston, Westbrook, Waterville, Sanford, and Saco. Saco, then as now, the best indicator of statewide support, gave more votes to Smith than to all her competitors combined.

But Margaret took none of this for granted and never stopped campaigning as she entered the general election phase of 1948. Although Republican enrollment figures favored her, she continued to canvass the entire state, working long and hard hours.

Her opponent, Adrian Scolten, a Portland dermatologist, had run unopposed. He ran a lackluster campaign that seemed at a loss for both issues and spark. The momentum Smith had developed in her crushing primary victory simply continued unabated through the general election. Lacking funds, cutting issues, and much in the way of name recognition, Scolten ran an epigonic, almost distant campaign. But Smith ran as if it were a very close election, keeping up the pressure and grueling schedule right up to the election.

Three months later, Smith demolished Scolten 159,182 (71 percent) to 64,074 (29 percent). She was on her way to becoming a true American legend. She summed up her feelings when she won: "I'm happy, I'm honored, I'm humble."[13] Her convincing victory was the largest senate margin run up in Maine until George Mitchell defeated Jasper Wyman in 1988 81 percent to 19 percent.

WHAT WERE THE KEYS TO VICTORY IN THIS ELECTION?

1. Her skillful treatment of "the woman's issue." She made any attack on her gender appear to be an attack on all women. She claimed no special status for herself based on her sex, but she insisted that her sex should not disqualify her from any political position.

2. Her hard work on the campaign trail. No candidate, male or female, in Maine political history ever worked harder or longer hours to achieve her or his political position.
3. Her excellent positioning on the issues. Her record became her defense. She turned attacks on her record around. Her campaign brochure defined her: strong on national defense, against higher taxes, a voting record "100 percent for the public, rather than exclusively for either Labor or Management," strong on education and housing, and very strong for social security and old age assistance, yet against "socialized medicine."
4. She was the Republican with a heart, a Republican with a blue collar background who understood working men and women and their plight and she was also against higher taxes, for more "efficiency" in government. Her blue collar background was crucial to her natural and political positioning. She was a woman of the people and had shared their concerns and poverty.
5. Her national exposure and press. After announcing she would cover the entire state of Maine within six to eight months, Margaret went on a European Inspection trip with the House Armed Services Committee. Political junkets now are common place for Maine politicians but then they were rare. To go to wartorn Europe and return with new knowledge made her in great demand as a speaker when she returned. She had projected herself onto the international stage, again, something we expect senators to do.
6. Her skilled use of imagery to reinforce her candidacy. Today candidates basically use television. She had to use print. This media is more difficult to control and develop. It takes a long time to cultivate reporters and they need constant "stroking" to keep them happy. It is much easier nowadays to simply project your own imagery on the television screen and control it absolutely.

    There are, for example, different images in the voters' minds for House, Governor, and Senate. Senators are seen as more independent, more worldly, more exposed to international relations, larger in stature than their counterparts as congresspeople.

    Bill Lewis should get a good deal of campaign credit for coming up with the idea for this effort; it paid off handsomely on the campaign trail. Margaret skillfully fitted herself into the national and independent image Maine people wanted for their senator.
7. Her positioning of herself as the underdog. We don't have solid polling data to support this claim, but it is unlikely she was ever very far behind—if behind at all—in any of her general elections and perhaps only behind in the early stages of the Republican primary of 1940 and again in 1948.

8. Her use of negative campaigning by her opponents to her advantage. She made her opponents appear to be underhanded, dishonest, and wrong. "Smears" later became any charges against her but that should not obscure the fact that there were a lot of genuine smears against her. For example, she had not broken up Clyde Smith's first marriage; he was divorced before she met him. But when her opponents charged this was true, she let it run until her opponents were associated with it, then and only then did she discredit the story by indicating she hadn't even known Smith until after his divorce.

9. Her use of her personal grassroots organization to counter Republican Party regular opposition to her candidacy. All Margaret's elections became a contest between "her people" and those of the Republican insider establishment. It was a "friendship chain" which any politician would envy. All candidates have a "personal following" which transcend gender, party, and the like, but Margaret made it into an art form. In 1974, James B. Longley and, in 1994, Angus King, followed directly in her footsteps by creating personal followings among Republicans, Democrats, and Independents to get elected.

10. She was a woman of accomplishments and she was skillful in displaying them prominently. Her campaign pamphlet for the 1948 Senate race, for example, says it all: "Don't Trade A Record for A Promise" and "The 'Can-Do' Candidate with the 'Can-did' Record."

    Today any political or media consultant would be pleased to come up with one such powerful slogan, let alone the two she ran on.

11. Most important of all, she made herself the centerpiece of the election. She dominated the election by being at its center and heart. She was, of course, aided by the fact that she was running against three men, but the popular governor Hildreth had all the power of statewide incumbency and should have been able to make this a referendum on his popularity.

    Margaret did not allow that to happen. She made herself the central issue. She made herself the ballot measure question to be decided. Was Margaret Chase Smith ready for and did she have enough stature for the U.S. Senate?

    Framed that way, the answer was yes so the election had to come out the way it did, once she became the central issue and answered these questions herself.

12. It must be added that her opponents helped in her victory. In politics, winners usually get more credit than they deserve and losers less but in this case the Republican "big men" helped her enor-

mously. Their basic strategy was flawed. Their tactics backfired. They concentrated on the wrong issue. By making her the issue, they gave her the chance to define what the election was going to be about.

13. Smith's use of campaign funds in 1948 was unique in her career. I am greatly indebted to Greg Gallant of the Margaret Chase Smith Library for pointing this out. In her runs for Congress, Margaret Chase Smith always made a point of not taking individual contributions to her campaign. And after 1948, she would revert to this pattern again.

According to Gallant, however, in 1948, Smith and General Lewis recognized that the senate race was different and if she were going to compete at that level, against all the opposition she faced, she would have to take personal contributions. He believes that Smith's contacts made through her service on the House Armed Services Committee put her in close contact with four important and well-to-do Princeton graduates who saw her promise.

Bernard Baruch and three classmates from Princeton University's class of 1913, including Wall Street financier Ferdinand Eberstadt, Secretary of Navy James Forrestal, and Clifford Carver, co-founder of the Penobscot Marine Museum, all came to support Smith's campaign financially in 1948 with Carver becoming her finance chair.

Gallant's point is that for this election and this election alone, Smith and Lewis recognized that they needed additional funds if they were to compete at the senate level against well-heeled and credible foes. Their strategy worked! The irony, of course, is that while this strategy was successful in 1948, when Smith was faced with her very formidable challenge from Congressman Bill Hathaway almost thirty years later, they did not return to that strategy.

WHAT IMPACT DID THIS
ELECTION HAVE ON MAINE POLITICS?

This 1948 Republican senatorial primary and subsequent September general election ended up being a very important watershed in Maine politics.

1. Most obvious, Margaret Chase Smith was the first woman in Maine and in the United States to run for the Senate "on her own," that is for a seat not previously held by her husband, and win.

She was also a new breed of Republican. Her reduced partisanship was seen in the voting records; where White and Brewster voted with their fellow Republicans 95 percent of the time, Smith came in at 75 percent.[14]

In the process, she became a powerful role model for young women all over America but especially in Maine. Both present U.S. senators, Olympia Snowe (1995 to the present) and Susan Collins (1997 to the present), grew up while she was a senator and both acknowledge her presence as a powerful image of what a woman could become on her own. Other women of both parties saw her as someone who had accomplished much on her own and without powerful backers or moneyed interests.

2. And less obvious, for in politics like art, context means a lot, she was a particular kind of Republican. While the Republican Party in Maine has traditionally been less conservative than Republican parties in other parts of the country such as the South or West, the center of Maine's Republican Party in 1948 was more conservative than Smith and her victory was to set an enduring pattern that remains in Maine—and other New England states—today. The major Republican officeholders are judged moderate as well as independent.

   She positioned herself and stayed "on message," as we would say today. "Each of us symbolizes something to Maine voters. My supporters say I am a symbol of a 'grass-roots' protest against political machines, money politics, and smears."[15]

3. And even less obvious to historians and commentators of the time, Margaret Chase Smith put together a campaign of personal following. She did not rely on Republican Party stalwarts in each and every town (many of them opposed her), but she worked hard to create her own following of Republicans, Democrats, and Independents. As Paul Mills points out, it was often asserted that there were three political parties in Maine during her era, Republican, Democrat, and "the Margaret Chase Smith people."

   This personalized style of campaign organization had occurred before but never to the extent she developed in the 1948 senate race. This "personal following" approach was to become a model for successful Republican candidates later in the century.

   Stan Tupper, Bill Cohen, Dave Emery, Jock McKernan, Olympia Snowe, and Susan Collins all ended up having personal campaign organizations rather than strictly Republican campaign organizations and Margaret was their model.

   This meant that as Republican Party enrollments shrunk, especially relative to the growth of Democratic Party enrollments, those candidates who adopted her model were less likely to suffer defeat and indeed, with the exception of Dave Emery and Susan Collins, none of the others ever lost a race. This was not by chance.

4. Margaret Chase Smith's 1948 run for the U.S. Senate also introduced some campaign techniques that were ahead of their time. For example, although today every serious candidate uses direct mail to tell groups of voters issue specifics of their positions, Margaret's campaign manager, Bill Lewis, was the first in modern Maine politics to pioneer the widespread use of this technique of targeted mailings. Previous Republican candidates had used mass mailings but these were seldom targeted to specific interest groups.

5. Her use of the electronic media (first radio and later, after 1954, television) foreshadowed the modern era as well. While it is true that she never used the 30-second commercial that is such a staple of the end of the century, she did adopt a very effective "end of the campaign" radio (later television) effort the night or the weekend before the election. She would purchase a half-hour of air time and speak to summarize her campaign efforts and, not incidentally, to brand any and all attacks on her as "smears."

   This technique enabled her to have the last word and turn any negative attacks on her to her advantage by categorizing them as "smears." No matter how legitimate the criticism, her labeling them as "smears" gave her the political high road. Since she mixed in refutable smears with irrefutable smears, she was able to paint her opponents with an effective negative brush stroke of her own.

6. Nobody in Maine politics—before or since—has been able to capitalize on negative attack as well as she. Her refutations of "smears" and her ability to turn attacks upon her to attacks upon her opponents are classics even fifty years later.

   To our ears today (and even in 1972), of course, some of this seems a bit heavy handed, old, and even querulous, but I believe that is because we are used to seeing much slicker television commercials, not because her half hours were less effective. We must remember that in 1948, television was a very new medium and most candidates did not know how to use it at all and many simply didn't see its potential. Margaret and Bill Lewis did and their early pioneering efforts in this media paid big dividends.

7. She really set a high national standard for Maine political figures, especially the women who were to follow in her footsteps. As Alice Fleming has so aptly put it, "Perhaps someday in the not too distant future, the United States will elect a woman President. When it does, Margaret Chase Smith will have the satisfaction of knowing that she was the one who led the way."[16]

3

The 1950s:

Edmund S. Muskie vs. Burton M. Cross

THE DECADE'S MATRIX

The 1950s began as the 1940s had proceeded, with complete Republican domination of the electoral process for the major political positions in the state. In fact, there was little on the political horizon to give Republicans pause. They dominated the landscape and expected to continue to do so. But the 1950s were to be a very different decade from the 1940s. Republican hegemony at the top of the ticket was to be challenged and, by the end of the 1950s, nearly totally defeated and in vast disarray.

There were few warning signs early in the decade, however, as the election cycle of 1950 continued to show Republican strength and Democrat weakness.

In 1950, incumbent Fred Payne defeated Leland Currier in the Republican primary for governor 62 percent to 38 percent and in the general election the Democrat Earl Grant and Leland Currier, this time running as a States' Rights Democrat. Payne received 60 percent of the vote to Grant's 39 percent and Currier's less than 1 percent.

In Maine's 1st CD, Robert Hale defeated Ray Stetson in the Republican primary 81 percent to 19 percent while Lucia M. Cormier won the Democratic primary with 71 percent over her opponent, Adrian Scolten. The general election saw the Republican Hale defeating Cormier 54 percent to 46 percent.

In the 2nd, and less Republican, CD, Charles Nelson was unopposed in the Republican primary while John Maloney got 77 percent in the Democratic primary as he defeated John Fortunato (17 percent) and A. M. Chiaravalloti (6 percent). Nelson, the Republican, captured the general election 58 percent to 42 percent.

Maine's 3rd CD, the so-called Bangor and Aroostook district, saw both
Frank Fellows the Republican and John Keenan the Democrat unopposed
in their party primaries with Fellows getting 63 percent of the general
vote to 37 percent for Keenan.

A special referendum in 1951 established the principle that direct initiative petitions needed to have at least 10 percent of the previous gubernatorial vote in order to go to the voters. This relatively low threshold for
ballot measure requirements was to have a profound effect on the political system of Maine in the future. By the 1990s, Maine had become a political system in which virtually every election cycle saw referenda of one
type or another.

The elections of 1952, while sustaining Republican dominance, contained in them significant seeds of change, change that would become
revolutionary in terms of a resurgence of the Democratic Party under the
leadership of Edmund S. Muskie.

In the 1952 race for governor, Senate President Burton M. Cross received 40 percent of the vote in the Republican primary compared with
Leroy Hussey's 32 percent and Neil Bishop's 27 percent. James Oliver,
who had served from 1937 to 1943 as GOP Congressman from the 1st CD
but was now a Democrat, was unopposed in his primary.

That fall, Cross received 51 percent of the votes for governor, defeating
Oliver (33 percent) but with Neil Bishop running as an Independent Republican getting 14 percent and Henry Bayker, an Independent, getting
less than 1 percent. Cross's thin majority and the continuing opposition of
Bishop both helped to set the stage for Edmund Muskie's eventual triumph in 1954. Neil Bishop was eventually to head up a strong "Republicans for Muskie" contingent in 1954 at a time when the Republican registration advantage was overwhelming. As we shall see in the concluding
section, it is instructive that Bishop's 35,000 votes received in the general
election of 1952 exceeded Muskie's 22,000 vote margin in 1954.

The 1952 race for U.S. Senate saw Governor Fred Payne win a close Republican primary over incumbent Owen Brewster (51 percent to 49 percent) while Roger Dube won the Democratic primary over Earl S. Grant
57 percent to 43 percent. Republican dominance continued in the general
election with Payne getting 59 percent of the vote to Dube's 35 percent
while Grant, running now as an Independent, received 6 percent.

The 1st CD again saw the strength of Robert Hale. He was unopposed
in the Republican primary and received 62 percent of the vote in the general election defeating his Democratic opponent, James A. McVicar.
McVicar, in turn, had defeated Adrian Scolten in the Democratic primary
62 percent to 38 percent.

The 2nd CD had the incumbent Charles Nelson unopposed in the Republican primary while Leland B. Currier received 59 percent of the vote

in the Democratic primary compared with A. M. Chiaravalloti who received 41 percent. Nelson was reelected over Currier with a comfortable margin of 67 percent to 33 percent.

The 3rd CD saw an unopposed Clifford McIntire and an unopposed Philip Sharpe contest the general election with the Republican McIntire getting 76 percent of that vote to 24 percent for Sharpe.

So after the first two election cycles of the 1950s, the Republican domination continued to be significant with Republicans having won all the elections held in 1950 and 1952.

But that pattern was about to be broken. A Rumford, Maine, native, Edmund S. Muskie, who had lost a 1947 race for Waterville mayor and who had served in the Maine legislature, was about to make a landmark in modern Maine history. He would run for governor and be the first Democrat since the Great Depression to be elected.

In the section at the end of the chapter on important elections, we will be focusing on the gubernatorial contest of 1954 but here, the bare outlines must suffice. It should also be noted that in 1953, the first TV station, WPMT Channel 53 came to Portland. Although WPMT soon went off the air, WCSH Channel 6 followed and was more successful. The next year, Channel 13, WGAN, and Channel 8, WMTV, came on the air. Maine's television age had begun.

Burton Cross, the Republican incumbent governor, was unopposed in his primary as was Muskie in his. In the general election, Muskie received 54.5 percent of the vote Cross's 45.5 percent. Muskie had begun an electoral revolution and would eventually lead the Democratic Party to parity with the Republicans and later, in the 1960s, hegemony over them. Much of this lay in the future, however, for Muskie's breakthrough election in 1954, while it made some other contests closer, did not break Republican control over the other offices.

In the 1954 Republican primary for U.S. Senate, Margaret Chase Smith easily defeated Robert Jones 83 percent to 17 percent. Paul Fullam, her Democratic opponent in the general election, was unopposed in his primary. She handily defeated Fullam in the fall 59 percent to 41 percent.

1st District CD races in 1954 were widely contested. Incumbent Robert Hale defeated J. Horace McClure and Ray Stetson in the Republican primary, getting 79 percent of the vote compared to 15 percent for McClure and 6 percent for Stetson. The Democratic primary saw James Oliver defeat Eli Gaudet 53.5 percent to 46.5 percent while in the general election, Hale narrowly defeated Oliver 52 percent to 48 percent.

Maine's 2nd CD was less contentious. Both Charles Nelson the Republican incumbent and Thomas Delahanty the Democrat were unopposed in their primaries, with Nelson defeating Delahanty in the fall 54 percent to 46 percent.

In Maine's 3rd CD, Clifford McIntire was again unopposed in the Republican primary as was Kenneth Colbath in the Democratic contest, McIntire being reelected 60.5 percent to 39.5 percent in the general election.

The year 1956 was to be a real watershed year in Maine politics. Obviously the Muskie election of 1954 could either be a one-time Democratic triumph in a Republican string of victories or it could be the beginning of a major trend. Previous Democratic governors in the twentieth century had been unable to institutionalize their success, either for themselves or for other Democrats, so the question did not have a ready or simple answer.

But Edmund S. Muskie was no ordinary Democrat. He was a party builder, an inspirer, a leader, and he proved it not only in 1954 but in 1956 as well.

Republicans were very anxious to defeat him and three candidates vied for the honor with Willis "Bill" A. Trafton (51 percent) defeating Philip Chapman (29 percent) and Alexander LaFleur (20 percent) for that honor but Muskie easily won reelection in 1956, getting 59 percent to Trafton's 41 percent.

Republicans maintained their hold on two of Maine's CDs, the 1st and the 3rd, but just barely in the 1st.

In Maine's 3rd CD, Clifford McIntire the incumbent and Kenneth Colbath, his Democratic challenger, were unopposed in their primaries, with McIntire winning reelection easily, 61 percent to 39 percent.

The 1st CD turned out to be the closest race of the postwar period. There, Robert Hale the incumbent (51 percent) fought off both James Day (38 percent) and William Veazie (10 percent) to capture the Republican primary but he was reelected over James Oliver by less than 1 percent in the general election after Oliver (56 percent) defeated Owen Hancock (25 percent) and Adrian Scolten (19 percent). Hale's margin of 29 votes set a record as the lowest vote differential in modern Maine politics and presaged Oliver's eventual triumph in congressional politics as a Democrat.

But it was in the 2nd CD that the Muskie revolution was first and formally institutionalized as Frank Coffin—Muskie supporter, confidant, and protégé as well as the party chair—defeated Roger Dube in the Democratic primary, getting 70 percent of the vote to Dube's 30 percent. On the Republican side, James Reid defeated Neil Bishop 61 percent to 39 percent as Bishop returned to the political fray after his initial support of Ed Muskie in 1954. A weakened Reid then lost a close vote to Frank Coffin, 53 percent to 47 percent.[1] The Democratic Party was on its way to true viability in the modern era as the Muskie revolution energized party faithful from one end of the state to the other.

The next year, 1957, saw two important ballot measures pass. In the first, the date of Maine's general election was changed from September to November, by a vote of 64 percent to 36 percent, and the term of governor was extended from two years to four, by a vote of 59 percent to 41 percent.

In 1958, having served two terms as governor and with his eye on the U.S. Senate, Muskie chose not to seek reelection and the open governorship was very attractive to Republicans and important to the Democrats to increase their sense of momentum. The Democrats prevailed.

Horace A. Hildreth, owner of several TV stations, successfully held off Philip Chapman in the Republican primary 62 percent to 38 percent and then went down to defeat at the hands of Clinton Clauson 52 percent to 48 percent. Clauson had earlier bested his Democratic primary opponent, Maynard Dolloff, 52 percent to 48 percent. The Muskie legacy continued.

The 1958 senatorial race saw the incumbent U.S. Senator Fred Payne defeating his Republican primary opponent, Herman Sahagian, 84 percent to 16 percent while Muskie was unopposed in the Democratic primary. In the general election, Muskie rather easily defeated Payne, despite his incumbent status, 61 percent to 39 percent.

Maine's 1st CD saw the triumph of James Oliver. Oliver, who had been a Republican congressman and subsequently became a Democrat, had already tried several times to be elected as a Democrat and 1958 proved to be his year. First, he defeated Bowdoin's football coach, Adam Walsh, 64 percent to 36 percent. Then, after Robert Hale had defeated two Republican primary opponents, Peter A. Garland (32 percent) and George E. Curtis (30 percent), with 40 percent of the vote, Oliver defeated Hale 52 percent to 48 percent.

Frank Coffin easily achieved reelection, going unchallenged in the primary and defeating Neil Bishop 61 percent to 39 percent in the general election after Bishop had dispatched Elwin Sharpe in the Republican primary 66 percent to 34 percent.

In Maine's 3rd CD, incumbent Clifford McIntire and his Democratic challenger, Gerald Grady, were unopposed in their respective primaries, and in the general election, McIntire won 56 percent to 44 percent.

The 1950s had been a decade of enormous change. Maine had moved into the national mainstream in terms of the timing of its elections and the Ed Muskie revolution had made Democrats competitive for the first time since the Great Depression. By decade's end, they controlled one U.S. Senate seat, the governorship, and two of the three congressional seats.

In fact, in the space of six short years, they had moved from a position of weakness and defeat to one of emerging dominance. Overall, the Republicans had won 16 of 23 major races but the Democrats had won 7 out of the last 14 in the 1950s.

How to Explain the Changes of the 1950s?

In some fundamental sense, Maine entered the national mainstream. Changes included making the chief executive position a four-year term, a big rise in Democratic enrollment and corresponding grassroots efforts, and the widespread use of TV as a medium—especially after Muskie's successful use of it in 1954.

For these reasons alone, the 1954 gubernatorial election becomes the most important contest of the decade, meriting a closer look on our part. It occurred during "the year of the hurricane" when Maine was struck by one hurricane (Carol) in August and another (Edna) just prior to election day in September.

SEMINAL ELECTION:
THE 1954 GUBERNATORIAL ELECTION

Born in Rumford, Maine, in 1914, Edmund Sixtus Muskie grew up in a six-family house in that somewhat grim mill town. His father was a Polish born tailor who changed his name from Marciszewski to Muskie when he emigrated to America to escape military service in the Czarist armies. He was respected but of modest means.

Muskie's childhood on the banks of the Androscoggin River, so polluted that it was black with lignin, often covered with foam, and smelled very bad, produced in him a lifelong interest in improving the environment. Concern for the environment, an appreciation of the value of education, and a strong national defense were to be important components of the Muskie agenda.

By all accounts, he was a quiet, thoughtful boy who read and studied a lot but who also played basketball and ran track. Muskie graduated from Rumford's Stephens High in 1932 and went to Bates College on a scholarship at the height of the Depression. Muskie worked hard, became class president, and made Phi Beta Kappa, graduating in 1936 before going on to Cornell University law school, again on a scholarship.

Muskie settled in Waterville in 1940 before joining the U.S. Navy in 1942. He served on various ships, including the destroyer escort the *USS Brackett*, in both the Atlantic and Pacific theatres. After the war, he returned to Waterville to practice law, later (1948) marrying Jane Gray with whom he would have five children.[2] For political insiders, the fact that she was both a Republican and a Protestant before she met him and that Muskie converted her on both counts suggests his early powers of persuasion!

In 1946, Muskie ran for the state legislature as a Democrat. Before his next legislative race in 1948, Muskie also ran for mayor of Waterville in

1947. This race was to be Muskie's only political loss in Maine, as he was defeated by Russell M. Squire, the popular proprietor of a women's clothing store. Reelected to the Maine House in 1948, he became Minority Leader among the small (1/6 of the members) Democratic contingent.

When party activists urged him to run for governor in 1954, Muskie only agreed after failing to get any other candidates to run. And Muskie ran primarily to help build up the party rather than with a reasonable expectation that he would be elected.[3] Muskie's low expectations seemed well grounded in reality. After all, the Republicans held a 260,000 to 99,000 registration advantage over the Democrats. Indeed, of all Maine's counties, only Androscoggin had a small Democratic plurality. The remainder were solidly Republican, including some like Hancock and Washington, with 4–6 to 1 Republican majorities.

Much has been written about the sitting governor Republican Burton Cross and his image problems during the 1954 campaign but Cross's frame of reference in that year reinforced his basic notion that he would be reelected. Cross was an archetypal Republican businessman. A successful florist, he worked his way through the Republican Party inner workings, becoming a state senator and then president of the Senate.[4]

This businessman into politician was a time-honored path for electoral success. Republican businessmen were thought to be better prepared than their Democratic counterparts for political leadership and Cross fit that pattern exactly.

Also, until 1954, Cross had never lost an election. His eventual defeat at the hands of Muskie was due to a number of factors, not many of which were apparent when the campaign began. In fact, there were many reasons why Cross could reasonably assume he would be given a second term by the people of Maine:

First, there was the huge Republican registration advantage. With 260,000 Republicans and only 99,000 Democrats, Cross certainly could look on the campaign basic matrix as being in his favor.

Second, no governor in the modern history of Maine had ever been denied a second term. Only in 1910 and 1914 in the twentieth century had sitting governors been voted out of office in a general election although Milliken was denied renomination to a third term in the 1920 primary.

Third, although regarded even by friends as somewhat cold and aloof, he was an able administrator. "He carved an impressive, progressive record overshadowed only by his ineptness in public relations."[5] Even the (then) staunchly Republican *Portland Press Herald* criticized the hamhanded way he ran his campaign, especially when he refused to debate Muskie during the campaign.

Fourth, unlike the first time he ran for governor, Cross was unopposed for the Republican nomination. Political operatives often look at unopposed candidacies in relation to other situations occurring in the same primary in order to gauge whether or not an officeholder or candidate is in trouble. There too, there was no cause for alarm.

While Muskie received 17,221 Democratic votes, when the votes were tabulated on primary night, Cross received 97,052 Republican votes. The total for Cross even exceeded the 96,457 cast for Margaret Chase Smith in the Republican primary for U.S. Senate (her opponent Robert Jones received 19,336).

Fifth, the national success of the Republicans under President Eisenhower gave Cross the sense that he could bask in the glow of Eisenhower's popularity and wrap himself in the cocoon of Republican virtues and policies. National Republicans thought Cross's reelection (along with those of Maine's three Republican congressmen and Senator Smith) would signal a strong Republican showing in the November elections.

Sixth, there was the logic of history. Over the previous 90 years, the Democrats had only captured the Blaine House on four occasions (1910, 1914, 1932, and 1934, plus twice as Fusion Democrats in 1878 and 1880). The most recent win had been during the Great Depression. Cross had accomplished a great deal as governor and had a most respectable record on which to seek reelection. Looking back at the historical record, Cross may have been overconfident about his reelection but the odds certainly seemed very much in his favor.

But this positive profile for Cross's reelection did not take into account Edmund S. Muskie. Muskie not only brought zest and high energy to his race, he also got many Democrats to see 1954 as a time to expand the party. Many were encouraged by the Democratic message that economic prosperity required a Democratic touch and that the out-migration of Maine's young people was due to Republican failures at the state and national level. Democrats at the state level thought these were meaningful issues that their exciting candidate for governor could get across to voters.

Muskie's race attracted a lot of political talent. With the triumph of Dwight David Eisenhower in 1952 ending Democratic control of the presidency, many Maine Democrats in Washington were out of federal patronage work and returned to the state. Many were anxious to get back into the political fray and the Muskie candidacy offered an excellent opportunity.

There were also some important newcomers to Maine's electoral politics. For example, Frank Coffin, another Bates graduate and prominent, successful Lewiston trial lawyer, was approached by Democratic State Committee Chair James Sawyer to serve as chairman of the Democratic state committee and later to help draft the 1954 platform.

Today the party platforms are not very important to the candidates running for office, but then they were taken much more seriously and regarded as standing for the candidate and he or she for that platform. Newspapers, in particular, held candidates accountable for their party platforms.

Coffin did such an excellent job with the platform that he was asked to stay on as state party chair. In early May, Coffin in turn recruited Don Nicoll of Buckfield, a former student of the man Muskie was to persuade to run for the U.S. Senate against Margaret Chase Smith, Professor Paul Fullam. Graduating from Colby in 1949, Nicoll also had a master's degree from Pennsylvania State College. At the time of Coffin's overtures, Nicoll was 26 and news director of WLAM radio and its UHF TV station. Coffin wanted Nicoll to build up the party's public relations and grassroots effort.[6]

Smart, aggressive, and energetic, Nicoll would later become Frank Coffin's administrative assistant in 1956 and, after Coffin was defeated in 1960 (when he ran for governor), Nicoll moved on to become Muskie's administrative assistant in 1962, replacing John Donovan. Nicoll had no previous practical political experience but quickly became an important part of the total Democratic resurgence.

The appointments of Coffin and Nicoll were critical to the Muskie effort. While most people think of most candidates as "running" their own campaigns—making decisions, carrying out strategy, etc.—the truth is that statewide political campaigns require a considerable amount of staff time and input. Candidates are on the road where they may have good ideas or bad ideas about how to proceed with the campaign. Most candidates require strong backup, not only to carry out the demands of the campaign but to keep the candidate focused on what he or she is doing.

Obviously, there would never have been a Muskie revolution in 1954 without Muskie the candidate. But it is fair to say that it would have been much tougher for him to succeed without the contributions from Coffin and Nicoll. They may have been "talented amateurs" but they made major contributions and were, together, the de facto campaign managers for the entire Democratic ticket.

Both were central to the campaign qua campaign and both played very important roles in making the campaign work on a day-to-day basis. Frankly, without them, it is doubtful Muskie would have pulled off his amazing upset, at least in 1954. Stated simply, if you take Coffin and Nicoll out of the equation, it is very difficult to imagine Muskie the winner in 1954.

From the first, Muskie and Coffin and Nicoll worked well together and John Donovan's analysis of the partnership between Muskie and Coffin rings very true. Not only were they good friends who worked well together, they provided a de facto alliance of the two wings of the

Democratic Party, the second- and third-generation Catholic immigrant Democrats and the Jacksonian or Yankee-Protestant Democrats.[7]

Muskie, Coffin, and Nicoll were soon joined by others, including Bates graduate John Donovan and Bowdoin professor Paul Hazelton. In 1954, Hazelton was Democratic chair for Sagadahoc County and would serve as Muskie's campaign manager in 1956. John Donovan, who would assist Frank Coffin in many ways, including speech writing, would later become Democratic state party chairman, run unsuccessfully for Congress in 1960, become Muskie's administrative assistant, and eventually serve in the Johnson administration before becoming a professor of government at Bowdoin College.

The Democratic team thus became a formidable one and as the race developed, the party builders concentrated heavily on the Muskie race, using the excitement he generated to expand the party base and to use that party base to promote Muskie. The resulting effort was quite impressive, given the situation that then prevailed in Maine.

We must remember that in 1954, the Democratic Party in Maine was moribund: "The treasury was exhausted; there was no permanent state headquarters, local Democratic committees existed in only 124 of the more than 500 Maine towns, the Democrats had guaranteed Republican control of the previous legislature by failing to recruit candidates in more than half the state's legislative Districts."[8]

Richard McMahon, a longtime Muskie friend, became his campaign manager and also traveled a great deal with Muskie, becoming what in modern campaigns would be called "the body man," the person with the candidate most, his driver and his aide, his confidant and pal. He was thus in a position to make many tactical and strategic contributions to the campaign.

McMahon believed that Muskie ran for governor only after he had asked many others to take up the banner and run for governor, only to be turned down. McMahon was then the treasurer of Waterville, a position with quite flexible hours, and he was Muskie's most frequent companion out on the hustings.

On the ground with Muskie during the initial political forays, McMahon saw Muskie the man as "set" by the time he ran for governor and believes that he found his stride quite early in the campaign and continued to build momentum throughout with his strong but commonsensical approach to politics.[9]

Muskie had youthful vigor, a good deal of charisma, and a feisty personality never better than when challenged. He loved the give and take of political exchanges with his audiences. Rather like Margaret Chase Smith, Ed Muskie enjoyed the zest of battle and was never better than when he was being attacked.

McMahon's description of the 1954 campaign highlights the hard work of Muskie, his excellent stump speeches, and especially, the frugality of the effort. In 1954, all five Democratic major campaigns (three congressional, one senate, and Muskie for governor) spent $18,000.

To make up for the lack of money, Muskie made himself into a good statewide campaigner by visiting Republican areas and going through workplaces and even door to door all over Maine. Muskie came to excel in what we today would call "retail politics," getting one voter at a time but hoping that one convert would speak favorably to many others.

While Muskie and McMahon were out on the hustings, Coffin and Nicolls were the organizers, fundraisers, and institution builders, creating the monthly "The Maine Democrat" newsletter to reach out to more than the regular party organization.

For Coffin's part, the 1954 Democratic Party platform he created was—and remains—a most impressive document. Even from a distance of 50 years, it is possible to see the genius of the effort. In the 1950s, party platforms were much more important than they are today when most candidates simply ignore most platforms and go their separate way, tied to their party platforms only when their opponents attack them.

The problem with most platforms today, of course, is that they tend to get written by party militants. Thus the most vocal and insistent party members gravitate toward platform activity and push for the "purest" form of planks. This generally means that Republican Party platforms are written by party regulars who are to the right of the party as well as the general population. By the same token, the Democratic Party platforms tend to be written by party regulars who are to the left portion of the party spectrum as well as the general population.

Both sets of party regulars seek purity and often would rather lose an election than have the candidates compromise on stalwarts' basic beliefs. But candidates would prefer to be free to adopt their own issue positions and be able to tailor their positions to what a majority of the electorate wants. This interplay between party activists and candidates is as old as party politics itself.

The 1954 Democratic Party platform, however, was not a partisan exercise. Under Coffin's able hand, it turned out to be a masterful blend of Democratic core issues and other positions that would appeal to the mainstream of the Maine electorate. Called "An Invitation to Better Government," it pinpointed problems (such as pork barrel appropriations for the highway department) and called for life improvements (such as expansion of unemployment benefits).[10]

Coffin took the party platform process "public," setting up forums open to all and sending questionnaires around, even to the existing Republican cabinet members, and made sure that the party regulars, while having input, did not end up creating an overly partisan or ideological document. By including public comment into the process, Coffin changed the political dynamic of the exercise. The resulting platform seemed "fresh" and "new" and stated "Maine needs a change." It thus captured a sense of renewal and needed change for the future. The platform also sounded some "Republican" themes such as a "complete reappraisal of the state tax structure" by "adequately financed independent Citizens Committees."[11]

Coffin was thus able to tap into the general malaise felt statewide. When completed, his platform offered something for everybody. There, for example, were planks to extend unemployment compensation, to increase funding for the University of Maine. But nowhere was the document shrill or highly partisan. It sounded good. It made sense. It left the candidate Muskie free to provide specifics and take advantage of local issues, enabling Democratic candidates to take many bread-and-butter issues to the Republican areas: better roads, more state aid for schools, improvements in the environment. It was a brilliant piece of work.

On April 8, in his hometown of Waterville, Muskie announced his campaign for governor, stating "Maine desperately needs two-party competition at the polls."[12]

He went on to say: "I will do my best to discuss the issues and conduct my campaign in such a manner as to contribute something substantial to the cause of better government, whatever the results of the election."[13]

Governor Cross immediately took a wrong turn, stating that he was "not concerned" about Muskie's candidacy and later gratuitously saying Muskie was not the strongest opponent he could have faced (although he did not stipulate who would have been stronger).[14]

For his part, Muskie began a basic, grassroots campaign. Although proud to be a Democrat and often pushing Democratic principles, he nevertheless was never harsh or shrill in his rhetoric. He made sure he visited rock-ribbed Republican areas as well as Democratic and swing Republican ones. In fact, Muskie, with his judicious and careful approach to finances, sounded like a small-town Republican on fiscal matters. He also ran as if he were concerned about every vote.

Muskie's message was populist but not alarmingly so. He refused to let himself be labeled a "New Dealer," the term then used by Republicans to call someone a "liberal." He was for change, but not radical change. His ideas made good sense and if voters initially discounted him for being a Democrat, they were soon won over by the commonsensical nature of his issues. He sounded like he was one of them. In today's jargon, he "connected" with the voters. Even if they disagreed with some of his stand, they were drawn to him.

Years later, Muskie would capture this dynamic when he said:

There was a closer tie between the candidate and the voters than you have now. There wasn't the cynicism and hostility you see today. I felt a part of them—the voters—rather than a member of a different class. There was a friendly, positive feeling between those of us who ran and those who voted for us.[15]

Muskie's vigor and leadership also dovetailed with new Democratic initiatives on the ground. For example, at the national level, the Democratic National Committee produced for the first time in 1954 a "Democratic Digest" that was promoted as a unique, unprecedented magazine that was an extensive, "how to" manual, providing all sorts of party-building tips. Each subscription added gained $1 for the person making the sale.

In its May 4, 1954 memorandum, the Democratic National Committee stated that "the principle of communication is meant to include publicity, propaganda, intelligence and press coverage of all types."[16] The Digest was to serve in all those capacities and gave the Democrats in Maine something to use in their grassroots efforts.

The Muskie campaign began to hit its stride when Muskie, aided by Coffin's issue information gathering, was able to focus on specific grievances in specific areas. In what I would term "the death of a thousand cuts," Muskie would attack Cross on a specific issue in a specific area. For example, in Aroostook County, Muskie would attack Cross for closing the Northern Health Institute or in Cumberland County, he would attack Cross for failing to support a grant of $10,000 to improve the port of Portland.[17] In Washington County, he charged that Republicans had made a biennial political football out of the Passamaquoddy tidal power project.[18]

Underlying these specifics helped Muskie make the more general point that Cross was out of touch and didn't care about the people who lived in various parts of Maine and his overall policies were forcing young people to leave the state and older people to despair. He successfully linked Cross to the generalized sense of malaise and stagnation. Muskie waged a vigorous campaign and kept a tough schedule, driving from one end of the state to the other.[19]

For his part, Cross seemed to do everything to play into Muskie's hands. First, he tried to ignore Muskie altogether, failing to respond to his charges until a lot of water was under the bridge. He didn't really begin his own campaign until the middle of August by which time Muskie already had significant momentum.

Second, Cross often went on the defensive, adamantly defending a position and refusing to back down on any past statement or action. The more Muskie attacked him, the more defensive he became. Often it was his style that grated. Even from this distance, Cross seemed arrogant and aloof. His nickname among Republican insiders was "Cross Bear," alluding to his crusty personality.

Cross acted aloof and almost disengaged from the campaign and refused to debate Muskie, saying: "I'll be happy to talk with Mr. Muskie anytime after the campaign."[20]

For his part, Muskie was not shy about attacking Cross and his policies, sometimes referring to his government as "a bland dictatorship."[21]

Some Republicans saw danger early on. For example on July 17, 1954, Margaret Chase Smith called the Democratic ticket "the strongest it has been in many years."[22] Many Republican insiders urged Cross to campaign more vigorously and take Muskie more seriously but he held back, refusing to debate or seriously engage him. By summer's end, many Republicans were alarmed but didn't know what to do. There was little in the way of an institutional memory on how to run a general election campaign.

I believe this was a very important factor in the Muskie victory. Success in the Republican Party had usually been decided more or less in private. A would-be candidate would normally have demonstrated success in business and would have satisfied the various power brokers within the party and thus winning the primary was tantamount to winning the general election. This meant that there was virtually no one in the party who had run a meaningful general election campaign against major opposition.

Even those Republicans who sensed the Cross campaign was heading downward had no frame of reference of how to correct it, no real time experience on how to turn around a general election campaign gone sour. There were, of course, no statewide polls to show where the real problems were, let alone how to correct them. The Republicans simply did not know how to run in a truly contested general election. They hadn't needed to since the 1930s and now, they didn't know how.

Some of the press sensed something was happening on the ground. The most important political writer in the state, Peter Damborg, writing for the Gannett papers, picked up the groundswell for Muskie, writing on August 21 that there was a "Nip and Tuck Battle for Governor."[23] Read in sequence, Damborg's reports on the campaign clearly outline a crescendo of Muskie support and Damborg came close to predicting an upset but never could actually bring himself to put that conclusion in print.

For his part, Cross was so overconfident that he predicted as late as August 31 he would win by 45,000 votes (he was actually to lose by 22,000).[24] He also exhibited a great deal of campaign ineptness and he seemed to have made a habit of saying the wrong thing at the wrong time. For example, the state of Maine was hit by an unusual hurricane in August 1954.

Hurricane Carol did a good bit of damage, although not as much apparently as Cross had anticipated because on a trip to the coast he said, "It's not as bad as I thought."

Of course to the people on the coast, it was that bad and then some. His remarks were given wide circulation in Maine and the Democrats lost no opportunity to make sure everyone, especially those living along the coast, knew about them.

The Democrats also made good use of television. This was really the first campaign in which TV was a factor since the first Maine-based TV stations had only made their debut in 1953. Coffin and Nicoll urged the party to put as much of its campaign funds as they could into television. With a half hour costing only $180, it was a very cost-effective medium and could be used to get the Democratic candidates directly into Republican households without the filter of a local, regional, or state newspaper. For many Republicans, it was the first time they'd seen Democratic candidates and Muskie's intelligence and knowledge came though very well on television.

Television also played an important role in one of the most important events of the campaign. Many accounts of the 1954 election stress some or all of the elements listed above. Few underscore one of the most important dimensions, however. The activities of Neil Bishop turned out to be central to the Muskie success even though Democratic loyalists—and Muskie himself—seldom acknowledged his importance.[25] A careful reading of the 1954 campaign progress can only lead to a conclusion that increases that importance.

Neil Bishop was a large man and a larger than life presence in Republican circles. Bishop was from Stockton Springs in Waldo County, now a swing, key predictor of the entire state, but then as rock-ribbed Republican as any county save Hancock, and his party credentials were as impressive. In 1954, Bishop was fifty years old and had been a state senator for four terms. His rural populism appealed to many in the inland areas of Waldo, Hancock, and Washington counties.

Paul Mills quite rightly points out that although he was then "conservative" to many Democrats and certainly would be so regarded today by contemporary activists and scholars, in fact, Bishop thought of himself as a "liberal Republican" and so identified himself in the state senate biographical sketches while he was in office. According to Mills, he and other Republicans of that day proudly referenced their affiliations with the old Bull Moose Progressive movement to distinguish themselves with the "conservatives" of the day.

Bishop had campaigned hard against Cross during the Republican primary of 1952, ending up with 36,931 votes to Cross's 54,865 and Leroy Hussey's 44,087. But when the primary was over, Bishop had not joined in support of Cross. Instead, he forced his way onto the ballot as an "Independent Republican" after the September 1952 primary, getting 35,732 votes in the four-way general election.

The bad blood between Bishop and Cross continued during the 1954 election cycle. As early as May 1, Bishop telegraphed his punch, telling the *Bangor Daily News*, "A Democratic victory in September 'might' improve both political parties," and saying of Cross, "He's weaker than he was two years ago and I never thought he was too strong then."[26] Bishop ended up heading "Republicans for Muskie." This was a most ironic piece of stage setting, for Bishop was eventually to run against Muskie during the 1970 election, but for 1954, it was to have significant impact.

In 1954, Bishop's support of Muskie was major news all across the state. On August 26, when he announced that he was voting for Muskie and leading a group known as "Republicans for Muskie," it was front page news in the *Portland Press Herald* and all across the state. He was the first major Republican to endorse Muskie, and his announcement was a huge political event.[27]

The *Waterville Sentinel* prominently displayed Bishop's charge that the Republican administration took Republican voters for granted.[28] The *Bangor Daily News* covered his attacks that party labels should not stand in the way of decency in state government.[29] For Republicans, the vast majority of eligible voters, Bishop had, in one stroke, helped to legitimize Muskie's central charge: that Cross was out of touch and not even doing a good job for Republican areas, let alone the whole state.

Today we are so used to "Democrats for Snowe" or "Republicans for Mitchell" that we could overlook the importance of "Republicans for Muskie." The mere fact of their formation was a very important milestone in the campaign and helped to legitimize Muskie in the eyes of Republicans all over the state. If such a party stalwart as Bishop (and he was soon joined by others) then rank-and-file could desert the party standard as well. A true populist in his own right, Bishop was not afraid to speak his mind: "Why," he asked, "this urgent cry for a new Governor? Because the present Governor has failed to invoke the good will of the people, they have lost faith."[30]

Bishop soon would be joined by State Senator Malcolm Noyes from Hancock County who on September 8 stated that he and others had formed "The Hancock County Republicans for Muskie."[31] Thus two of the strongest Republican bastions both provided party leaders who were now opposed to Cross's reelection. It was an ominous sign that Cross and those around him downplayed and ignored—to their subsequent peril.

Bishop's support was front page, statewide news. But he went even further. On September 6, Bishop went on Bangor TV station WABI to publicize his support for Muskie and to raise money for further TV broadcasts. The appearance was sponsored by the Waldo County Republicans for Muskie Club, The Hancock County Republicans for Muskie Club, and the Statewide Farmers for Muskie Club with tacit and financial support from the Muskie campaign. It is now clear from the historical record that the Muskie forces knew more about the Bishop effort and did more to subsidize it than previously thought. The efforts of Eben Elwell, Democratic Party chair in Waldo County, were critical in this regard.[32]

The decision of Bishop and other prominent Republicans to go for Muskie was a crucial turning point in the campaign.

This is especially the case when you think that Bishop's 36,000 votes in 1952 eclipsed by 14,000 votes the 22,000 margin of Muskie's eventual victory in 1954. Now, there is, of course, no one-to-one correlation between these numbers but they do show two important aspects of the situation:

First, Bishop was an authentic populist with a statewide following and his support of Muskie served to legitimize Muskie's candidacy for many Republicans. They could not reject him out of hand if someone like Bishop had urged them to support him. They at least had to take a look at Muskie. Many then liked what they saw.

Incidentally—to show his staying power on the Maine political scene— Bishop would run for major office several times in the future: first for Congress in Maine's 2nd CD in 1956, losing the primary to Hallowell State Senator Jim Reid, then in 1958, winning his Republican primary with 66 percent of the vote (against Elwin Sharpe) and eventually losing to Coffin 61 percent to 39 percent; then in 1970 he would run against Ed Muskie for the U.S. Senate, losing 62 percent to 38 percent after defeating Abbot Greene in the Republican primary 60 percent to 40 percent.

Second, the numbers showed that Cross was not able to readily respond or to make up for these defections. Cross finally began his campaign in earnest after some Republicans blamed Republican Party Chair John Weston for the slow pace of the campaign. Cross did get a firm endorsement from Senator Smith, and national Republicans such as Vice President Nixon appeared for him on WGAN-TV as Cross stepped up his appearances and did a preelection eve half hour of TV. For his part, Muskie kept up the pressure right through September 12, campaigning vigorously the last ten days before the election and using a TV and radio burst during the last three weeks.

Hurricane Edna hit just prior to election day with 90 mph winds and downed power and phone lines. Democrats worried that voter turnout would be low and that Muskie would suffer as a result. Republicans worried that since they had so many more voters, they would be hurt worse than the Democrats by the storm.

But the election turnout was above that of 1952, with almost 250,000 voters casting their ballots. Muskie received 135,673 to 113,298 for Cross, a 55 percent to 45 percent upset victory.

That victory was and remains awesome in its dimensions.

Franco Americans turned in large percentages for Muskie. He carried Lewiston/Auburn with 66 percent of the vote and Biddeford/Saco with 76 percent. Muskie carried his Democratic base with a vengeance (although we need to remember how small that base was in 1954, only Androscoggin having a Democratic majority).

He not only beat Cross by 22,000 votes, 55 percent to 45 percent, he did so by beating him solidly in Republican strongholds such as Waldo County, home of Neil Bishop. Kennebec, Penobscot, and York, all of which had Republican majorities, went for Muskie and of the five most populous counties (Cumberland, Penobscot, Kennebec, York, and Androscoggin), only Cumberland went for Cross.

All over the state, many towns with big Republican majorities went for Muskie. He even carried Skowhegan, the hometown of Margaret Chase Smith! He had broken through Republican defenses and scored all across the state.

Speaking after his victory, Muskie sought to put his revolution into perspective, "We of the Democratic Party can be proud of our traditions. We are the oldest Party. We have a great past. But most important, we have a future. Our future is assured because we are constantly developing new ideas, new leaders, and new enthusiasms."[33]

Yet although the 1954 vote was not strictly anti-Republican, its impact showed up in the weakened nature of the Republican winners as many Maine voters split their tickets. Margaret Chase Smith was reelected with 59 percent of the vote compared to Paul Fullam's 41 percent. Nevertheless, this was down from her previous Senate margin of 71 percent to 29 percent.

In Maine's 1st CD, Robert Hale only narrowly beat James Oliver 52 percent to 48 percent. In 1952, Hale's margin had been 61 percent to 39 percent. In Maine's 2nd CD, Charles Nelson won 54 percent to 46 percent. In 1952, Nelson had won 68 percent to 32 percent. In Maine's 3rd CD Clifford McIntire got 60 percent of the vote compared to Kenneth Colbath's 40 percent while earlier in the 1952 cycle, McIntire had garnered 76 percent of the vote to 24 percent for his opponent. Thus one can see for the first time in post–World War II politics in Maine, not only a major Democratic victory but the pull of Democratic coattails as well.

Although many regarded the 1954 results as a fluke, Republicans had taken a considerable hit in the 1954 elections. That hit and the follow-up victories of the Democrats in 1956 were to put the Republicans on the defensive until 1972. It amounted to nothing less than a revolution in Maine politics.

WHAT WERE THE KEYS TO
VICTORY IN THIS ELECTION?

1. Muskie believed in himself and the rise of the Democratic Party. Initially he may not have expected to win when he began the race but he was determined to broaden the base of support for "Democrats" and the "Democratic" agenda. But as the campaign wore on, he gained confidence in his ability to actually win and projected an aura of confidence throughout the rest of the campaign. He was a man on a mission and his sense of purpose helped people accept his positions on issues. He had confidence and that confidence grew on the campaign trail. Muskie was working for himself and something beyond himself.

2. Muskie took himself and his campaign to places where Democrats had never been seen. He was determined to have Republican areas see a Democrat in the flesh and to see that not all Democrats had a socialist or quasi-socialist agenda. This coupled with wise use of television enabled Republicans to see a Democratic candidate for major office, often for the first time. In our age, this would seem simply a commonsensical way to campaign but prior to Muskie, many if not most Democratic candidates stayed out of Republican areas, especially the small towns and thus made of their campaigns self-fulfilling prophecies of defeat. Muskie's outreach strategy paid off.

3. He campaigned as if he were running for a local election in each town he visited. Many previous Democratic candidates had been content to express themselves through newspapers and radio addresses but not actually go to many of over 400 towns in Maine. But Muskie did more than simply go to the many Republican small towns, he went there and talked about local issues (or the ramifications of statewide or national issues on the locales he visited). He ran, one wag said, "as if he were running for selectman." This proved to be a very effective campaign style.

4. Muskie was surrounded by talented people. Unlike Margaret Chase Smith who was very much a loner (with her consort and administrative assistant, Bill Lewis), Muskie attracted and utilized many talented people. The chairman of the Democratic Party was the Lewiston lawyer Frank Coffin. Coffin would later run for Congress in Maine's second district and be elected in his own right in

1956. He later went on to be a federal judge. We have already mentioned his contributions and those of Don Nicoll. But there were many others, as Muskie's vigorous campaign attracted many new volunteers and energized older ones.

5. Muskie was helped not only by the lackadaisical attitude of Cross but by the general apathy of the Republican Party in general. One hundred years of political domination had led to a self-satisfied and complacent political structure on the part of the Republican Party in Maine.

   Republicans expected to win all elections. They had an attitude that they were the rightful rulers of Maine and having had a virtual monopoly over the major state offices, they often acted arrogant and high handed. Muskie played to the resentment others had of this style.

   Perhaps even more fatal was the Republican sense of entitlement and the refusal of the Republican leadership to believe they could lose until it was too late. They simply were unable or unwilling to transfer their skills at winning primaries to winning general elections until it was too late.

6. Muskie was also helped enormously by Cross's amazingly inept campaign. Beyond the general Republican malaise, there was the very poor campaign of Cross. In politics, it is often said "it takes two to tango" meaning that a good campaign can come up short if the opposition also runs a good campaign. Muskie was greatly helped by Burton Cross's series of blunders and his basic attitude toward the election—that he was "owed" a second term. By insisting that Muskie was simply an irritant to be endured, not to be taken seriously, Cross directly aided and abetted Muskie's rise to political power.

7. Ed Muskie was extremely fortunate that Neil Bishop—at least briefly—took a liking to him and supported him for governor. There can be no question but that Neil Bishop was instrumental in putting Muskie over the top. Doug Hodgkin conclusively proves this in his "Transfer of a Personal Following" by indicating that the Democratic percentage point increase from 1950 to 1954 in "Bishop" towns (where Bishop had received more than 40 percent of the vote for governor in 1952) was 27.2 percent compared to only 8.6 percent in non-Bishop ones.[34] Hodgkin also demonstrates Bishop's statewide delivery of critical farmers' votes.

   Although Bishop would become disenchanted with Muskie and run against him for the U.S. Senate in 1970, in 1954, his support was critical to Muskie's success.

8. Muskie made good use of local/county issues. He tailored his message to the part of the state he was targeting. Coffin would send out

postcards to discover what was on the minds of people in specific parts of the state before Muskie visited them. Coffin's "polling" was a true advance in the art of political campaigning in Maine and gave the candidate a big edge in local settings where he already knew what was on the people's minds.

This is a corollary to the point raised in number 3. Not only did Muskie campaign as if he were in a local election, he knew what was on the minds of the people where he was speaking. In Aroostook, for example, he hit Cross hard on the closing of the Northern Maine Sanatorium; in Washington County, the lack of development; in Portland, the failure of the Cross administration to secure funding for its port.

9. Muskie tapped into two powerful psychographic dimensions of Maine, the subculture of the "good old boys" and the "Wild, Wild East." Many observers have commented on this dimension. These are two concepts that I have developed to explain the importance of the image of Maine as a "wilderness" and the men and women who are at home in the great north woods.

Muskie fit into them with ease. He wore plaid hunting shirts and did enough bird hunting to qualify as a "good old boy." He could speak with knowledge about trout fishing. Plus he held a strong friendship with such well-known sports figures as the Augusta dentist and national leader of the National Rifle Association (NRA), Alonzo "Gus" Garcelon. Garcelon was subsequently one of the founding fathers of the Sportsman's Alliance of Maine. Until the day he went to the great woodcock cover in the sky, Garcelon kept a picture on his wall of Muskie, several dead pheasants, and the dog who retrieved them.[35] Many campaign shots of Muskie in casual, L.L. Bean hunting garb showed he wasn't a city slicker or some urban socialist.[36] Indeed, the Muskie archives at Bates College prominently displays another campaign photo of "Big Ed" afield with hunting dog and pheasant (while his wily companion holds the much harder to hit partridge). Muskie knew how to strike a chord with those who hunted and fished in Maine.

10. Frank Coffin's soundings of the various counties, what today we would call "rolling focus groups." As mentioned above, while not scientific polls in the sense of being randomly generated or balanced by demographic groups, they nevertheless gave Muskie a huge advantage over Cross in knowing what issues were on the minds of the people in which areas. But there was another dimension: Muskie's receptivity to those concerns was also a vital ingredient. All candidates have feedback from the field. Not all "have their ears on" when they get it. Muskie excelled at getting

his audience's reaction to a point made and tailoring it to his next campaign stop.

11. Earlier, we discussed the importance of the Democratic Party platform in the election. Here we simply need to reiterate its very positive impact on the electorate and the cords that it struck in the various segments of the Maine population. It was a great document on which to run, with little of controversy and yet a lot of challenges to the status quo. In effect, Muskie was to end up running, as the platform itself asserted, against the status quo and toward a better future. The platform was a document for reform, but it was also a call to political action with a better future at the end. Cross offered competence and past performance. Muskie offered a better future.

12. Wise use of television. In 1954, Maine had five television stations, one each in Lewiston, Presque Isle, and Bangor and two in Portland. Muskie, Coffin, and Nicoll made excellent use of television. They were, in their own words, "skillful amateurs" who used the new medium with great effect. They began the campaign with it and ended with it and also used radio to get out their message. Under Nicoll and Coffin's direction, the entire Democratic slate was able to be heard five times during the last three weeks of the campaign, individually minutes at a time, collectively in fifteen minute slots.

In terms of TV, it must be remembered that the technology of this period was, by our standards, very primitive—TV commercials had to be live because there was no easy way to record them prior to air time. Democratic commercials aired in all four media markets, Portland, Bangor, Lewiston, and Presque Isle. This TV effort, coupled with extensive use of live radio in the closing weeks of the campaign, gave the Democrats statewide punch at a time when the campaign was coming to its climax.

Republicans used TV too, but for the fledgling Democratic Party, TV was even more important since it brought the images of Democratic candidates to places where no Democrat had ever been seen. There was a potential audience of 400,000 people in 1954 and the newness of TV ensured that many people watched whatever was on and TV was inexpensive. Television enabled Muskie to reach many people he would never meet and reinforce his likeable image with those who had encountered him already on the campaign trail.

Muskie used television far more effectively than did Cross in getting out his message and the sight of Muskie on TV did a great deal to allay Republican voter fears that he was "different" from them. Cross would follow in the footsteps of Margaret Chase Smith and rely on a much smaller number of longer TV appearances at the end of the campaign when, it now seems likely, voters had already made up their minds.

13. Muskie's campaign style. When it came to "retail politics," Muskie excelled. He liked meeting people and carried a message that was appealing and the very fact he was bringing his message to individual voters—and expecting them to widen his area of support— was very much in the tradition of Margaret Chase Smith.

    His youthful, vigorous style with a ready smile and delight in mixing it up on the stump endeared him to many voters. Muskie was feisty and combative, relishing the thrust and parry with his audience. Mainers responded to his style and liked his basic personality. Today, we would say that psychographically, Muskie connected with the voters.

14. The times. The early 1950s were a good time for new ideas and new faces. Maine was in the doldrums, economically and psychologically. In terms of per capita income, the state was dead last in New England. Times were tough. The future looked bleak. Stagnation seemed the norm. Muskie offered confidence and hope, two very appealing elements to a state with high unemployment and few positive prospects for job creation.

    Moreover, the lack of job opportunities meant that many young people were leaving Maine. Muskie tapped into this concern with vigor and dispatch and the out-migration of Maine's young people became a cornerstone of this campaign.

15. The Democrats made excellent use of what is today called "opposition research." Both at the state and national levels, they studied the extreme positions and mistakes of their opponents and their campaign literature often seemed geared to the national level as if they were running against the national Republicans. Any woes in Maine were linked by the Democrats of 1954 to both the national Republican leadership and the state Republican leadership.

    Muskie could call up a number of Republican positions and attack them in his basic stump speech that he altered from place to place depending on the audience.

16. Muskie hit upon a "fairness" theme that worked extremely well for him as a basic underlying construct of his campaign. He stressed the need for Maine to be a "two party state." He insisted that competition was good for political campaigns as it was for business and that Maine needed the competition to get the best people elected to office and the best ideas actualized.

    The Donkey Serenade of January 1954 stated the basic theme: "incumbency by one political party breeds laxity and moral decay."[37]

The last shot of the Muskie for Governor effort included a flyer that asked, "Is there anything wrong with two strong parties, that which the Constitution advocated?"[38]

So from the beginning of the campaign to the end, there was a constant underscoring of how the political system would be better if it were more balanced. Like Margaret Chase Smith raising the issue of her gender while discounting it, Muskie raised the issue of competition qua competition and acted as if he—along with America's Founding Fathers—had invented it.

17. Finally, there is an underlying cultural element that played a factor and I am indebted to Don Nicoll for this observation. To the major Democratic actors in the 1954 election, the twin events of the Great Depression and World War II led to an assessment that there was both nobility and need in public service and a "can do" attitude.

They said, "We have lived through these cataclysmic events, we can make a difference, we can change things." This belief, coupled with a commitment to public service, drove people who were not actually seeking political careers to end up having important ones. Those who participated in the Muskie revolution believed they could make a difference—and they did.

WHAT IMPACT DID THIS ELECTION HAVE ON MAINE POLITICS?

1. The Muskie revolution changed the nature of Maine politics for the rest of the century. Remember that the Republicans had won every major election from 1940 until 1954.

Now they were to lose a majority of those elections from 1954 until 1972. The Muskie revolution was just that: a revolution. He changed the cognitive political map of Maine once and for all. Democratic enrollment grew and grew until they eventually surpassed the Republicans by 1978.

At the same time, Paul Mills is quite right that Muskie's victory did not "come out of nowhere." He cites the 1950 performance of Lucia Cormier and her 46 percent of the vote against Republican incumbent Robert Hale as well as the achievement of Davis Clark—a virtual unknown—who received 39 percent of the vote against millionaire incumbent governor Horace Hildreth in 1946 as examples. Mills also is quick to point out that during the Depression, Louis Brann was a two-term governor and the Democrats won two out of three congressional races so there were some precedents for Muskie and Coffin's triumph. Harold Dubord, who nearly won a U.S. Senate seat, later recruited Muskie to run for the legislature in 1946.

2. Muskie's victory was not his alone. He led it. He drove it. He brought its first success. But the Muskie revolution was not just he and his charisma but the institutionalization of the Muskie revolution. Muskie's victory led to a revolution. It was nothing less than that for like all good revolutions, it attracted new players with new agendas and styles. Muskie's victory in 1954 led to Frank Coffin's congressional victory in 1956 and both were followed up by Muskie's successful senatorial bid in 1958.

   Muskie the party builder revolutionized politics in Maine by bringing Democrats up to parity with Republicans in terms of office holding power and eventually, in terms of enrollment. New voters were more likely to become Democrats; older voters who passed away were more likely to have been Republicans. The basic "terms of trade" for the two parties had changed decisively. Muskie's victory and subsequent party building remains the single most important influence on post–World War II politics in Maine.

3. Muskie's victory was to reverberate for decades to come, attracting to the Democratic standard a host of talented new players who would be elected in their own right. Officeholders such as Peter Kyros, Ken Curtis, Bill Hathaway, John Martin, and others owed their subsequent success to the Muskie model.

   Doug Hodgkin calls it a "breakthrough election" and a "realigning election" in which the fundamentals of Maine politics were changed.[39] He is correct.

4. The Republicans were pushed onto the defensive from 1954 until 1972. Muskie's coattails became very important. In 1958, for example, he ran for the Senate and beat Fred Payne by 61,000 votes, and into office rode "Big Jim" Oliver as a Democrat.

   Jim Oliver had served three terms as a GOP congressman being elected in 1936, 1938, and 1940 before losing his bid for reelection in 1942. In 1952, he ran for governor as a Democrat and was unsuccessful. He then sought a seat in Congress as a Democrat in 1954 and 1956 and lost both times. He finally won in 1958 with Muskie at the top of the ticket (only to be defeated for reelection in 1960). Muskie also helped Clinton Clauson get elected as governor. Clauson stayed as close to Muskie as he could get the entire campaign, often giving speeches that sounded to the casual listener as if they were Muskie's own.

5. The Democratic team's use of TV in the 1954 election set in motion an ever widening use of that medium in Maine politics. Muskie's use of television in 1954 led to more and more use of that medium,

not just 15 minutes or half-hour programs at the end of the campaign but with 30-second and one-minute commercials during the campaign.

At $100 to $200 a slot, TV commercials were very cheap and the Muskie team's use of them was to accent their utility for the future. Unfortunately, the cost of television time skyrocketed and skyrocketed again until today, television time is by far the most expensive part of any successful statewide candidate's budget.

6. Frank Coffin's "polling" of issues was a huge step forward in the art of political campaigns and foreshadowed the coming dominance of professional polling techniques in the 1970s and beyond. These early "polls" or "rolling focus groups" were not scientific and didn't use the sophisticated techniques of cross-tabulation and regression analysis but they gave the candidate a "feel" for the area he was about to visit.

It also meant, in the skillful hands of Coffin, Nicoll, and others, that each locale's burning issue or issues were in the hands of Muskie and gave him a considerable advantage over Cross who, throughout the campaign, always seemed on the defensive. Muskie used "the death of a thousand cuts" to constantly attack him on local issues in the locales where they mattered and then moved on to new areas and new issues before Cross could even respond to the first attacks.

7. Looking at the 1954 campaign in its entirety, one is struck with the importance of the daily and weekly press. This importance did not begin with the 1954 campaign and did not end with it, but by the time of the Cohen counterrevolution of 1972, print coverage had already diminished to the point where it was not possible to win a campaign on the basis of daily and weekly newsprint reporting.

Today, it would be impossible to run the type of campaign that Muskie, Coffin, and Nicoll put together. The newspaper reporters of today—as well as their editors—simply would not cover the race the way they did earlier. For most major newspapers in Maine, political campaigns are not worth covering in their ebb and flow, only in the generic sense of press conferences and polls. Newspapers today simply do not follow the campaigns and send reporters to cover only very high profile events.

Muskie's attacks on Cross were front page or at least prominently displayed items virtually every time he spoke or sent in a press release. Today, newspapers simply put such items in little campaign boxes and bury them in the back of the paper, consigning virtually all press releases to these out-of-the-way locations. They treat all press releases and all speeches virtually the same: as hardly worthy of note. Even more perniciously, they tend to seriously undervalue press releases from challengers, making it much more difficult for them to break through to get at the incumbents.

Moreover, while an AP or print reporter might take a one-day swing with a candidate to get the "flavor" of his or her campaign, no news organization would follow the candidate around as did the reporters in 1954.

Peter Damborg of the Gannett papers gave readers a week-by-week sense of what was happening and in fact, even after fifty years, it is possible to feel the momentum build for Muskie in Damborg's coverage; even though at the very end he didn't quite dare call it definitely for Muskie, he did capture the dynamics of Muskie's surge and the overall race.

Regrettably, this print coverage is long gone in Maine politics and has been replaced by made-for-TV public appearances and the 30-second commercial. Newspaper editorials decry the high cost of campaigns and the overemphasis on television, but newspapers themselves are the major reason for these developments. They simply do not pay enough attention to most political campaigns to give their readers anything but the most epigonic of coverage.

Finally, as we leave the world of the 1950s, we should provide a word of praise for Cross. He refused to change his positions to suit the polls (he took none). He refused to trim his sails (even when urged by supporters). He refused to back off positions he believed were correct. He was proud of his record of accomplishment (and had every right to be). He did it his way.

Cross stands with other candidates and officeholders in Maine history such as Dave Emery and Bill Hathaway who, when faced with defeat, chose to be true to themselves, their positions, and their beliefs. Cross felt he had done a very good job as governor and he stuck with that belief right through the election. He refused to change his campaign style. He lost to the "campaign of a thousand cuts" but he didn't lose his sense of self-worth.

4

The 1960s:

Kenneth M. Curtis vs. James S. Erwin

THE DECADE'S MATRIX

I f the 1940s were the years of total Republican dominance and the 1950s a time of transition for Democrats, then the 1960s were the Democrats' most successful decade of the postwar period. It ended with the Democrats controlling the governorship, both congressional seats, and one of two U.S. Senate seats.

The decade did not start off that way.

In the governor's race of 1960 (to fill out the unexpired term of Clinton Clauson who had died in office), John Reed, who had been unopposed in the Republican primary, and Frank Coffin, who had given up his congressional seat to run for governor, met, with Reed (53 percent) narrowly defeating Coffin (47 percent).

And in the race for U.S. Senate that year, the incumbent Margaret Chase Smith handily outpolled Lucia Cormier 62 percent to 38 percent.

Moreover, the Republicans surged in the three congressional races. Peter Garland defeated the incumbent James Oliver in the 1st 54 percent to 46 percent, while in the 2nd, Stan Tupper won the Republican primary over Roy Sinclair 57 percent to 43 percent and his eventual Democratic opponent, John Donovan, defeated Roger Dube 76 percent to 24 percent. Tupper (53 percent) went on to defeat both Donovan (46.5 percent) and Dube (0.3 percent) who continued after his defeat in the Democratic primary. In Maine's 3rd CD, Cliff McIntire handily won reelection over David Roberts 64 percent to 36 percent.

The 1962 election for governor went to John Reed by the narrow margin of 50.1 percent to 49.9 percent over Maynard Dolloff after Dolloff had defeated Richard Dubord in the Democratic primary 50.3 percent to 49.7 percent. Dolloff set a Maine record for the narrowness of both his victory and his defeat.

The congressional scene in Maine changed significantly in 1962, as Maine, having lost population relative to other states, gave up one of its congressional districts.

In the two remaining CDs, Republicans won both. Stan Tupper easily defeated fellow incumbent Peter Garland in the Republican primary 62 percent to 38 percent in the 1st CD while Thomas Maynard defeated Clyde Bartlett 57 percent to 43 percent in the Democratic contest.

The general election went to Tupper, 60 percent to 40 percent over Ronald Kellam, after Maynard experienced a heart attack and resigned. He lived for several more years and ran as an antiwar Independent candidate in 1966.

In Maine's new 2nd CD, Cliff McIntire continued his winning ways, defeating William D. Hathaway 51 percent to 49 percent.

Republican dominance over the first two election cycles of the 1960s, however, was severely challenged in the 1964 contests.

Cliff McIntire, seeking to move up from his congressional seat, was defeated by Ed Muskie in the race for U.S. Senate 67 percent to 33 percent.

William Hathaway defeated his Republican challenger, Kenneth MacLeod, 62 percent to 38 percent for Maine's 2nd CD after MacLeod had successfully defeated Herbert Silsby 62 percent to 38 percent in the Republican primary. The Democrats were asserting political power all across the board.

In Maine's 1st CD, incumbent Republican Stan Tupper defeated his Democratic challenger Kenneth Curtis 50.1 percent to 49.9 percent after Curtis beat Henry Desmarais in the Democratic primary 66 percent to 34 percent.

Paul Mills has perspicaciously pointed out that 1964 witnessed the Democratic seizure of the state legislature for the first time in 50 years and the first time that both houses were under Democratic control in 54 years. This gave the Democrats a fine recruiting ground for future candidates with Secretary of State Ken Curtis, Senate President Carlton Day Reed Jr., and House Speaker Dana Childs, all of whom would contend for the party's gubernatorial nomination in 1966.

The 1966 cycle saw Governor John Reed challenged by James Erwin in the primary and by Ken Curtis in the general election. Reed defeated Erwin 60 percent to 40 percent but lost to Curtis 53 percent to 47 percent after Curtis had eliminated two challengers in the Democratic primary, taking 57 percent of the vote over Carlton Reed (25 percent) and Dana Childs (19 percent).

In the race for U.S. Senate, Margaret Chase Smith easily won reelection, defeating Elmer Violette 59 percent to 41 percent. Violette gathered 45 percent of the vote in a three-way race for the Democratic nomination, turning back Plato Truman (39 percent) and Jack L. Smith (16 percent).

Maine's 2nd CD saw the reelection of William Hathaway who took 57 percent of the vote from his Republican challenger, Howard Foley. Hathaway was to win reelection to the House twice more before going on to defeat Margaret Chase Smith for the U.S. Senate in 1972.

When Stan Tupper chose not to seek reelection, the open 1st District seat attracted a host of aspirants. On the Democratic side, newcomer Peter Kyros received 60 percent of the vote to 41 percent for Eben Elwell and 9 percent for Carlton Mendell. The Republican primary contest was one of the most crowded in Maine history. In it, Peter Garland (25.4 percent) narrowly defeated George Kittredge (23.5 percent), Ralph Brooks (21 percent), Ralph Lovell (8.7 percent), Cedric Thomas (7.8 percent), Frank Rodway (7.2 percent), and Frederick Halla (6.1 percent).

In the general election, Peter Kyros received 50.4 percent of the vote to 45.2 percent for Peter Garland and 4 percent for antiwar Independent candidate Thomas Maynard.

In 1968, both incumbent Democratic congressmen won reelection. Although Peter Kyros had competition in the Democratic primary, he easily defeated Plato Truman (16 percent) and David Graham (10 percent).

The Republican contest saw Horace Hildreth (66 percent) defeating Dave Ault (18 percent) and Gary Merrill (16 percent). In the general election, Kyros bested Hildreth 57 percent to 43 percent.

The 2nd CD saw the popular Bill Hathaway defeat his Republican challenger Elden "Denny" Shute 56 percent to 44 percent.

Both Shute and Hildreth were attractive candidates who ran vigorous campaigns. Democratic success was undoubtedly helped by the fact that Ed Muskie was on the national ticket as vice president. This was the first time since 1896 (when Arthur Sewall was on the Democratic ticket with William Jennings Bryan) that a Mainer was on the national ticket of one of the major parties.

Thus Democratic dominance continued to assert itself in the final election cycle of the 1960s, with the still minority party ending up by holding both House seats, the governorship, and one of the U.S. Senate seats. They were poised to sweep the board in the 1970s.

SEMINAL ELECTION:
THE 1970 GUBERNATORIAL ELECTION

On its face, it might seem strange to study an election that took place in 1970 as crucial to understanding the 1960s. But in fact, there are a number of reasons why the 1970 election belongs with the 1960s and was to be the last election of a political era.

First, the 1970 election cycle was to see the Muskie revolution in its final full flower, with the Democrats winning all of the major elections held that year. 1970 was the last year the Muskie coattail effect could be seen in such clear perspective.

Moreover, and related, that coattail soon would be institutionally eliminated with the abolition of the "Big Box" mode of voting whereby a voter could vote a straight party ticket simply by choosing a single, partisan "Big Box" at the top of the ballot. This had helped the Democrats build on their election success of 1954 and expand the Muskie revolution to its full potential.

Second, after the next election cycle began (in 1972) the Democratic upsurge that had characterized the previous decade abated, and the Republicans once again went over to the offensive, winning a majority of the major races that decade.

In 1970, however, the Democrats' momentum seemed unstoppable and likely to overwhelm even the longtime Republican champion Margaret Chase Smith (which would actually happen in 1972). As things turned out, 1970 is the last chance to see the Democrats totally in command of the political driver's seat. There was a Republican resurgence in the making for the next election cycle.

Third, 1970 was also an election that was part of a space-time continuum that began in 1966 with the election of Ken Curtis as governor of the state. Curtis, who served in between the Republican John Reed and the Independent James B. Longley, was one of the most important governors in postwar Maine.

Curtis was to have a most profound impact on the course of state government in the Pine Tree State, perhaps even more profound than that of Ed Muskie, if not in terms of the political election dynamics than in terms of governance. Under Curtis the state took over funding of education throughout the state. During his time in office, state government began its modern expansion, an expansion in the size, scope, and cost of government that went on unabated until the first administration of Angus King, resuming its financial expansion during his second.

Only then, in 1999, was it possible to state that, in terms of personnel, the size of the state government had shrunk. For the thirty-year period 1966 until 1996, the size of state government showed a continual expansion. Not even under the much-heralded administration of James B. Longley (1974 to 1978) did the actual size of government in Maine shrink. Longley did reduce the size of the biennial increase but he did not prevent or reverse that increase from continuing unabated.

The gubernatorial election of 1970 was thus logically and logistically part of the decade of the 1960s, since the election of Curtis and his changed approach to government (Muskie had taken great pains to govern more as a tight-fisted Republican) represented a true watershed in Maine politics.

Elected by a vote of 53 percent to 47 percent in 1966 and reelected by a much narrower one (0.1 percent) in 1970 after passage of the state income tax, Curtis transformed the nature of Maine government. His successive administrations made the modern state what it is today with its cabinet system, extensive bureaucratic apparatus, and central planning for education, income redistribution, and environmental protection concerns.

Exuberant, open, and a true compromiser, Curtis shaped the character of Maine state government as no one before and provided the impetus for its growth. In doing so, he responded to the deep felt needs of Maine people and set in motion the course of modern government in Maine.[1]

Often without realizing the true extent of his contributions, current Republicans and Democrats and Independents fight over his legacy virtually every election cycle. His legacy usually wins.

Born in Leeds in 1931, Ken Curtis graduated from the Maine Maritime Academy in 1952. His initial political activity came while attending the Portland University School of Law (now the University of Maine Law School) when he worked on the congressional campaigns in 1956 (unsuccessful), 1958 (successful), and 1960 (unsuccessful) of James "Jim" Oliver.

Deciding to run for Congress himself in Maine's 1st Congressional District during 1964, he challenged Maine's popular Republican congressman, Stan Tupper. Curtis ran hard and well, generated a lot of enthusiasm, and, riding on the substantial coattails of President Lyndon Johnson (who carried Maine by over 150,000 votes) and Senator Ed Muskie (who carried Maine by 130,000 votes), lost to Tupper by a few hundred votes.

Now clearly enthusiastic about the political life, Curtis became Secretary of State and ran for governor in 1966, handily winning the Democratic primary over Speaker of the House Dana Childs and President of the Senate Carlton Reed.

John Reed, the incumbent Republican governor, was a very likable, amiable fellow who enjoyed politics the old-fashioned way: with lots of public speeches and travel around the state. One of his nicknames became "Reed the Ribbon Cutter" due to his penchant for ceremonial appearances.

Younger and more politically focused—and armed with his own political polling as well as the issues raised by the Muskie revolution—Curtis went on the offensive against Reed. He produced a "Maine Action Plan" that he said would stimulate economic development and keep more of Maine's youth in the state. He also promised that he would not press for a state income tax for at least two years and charged that Reed had favored an increase in the state sales tax. Curtis finished strong and won 53 percent to 47 percent.[2]

While Curtis did keep his electoral promise by not raising the income tax during his first two years in office, he did turn to the income tax as a source of state revenues in 1969. With the support of moderate Republican legislators such as Harry Richardson, Dave Kennedy, Richard Hewes, Bennett Katz, Joe Sewall, Roosevelt "Rosy" Susi, and Ken MacLeod, Maine's first income tax became law.

Its passage was to come back to haunt Curtis in his bid for reelection and the debate about the expansion of state government (which the income tax fueled) became the central focus of the campaign, nearly costing Curtis a second term.

According to Curtis's only biographer to date, Kermit Lipez, by the time he ran for reelection, Curtis had taken three major unpopular stands, one for gun control, one for a proposed oil refinery, and one for the personal income tax that he had signed into law during the 104th Legislature after promising no new taxes. Lipez sees this issue cluster as putting Curtis deep in a political hole.

During his first term, he also had irritated many gun owners with his stand in favor of gun control. While the reforms may seem modest enough today—prevent convicted felons, drug addicts, and those in mental institutions from owning weapons—at the time, they were quite controversial. Lipez points out that not only did the NRA and Republican Attorney General Jim Erwin testify against the proposed legislation but so too did Curtis's own Commissioner of Inland Fisheries and Wildlife.[3]

Curtis also upset environmentalists in the state with his strong support in January 1970 for a proposed oil refinery at Machiasport by Occidental Petroleum. The 300,000-barrel-a-day refinery idea touched off a firestorm of opposition led by the *Maine Times*, a newly established but respected weekly voice for Maine's environment. In the general election, Curtis would end up losing many of the coastal communities by wide margins.

In fairness, however, it must be said that Curtis balanced his support for an oil refinery at Pittston with important environmental legislation, including the passage of the Land Use Regulation Commission (LURC) and other far-reaching environmental laws (such as the oil conveyance act, passage of various air and water pollution abatement legislation, and the site selection law). On balance, since the refinery was never built, his environmental legacy must be seen as significant and positive.

Prior to announcing his reelection bid, Curtis commissioned a poll by the respected national consultant, the late Oliver Quayle. Quayle's findings would have made a lesser officeholder throw in the towel. In the possible reelection matchup with Jim Erwin, Curtis trailed Jim Erwin, the most likely Republican candidate, by 28 points and Quayle told Curtis he'd never seen an incumbent in more trouble.[4]

In fact the numbers were so bad that Curtis didn't even share them with Senator Muskie although he did offer to get off the ticket if Muskie thought he should. Muskie replied, "There is no one else."[5]

Ironically enough, however, the negative polling numbers were interpreted by Curtis as being true since he knew he had aroused a lot of opposition with his stands. But Curtis took personal solace from the information that more voters thought he could do a better job than Erwin as governor, despite his lower numbers in the political matchup.

Looking at the five managerial and issue aspects of being governor, voters chose Curtis over Erwin, 2–1. Curtis felt that once the voters' wrath over the income tax died down, it was this dimension that would rise to the surface of voters' minds. He therefore began to put on a good campaign face and stress his accomplishments, telling the *Portland Press Herald* on January 30, 1970: "Maine has grown so well that we are in better shape than we ever were to face adversity." He also went on to underscore the significant strides Maine had made in terms of pollution abatement, citing the $50 million bond issue, the largest bond issue in the history of Maine.

On February 18, right after Republican James Erwin announced his candidacy, Curtis followed up by setting his priorities for the next Legislature: establishment of a Medicaid program, property tax relief for the elderly, accelerated expansion of vocational training facilities, and further tightening of pollution control laws.

However, Curtis was soon challenged within his own party. Plato Truman, the colorful and perennial candidate and one-time state representative from Biddeford, had previously run for Congress, governor, and the U.S. Senate. Plato "Two Great Names, One Great Man" Truman was not considered a threat by Curtis or any of the Democratic establishment.

But as Donald "Don" C. Hansen, political writer for the *Portland Press Herald* and *Maine Sunday Telegram,* noted early in the campaign, although Truman couldn't win the primary, he would do great damage "because his campaign is going to firmly connect Curtis and the new state income tax in the voter's mind."[6]

Curtis made a conscious decision not to "contest" Truman and made no effort to combat his attacks with TV commercials or even many personal answers. Curtis claims he was not upset by Truman's billboards because he was hearing the antitax complaints everywhere he went anyway. But early voter reactions were so negative that Curtis began to campaign at mill and plant gates in the early morning rather than later in the day when union members were more hostile.[7]

Plato Truman did cause Curtis supporters much heartburn, however, and cost Curtis a lot of popularity by running a strong, vigorous antiincumbent race based on his opposition to the state income tax. "Stop the

Curtis Tax" became his rallying cry and he spent considerable money on billboards across the state attacking Curtis and his income tax.

Even right up until election day in November, press accounts continued to speak of the effectiveness of the Truman message concerning taxes.[8] Truman's tactic and central message struck a chord with conservative Democrats.

In addition to criticizing the governor on taxes, Truman also went after him on the environment: "I flatly oppose the idea of big oil refineries, aluminum plants and so forth for the Maine coast. You can talk about jobs all you want but what good are they if the whole area is ruined by air and water pollution? That's not economic progress."[9] Truman hammered away at Curtis for nearly six months.

For his part, while Curtis did not launch a big "public" campaign against Truman, he did use the power and visibility of his office to stay in the news and make points against both of his opponents although he seldom mentioned them by name at this stage of the primary season.

In the end, Truman ended up doing extremely well in a Democratic primary, getting the highest total ever gained against a Democratic incumbent since World War II. Truman got 36 percent, a huge number against any incumbent. Worst of all, according to Lipez: "A mediocre, one-issue candidate had exposed the governor's vulnerability."[10]

Truman's showing would eventually force Curtis to spend valuable campaign time in the general election campaigning in Democratic strongholds such as Biddeford, Lewiston, and Waterville (where Truman had polled nearly half the vote) to repair the primary and income tax damage. Erwin took Franco American opposition to the income tax as solid support for his candidacy but in the end, when the election finally came, the Franco American communities across the state stayed firmly in the Democratic column and returned to support Curtis.

In fact, even though he lost the primary, Truman was prepared to continue the struggle against Curtis by staying in the race as an Independent (which was possible until 1971 when the Legislature enacted the so-called sore loser law prohibiting candidates who lost in the primary from contesting in the general election as Independents). He circulated petitions and turned in enough signatures to stay on the ballot. Republicans were only too happy to help circulate his petitions.

Only when Democratic Party Chair Severin Beliveau and the Democrats challenged the validity of many of the signatures and threatened to go to the attorney general with the case did Truman back off and withdraw them from the Secretary of State's office.[11] Truman formally withdrew on September 1.

Had Truman stayed in, it is doubtful Curtis could have won, both because Truman would have sapped his strength in the Franco American strongholds such as Biddeford and Lewiston but also because Truman was rich enough to afford his own media budget to keep attacking Curtis and doing Erwin's work for him.

Curtis was thus very much on the defensive when the general election contest began; his slogan "Ken Curtis Means Progress for Maine" seemed at odds with the electoral mood and he was forced to defend it and himself at many points in the campaign. The slogan was dropped after the primary, replaced by the much more appealing "Curtis Cares" that far better fit the policies and persona of the candidate.

For their part, while this was going on, many Republicans were simply licking their chops and enjoying the spectacle of a well-off Democrat attacking the sitting governor with their issue—taxes. They couldn't wait for the general election and the opportunity to retire Curtis and install a Republican governor again.

Certainly nobody enjoyed it more than the major Republican challenger. The Republican candidate was 49-year-old World War II veteran James "Jim" Erwin, the state's capable and respected attorney general. A graduate of Dartmouth and Columbia University Law School, he had been elected to the Maine Senate in 1960 and after being defeated for re-election in 1964, subsequently was elected to the Maine House.

Courtly and handsome and sure of his own abilities, he has reminded some of Tom Dewey, the Republican candidate for president in 1948 who had a huge lead early on but eventually lost to Harry S. Truman. Like Dewey, Erwin gave off a sense of entitlement. He deserved to be governor. He was a good man and an honest, capable one with considerable executive ability. He expected to be elected—and in most post–World War II Maine situations, he would have been.

Erwin had previously run for governor against John Reed, losing the 1966 Republican primary but garnering a very respectable 40 percent of the vote. Today in political circles, Jim Erwin stands as one of the half-forgotten and often-maligned political figures in Maine history who are remembered more for their defeats than for their victories. The full story of his candidacy needs to be told for although he lost three times, he remains a person of substance and character.

In his political life, Jim Erwin was a tough, no-nonsense, stand–up candidate. He had a penchant for not suffering fools gladly and he spoke his mind on controversial issues. He was not always at ease on the campaign trail, not mixing easily with "street people." His prep school, Ivy League background seemed to inhibit his ability to relate easily with many working class voters. Erwin was also something of an anachronism in that the value of modern campaign techniques was not apparent to him and the major changes in campaigning since the Muskie revolution eluded him.

At the same time, it should be pointed out that in 1970, there were no role models in the Maine Republican Party to point him in other directions. Republicans were used to fighting hard for the party's nomination and then often coasting to victory just by being that nominee. Winning a general election, and courting Independent and Democratic voters, was not something about which they knew a great deal.

Erwin campaigned on the issues, on his competence, and on his sense of self. He did not place much stock in polls or focus groups or scientific scheduling or segmentation analysis or image enhancement or political makeovers. When presented with polling numbers, even his own, he seem to ignore their import and meaning.

Erwin didn't see much value for television in his political campaigns either. There is considerable irony here for Erwin was a handsome, strong candidate whose whole image would have been perfect for a major TV effort. Erwin would have been stunning in a series of 30-second spots and had he used this tool effectively, he probably would have been elected rather easily.

Instead, Erwin believed in hard work, long schedules, vigorous campaigning, and grassroots organization. He estimated that during the 1970 campaign he shook roughly 50–60,000 hands and campaigned vigorously from one end of the state to another.[12] In this regard, Margaret Chase Smith was his role model and he worked very hard, putting in long hours on the campaign trail. She didn't need pollsters, media consultants, and segmentation analysis; why should he?

Erwin also had a lot of support among young Republicans. His own relative youth and his dynamic approach to grassroots politics appealed to many. He energized a whole generation of young activists including his son Jim Erwin Jr., Gordon and George Smith, Evan Richert, and Dave Emery, who after running for the Maine House and winning the Republican primary was unopposed in the general election and went door to door in his district for Erwin.

These young people helped sustain Erwin during the tough times on the campaign trail and after and to this day, he credits them with working as hard as he—not a minor compliment.

There were many issue dimensions to Erwin's campaign when it started. His personal platform and agenda was many faceted, not one-dimensional, although the Democrats later were very successful in making the focus of the election a simple referendum on his claims that the state budget could be cut by 10–20 percent. The process of focusing on Erwin's statements and credibility became the central facet of the Democrats' 1970 campaign. This happened even though Erwin made many valid points about expanding the educational system of Maine, opposing the proposed oil refinery, reducing crime, and putting Maine on solid economic footing. Erwin ended up being on the defensive.

It didn't start out that way.

Announcing on February 16, 1970, Erwin stressed "4 Burning Issues." They represented a holistic program with a positive set of messages for voters. The first "burning issue" was that the state was "rapidly spending itself into a position of fiscal irresponsibility" with Erwin claiming that "accountants and businessmen all over the state say Maine could have 10–20 percent savings in the running of state government."[13]

He also made civil rights one of those burning issues, expressing dismay that "Maine had not been able to better the lot" of the state's blacks and Native Americans and calling for an end to their second-class treatment in the state of Maine. He wanted the state to give the Native Americans of Maine both significant land and home rule. These concepts were considerably ahead of the times.

Erwin then called for a rethinking of educational priorities to place more emphasis on vocational training and wanted greater emphasis on bringing smaller, nonpolluting companies to Maine: "We don't want these giants belching their pollution into our clean air and dulling our blue skies."[14]

Lipez quite rightly points out that Curtis had already "named the first black to the University of Maine's Board of Trustees, an Indian as Commissioner of Indian Affairs and . . . a Franco American as chief justice of the Maine Supreme Court."[15] But Erwin's platform was a strongly worded, progressive, even "liberal" message for a Republican of the day. And by opening up on Curtis with regard to the environment, Erwin gave notice that he was not going to concede any issues to Curtis or the Democrats.

Erwin was ahead of his time in judging the Maine voters' psyche, opposing an oil refinery on the Maine coast and supporting civil rights. He had a much stronger record and issue stance on the environment than he is given credit for. Forty years later, we need to be reminded that in those days, Democrats were more likely to be in favor of big development projects (such as the Passamaquoddy Tidal project, the Dickey-Lincoln Dam, and oil refineries) than their Republican counterparts.

These big projects were to be opposed vigorously by what became the environmental movement and Republicans were very much in the forefront of these initial oppositions to them. Of course, Curtis was not alone in this regard, supported as he was by similar views held by Ed Muskie and Bill Hathaway.

Erwin also was disturbed about the rising crime rate in the country and the expansion of the drug culture. He believed he had done a good job fighting both with the limited means at his disposal as attorney general. He had expanded that office and improved law enforcement although ironically enough Curtis would eventually score significant political points by charging that Erwin had greatly expanded the size of the attorney general's operation.

Erwin's initial program offering was strong, progressive, and wide-ranging. It was an excellent challenge to Curtis and, in terms of positioning, should have served Erwin well. Had Erwin been able to make the campaign revolve around his entire platform, he would most likely have prevailed.

But Curtis and the Democrats were to be very successful in getting the election to hinge on some of Erwin's claims and his difficulty in proving them, thus changing the framework of the debate from Erwin's positives to what would become his negatives.

For all his strong points and substantial issue support, Erwin was to run a poor election campaign and he was to get little help from the Republicans. I say "poor" not because he didn't work hard or have good issues or was a flawed candidate. I say "poor" simply because Erwin's campaign was old-fashioned and did not take advantage of modern campaign techniques that the Democrats were to use so effectively. Most of his major speeches were delivered to Rotary and Kiwanis clubs, for example, the vast majority of whose members were already going to vote for him.

Sixteen years after the Muskie revolution began, the Democrats were used to employing and integrating modern campaign techniques, especially television, polling, and scientific scheduling, in a way Republicans were not and there was no cadre of Republican professionals to match the Democratic pool of campaign consultants and experienced, successful political operatives in 1970.

Erwin's campaign manager was Robert Fuller, a nice man who could and did raise a lot of money for the campaign. He had no experience in running a campaign and no frame of reference to use to insist on being able to hire professionals to assist his effort.

For his part, Curtis proved adept at shifting campaign strategies as time went on. His campaign team, led by coordinator Neil Rolde, simply had a better feel for statewide electoral politics than their Republican counterparts. For example, when Curtis initially appeared at plant gates during the day in the spring, workers threw his campaign literature into the mud as a protest against the income tax so Curtis came to the plant gates very early "when they weren't so aggressive." He also remembers getting very negative receptions at Bath Iron Works: "The union leaders invited a lot of guys to the meetings, hardly anyone showed up."[17]

Curtis also ran his campaign schedule more scientifically, asking questions such as: Where do I need to spend time? Where does my polling say I'm the weakest? Where do I need to mend fences? Which are the Democratic communities I need to target in order to get back my base? How much time is available to me? How should I allot my time?

He then developed a good campaign technique for getting a lot of mileage out of those visits. Then it was traditional to go to a location and spend a whole day. Curtis did it with half days, getting the most bang for his buck and then moving on.

Remember that in any campaign the most valuable commodity is the candidate's time. You can raise more money, you can recruit more volunteers, you can come up with another press conference or position paper. But you can't get back the candidate's time. That is the one crucial ingredient that is self-limited.

For his part, Erwin was a vigorous campaigner and he worked hard to visit communities all over the state. With Curtis in deep trouble and attacked by a vigorous challenge within his own party, the spring of 1970 looked splendid to Erwin. He was a strong candidate against a much-weakened incumbent. He had a strong message that seemed to play into the public mood against the income tax.

Erwin did not have significant Republican opposition and in the Republican primary of 1970, he would soundly defeat Calvin Grass from Sebago Lake, a professor at Gorham State College, 89 percent to 11 percent and thus move into the general election with considerable momentum.

But Erwin had already made a couple of major mistakes. The first was the nature of his campaign. The second was coming out so forcefully against the increases in the state budget and then claiming specific redress was possible.

From the beginning, Erwin stood solidly against the Curtis view of state government. He opposed the expansion of state government under Curtis and insisted that the state government could be cut by 10–20 percent by "trimming the fat." Since the state budget was $323 million, this meant Erwin would have to cut between $32 and $64 million so the Democrats could hammer Erwin over and over, demanding where he was going to cut programs and spending.

It is more than probable that a majority of Maine people agreed with Erwin at least in the abstract for the income tax was not then popular (although it would become far more popular when it was challenged by a repeal campaign in 1971).

But a very important campaign principle was at stake here. Successful campaigns are usually long on concepts with few specifics and this was a concept that would come back to haunt Erwin as the campaign progressed and put Erwin, not Curtis on the defensive.

The problem for Erwin quickly became one of specific examples. Many, even a majority of Maine people may have liked the idea of cutting taxes and the size of state government in the abstract and had only vague notions about how this could be accomplished. But by giving a specific figure—10–20 percent—Erwin had turned the terms of the debate around. It put him in the position of showing how he would do this.

But Erwin was unable to offer many examples as to how this would be done. The more the Democrats asked him for specifics as to how he would cut the budget that amount, the more on the defensive Erwin got. Eventually, after his surrogates had softened Erwin up with relentless attacks on his credibility, Curtis was able to put Erwin on the defensive in various debates by calling upon him to do so.

It is, of course, easy to run against government waste and inefficiency and many if not most candidates do so in every election cycle. The successful ones simply pick a couple of egregious examples of waste and use them as metaphors for that waste. Think, for example, of the Pentagon and its $500 toilet seats and how effective that word picture is as an example of governmental waste! Think of Ronald Reagan and a few simple "examples" which he turned into metaphors for all government waste.

But this is not what Erwin did. He was too intellectually honest for that. He came out early and often with a huge claim but then failed to give the public enough credible specifics to support it. By late in the contest, he had lost a great deal of credibility. The 1970 Republican gubernatorial race is a strong validator for one of my favorite political propositions: "All the big mistakes are made early."

Erwin's very honesty and forthrightness got him into electoral trouble and could not get him out of it. Like a ubiquitous tar baby, the issue followed him throughout the campaign and he could not disengage from it. Of course, the Democrats would not let him no matter how hard he tried. No matter how many times in July, August, and September Erwin talked on other subjects such as preserving the environment, strengthening the Equal Rights Amendment, and preventing crime, Democrats kept their attacks centered on his claims of cutting state government.

Thus with hindsight, it is also possible to see that Erwin made a huge and ultimately fatal mistake in coming out so early with strong statements about what he could do in cutting the budget and the size of government.

Had he been more vague in his early campaign statements or come out with them much later in the general election, he could have avoided giving the Democrats so much time and opportunity to refute his central claims. His early telegraphing of his campaign strategy was poor timing and would come back to haunt him.

It also gave the Democrats the opportunity to marshal all the institutions and groups who perceived that they would lose services or funding: those in the educational system, including local schools and the university system, and state employees, those connected with the welfare bureaucracy and other state services.

Ironically, moreover, Curtis would eventually be able to strike back with the notion that Erwin had increased spending in the attorney general's office by 120 percent during Erwin's two terms.[18] Erwin had made a major mistake in making a high profile claim he couldn't—or wouldn't—substantiate until right before election day. He had given the Democrats an opening to reduce his lead and undercut his credibility.

But remember, all of this unraveling of the Erwin lead lay in the future. In July of 1970, Erwin looked like a winner and Curtis looked like a loser. Erwin was still probably 20 points ahead and Curtis had major fence mending to do, both with his Democratic base and with Independent voters as well.

The 1970 gubernatorial campaign qua campaign had yet to play out.

The summer brought great personal tragedy for Curtis when in late July his eldest daughter, 11-year-old Susan Curtis, died. Out of respect, Erwin stopped campaigning and did not resume his efforts until Curtis did at the end of July. As for Curtis, Democratic insiders say, understandably, he did not regain his political stride until after Labor Day.[19]

The loss of one's beloved child is one of the most horrible blows fate can deal a person and to be struck with that trauma and its concomitant pain and suffering in the middle of an already stressful political campaign would have felled a lesser person.

It may also have been that Curtis was able to throw himself into the campaign with vigor as a way of dealing with his tremendous sense of loss.

In any case, Curtis began to campaign much more vigorously and seems to have gotten more focused on winning. Working off his slogan, "Curtis Cares," Curtis and his heightened interest got his staff more fired up. Neil Rolde as campaign coordinator became more visible and active. Advertising on TV and radio and in newspapers picked up. The campaign used the Orono graphics firm headed by Kenneth Jacobs who, along with Rolde, designed most of the printed material. TV visuals were done by Sid Aronson, who also did campaign films for Senator Muskie.

Rolde also cranked up the highly effective "campaign caravan" technique that had the governor and a small motorcade showing up in a neighborhood with a loudspeaker truck welcoming everybody to "Come and Meet Governor Curtis."

The governor would get out and meet the people and aides would hand out balloons and campaign literature. These bursts of campaign energy were very effective in creating a sense of accomplishment and ubiquitousness that helped get the Curtis campaign back on track.

Curtis got some help from Republican quarters as well. The Republican Executive Council's initial reluctance to confirm Curtis's nomination of Justice Armand A. Dufresne Jr. to become chief justice of the Maine

Supreme Court certainly served to galvanize Franco American opposition
to the Republicans. Although Dufresne would be confirmed before election day, the damage was done. In Lewiston, which Curtis had only carried 4,178 to 3,735 against Plato Truman, Representative Louis Jalbert declared, "The Republicans have just won the election for us," reported Don
Hansen.[20]

A Dorr Research Corporation of Boston poll done for Erwin in late August was also cited by Hansen. It showed Erwin leading Curtis by 46 percent to 39 percent with 15 percent undecided. Hansen rightly believed
that if the election had been held that day Erwin would have won but he
also had picked up on the momentum swinging toward Curtis. And had
he known that Erwin's 28 percent point lead had shrunk to 7 percent, he
would have been even more forceful in his sense of the improvement in
Curtis's fortunes.

The first televised debate between the candidates was held on September 24 and carried statewide on Maine's Education Television Network. It
was also rebroadcast later. Wide ranging and decorous, the debate
showed the candidates in sharp relief with both sticking to their basic
campaign themes.

According to the *Maine Times*, a focus group of voters indicated that
Curtis had won the debate.[21] Most observers at the time seem to have felt
that Erwin appeared awkward and not in command while Curtis appeared more poised and straightforward. In any case, Erwin also believes
Curtis won that first debate.

Erwin may have been overprepared, for Curtis came across looser and
more poised. Jim Brunelle blamed both overpreparation and a poor
makeup job that left Erwin looking "somewhat pasty and plastered
down. He was stiff and unsmiling throughout the telecast."[22]

I have seen this many times; the better prepared candidate often does a
poorer job if he or she is overprogrammed. Or the more intellectual or bet-
ter-versed candidate comes across as less appealing than his or her rival.
Most candidates want to take too much time off the campaign trail to
"prepare" and political consultants and campaign managers always need
to guard against this tendency.

Getting a candidate ready for a debate is a true art form, often misunder-
stood by candidates, their significant others, and various hangers-on, all of
whom push for more "prep" time. It is almost always better to have the candidate rested and refreshed but still grounded in the realities of campaigning, rather than being stuffed like a Strasbourg goose force-fed to produce
larger livers. Let them come off the street relaxed and smiling and forget all
the background information they won't be able to use anyway.

Be that as it may, reading the transcript of the debate provided by the
Maine Sunday Telegram of September 27, 1970, one does get the impression

that Erwin was on the defensive, especially with regard to cutting the costs of government, when the moderator Federal Judge Edward Gignoux asked him: "Mr. Erwin, back at the beginning of your campaign you discussed a 10 percent or $32 million cut in the state budget that you felt could be accomplished. At that time you said you would identify specific areas where you felt the budget could be cut. Are you ready yet to identify these areas?" Erwin responded: "Let's restate that. I'm talking about an objective. The objective might be 10 percent, it might be 9 percent, or 11 percent. No one can be specific about it. I'm not going to say to you that I am prepared to cut any service. I'm not going to say to you, and I never have incidentally, that I am going to cut jobs."

Erwin then went on to say he would not necessarily cut programs and people to which Curtis replied: "I agree with the attorney general that he did say that he would not touch people or programs, which makes it a rather impossible task from my viewpoint."

Curtis also ended up firmly in support of the income tax, saying, "If I had it to do all over, I would certainly support the income tax again. . . . "

But despite Curtis's performance in the debate, many Democrats were still worried. Some Curtis partisans credited Erwin's continuing lead to his "brutally effective television spot" that showed a picture of Ken Curtis's 1966 flyer against John Reed, quoting, "Ken Curtis Stands Firm Against Major New Taxes."[23]

By attacking Curtis's credibility, Democrats felt Erwin was making a telling thrust. But Erwin didn't believe that the TV ad was working and didn't keep it on the air very long. He simply didn't believe that TV was that effective in telling his story.

The governor struck back with his own one-minute commercial. It featured him "to camera" speaking directly to the audience, telling why it was necessary to go to an income tax instead of a sales tax because Curtis believed that income taxes were fairer than sales taxes.

The Erwin team failed to realize the importance of their own TV ads and instead seemed bent on frittering away campaign resources on frivolous activities.

For example, Republican operatives planted several hundred pounds of rye grass all over the state. Rye, which stays green long after other grasses have faded in the fall, was used to spell out Erwin's name at various points all over the state, including "the front lawn of the Democratic Party headquarters in Augusta" and key locations in Houlton, Ft. Kent, Portland, Caribou, East Millinocket, Waterville, and Winslow.[24] It is difficult to imagine a bigger waste of campaign time and effort although someone undoubtedly thought it was a great idea at the time!

Despite the September and early October TV ads where Curtis made up some ground, two weeks before the election an Oliver Quayle poll paid for by Senator Ed Muskie showed Erwin still with a substantial lead, 44 percent to 31 percent with 25 percent of the electorate undecided.[25] Although I tend not to believe these numbers because I think Erwin had already slipped much farther, they did have a galvanizing impact on Curtis.

Stung by these projected results, Curtis turned up his daily campaigning a notch and began to work 15- and 16-hour days. He had lost a close race before, the congressional contest against Stan Tupper. In that 1964 race he had been ahead and had been outworked by Tupper in the closing weeks of the campaign, losing a very close race 50.1 percent to 49.9 percent. Curtis was determined not to let that happen again and I believe that he had learned a great deal from his previous narrow defeat and pulled out all the stops to prevent it from happening again.

For his part, Erwin continued to work hard as well, but his campaign seemed flat and epigonic at the end, with no finishing kick or punch to persuade undecided voters to turn out a previously popular incumbent. His—and the overall Republican campaign apparatus—did little to target undecided voters while the entire Democratic slate was putting on a full court press and upping their TV buys.

Erwin felt he had stated his case before, vigorously and often, and, although he did not know it, he was losing ground relative to Curtis. He continued to believe right up until the end that he was going to win because he should win.

Five days before the election, Erwin finally offered a program of administrative savings but it was attacked by the press and by Democrats. Erwin had made what was his best case already and it was not resonating with enough voters. At the end, he had lost momentum and was not sure how to regain it. He ended up the 1970 campaign on the defensive, exactly in the position Curtis had been when it began.

The candidates had a second debate, on October 30, 1970. Liberal political columnist Jim Brunelle focused his story on Curtis's challenge to Erwin to prove that he could cut $34 million. Erwin responded that "it may be impossible . . . but Nebraska did it." To which Curtis replied, "This is Maine, not Nebraska."[26]

Incidentally, although Curtis thought he'd done "all right" in both debates, Erwin thought he lost the first debate and tied the second. This was not a ringing self-endorsement for a challenger.[27]

Meanwhile, the Democrats continued to blitz the airwaves with a heavy buy of commercials the last several weeks of the campaign. And Curtis ended with his most telling argument: "Nobody likes taxes. But you can't have schools without paying for them. You can't operate a mental institution, or have old age assistance, or aid to the blind, or good roads, or an environmental improvement commission, without paying for them.

"All during the campaign we have tried to level with the Maine people. We have tried to tell it like it is. What we have said is not always what people have wanted to hear, but nevertheless, we have attempted to deal with the realities of state government in as simple and as concrete a manner as possible. We have been consistent. We have not sought to mislead or to paint a picture rosier than it can possibly be. I believe that Maine people appreciate this straight talk."[28]

For his part, Erwin was hurt by a lack of any significant television presence in the closing days and, in more ways than one, he was the victim of the long coattails of Ed Muskie. Subsequent research (by a Democrat, George Mitchell) was to show just how strong and long those coattails were and as the Democrats surged in all races during the final weeks, the Republicans and Erwin fell back.

Republican candidates had taken their best shot and were trying to ride out the storm. They had no finishing kick, no flurry of late television, no last-minute rejuvinating ploy to get them back on track. In campaign parlance, they finished up flat.

On November 1, 1970, Erwin and his wife, Anne, and family appeared on WGAN for a half-hour program with Margaret Chase Smith. Arranged by humorist John Gould, the joint appearance was for Erwin the highlight of the campaign, yet in many ways it was emblematic of the problems his campaign faced during the whole election.

While the half-hour election eve television appearance had long been a staple of the political repertoire of Margaret Chase Smith, its era had passed, its efficacy overcome by a flurry of 30-second ads well before the closing days of a campaign.

Contrary to popular belief, the vast majority of campaigns are decided long before the final days with winner and loser locking into place well in advance of voting day. Few voters, even political insiders, would watch an entire half hour devoted to a single candidate talking.

Jim Erwin was following an old-fashioned Republican campaign model and that model was itself going to come back to haunt Margaret Chase Smith; she would lose her senate seat during the next election cycle in 1972, refusing to move to the new, much more powerful 30-second television commercial.

Ironically enough, Robert A. G. Monks who was to challenge Smith in the 1972 Republican primary—despite bringing modern campaign techniques to Maine Republicans—also eschewed the 30-second commercial in lieu of a series of these half-hour "specials." He would lose badly in that primary even though Smith herself was a spent force by the time of the general election.

Curtis raised more money and spent more of it on television. Erwin raised less money and spent more of it on grassroots activities. Ironically,

Erwin relied on his personal appearances and the daily coverage of the press to bring his message to the people, not the 30-second commercial that he would have controlled far better and that would have had far greater access to the voting public.

It is hard to understand how such a hard-headed, realistic, politically experienced man could have such a negative view of the free press and yet seem to rely on them to carry the truth of his message. Jim Erwin desperately needed the medium—television—in which he had such little faith.

On election day, Curtis received only 890 more votes than Erwin out of 325,000 cast.

The election of 1970 turned out to be one of the closest major elections in Maine history.

For years afterwards, some speculated that if Erwin had gone on vacation for much of the campaign season, he—not Curtis—would have emerged victorious. This is probably an unfair analysis of the dynamics of the race because Erwin did offer a fitting contrast to Curtis right up until the very end. It's just that in the final analysis, enough things broke Curtis's way to ensure his narrow victory.

The election of 1970 was a Democratic sweep in the state of Maine. It was a party triumph. Senator Muskie headed the ticket with 62 percent of the vote over his old ally Neil Bishop who got 38 percent. Maine's two Democratic congressmen were reelected by huge margins. Peter Kyros carried the 1st CD with 59 percent of the vote to 40 percent for Ronald Speers and .1 percent for write-in candidate Elwin Sharpe. William Hathaway led the ticket with 64 percent over Maynard Conners who received 36 percent.

All major contested races had gone to the Democrats. Thus by January 1, 1971, only Margaret Chase Smith—who was not up for reelection—stood as a Republican in Maine's major political profile.

In that context, Curtis's 50.1 percent to 49.9 percent triumph was considered a marvel and the 890 vote margin led almost immediately to a recount. The next forty-two days saw the Republican and Democratic parties and their lawyers locked in a furious duel to ensure their candidate was sworn in as governor.

The recount itself lasted from November 23 until December 15th and Curtis was eventually sworn in on January 7.

It is also apparent that Curtis benefited from the straight party votes for the Democrats that cycle with Senator Muskie getting nearly 62 percent of the vote and Congressman Bill Hathaway getting 64 percent and Peter Kyros 59 percent. He needed every single one—but never looked back and went on to become one of Maine's most popular and enduring public figures.

For his part, Jim Erwin would run for governor once more, in 1974, winning the Republican primary but losing to a surging James B. Longley.

Longley's story and that of Maine's other Independent governor, Angus King, will be told in the chapter dealing with the 1990s.

In our analysis of the elections of 1948 and 1954, we saw a pattern of factors working for Margaret Chase Smith and Ed Muskie. When we totaled up the factors, we saw how it was the cumulative effect of a number of them that produced such a conclusive set of outcomes.

The 1970 gubernatorial race in Maine was different. The vote was so close and the outcome so hotly contested—both before and after election day—that there was a less clear picture of electoral domination. When a race is as close as the Curtis-Erwin struggle of 1970, one has a tendency to look at each factor isolated under a magnifying glass, to isolate this aspect or that dimension and give it overmighty power.

This is no less true for the participants than those who later analyze those factors. This is especially powerful for the losing candidate. While the winner—in this case Curtis—can sit back and say, "Whew, we won," and be thankful for each piece of the puzzle, adding, "Glad we had that on our side" or "It was important we did that," the loser is faced with a multifaceted replay in which any of a great number of variables could have made the difference.

Even with the aid of hindsight, it is difficult to put these variables in proper perspective. But it can be done. The section that follows gives a full listing of the various variables listed by the candidates and by reporters and later writers, but it will end with my assessment as to which of the factors ultimately was decisive.

WHY CURTIS WON

1. The role of the press. Losing candidates often blame the press for their defeats. Usually they are not correct. But in the election of 1970, Erwin's claim that the press didn't like him and covered his campaign accordingly rings somewhat truer than normal. The working press didn't seem to like him and many took glee in his downfall. The working press also seemed somewhat more skeptical of Erwin's claims than those of Curtis.

   As the candidate himself put it years later, "I avoided the media. I didn't like them and they didn't like me, in retrospect I wish I had formed a more beneficial relationship with the media. I think that really hurt my campaign."[29]

   Erwin did find some political reporters such as Don Hansen "fair and objective" but had some strong evidence that some in the media really were against him. For example, according to Erwin, Jean Gannet Hawley, owner of the Gannet Newspapers including the

Maine Sunday Telegram and *Portland Press Herald* as well as a TV station in Portland, appeared at one of Erwin's press conferences and said she was going to run a headline calling him "a horse's ass."[30]

Certainly her ownership of the paper and her views about Erwin came into play later in the campaign when both the *Portland Press Herald* and *Maine Sunday Telegram* endorsed Ken Curtis for reelection. So there can be no question but that Erwin was right; some in the press, including some powerful people in the press, were against him. Also, according to Erwin, he managed to make Lillis T. Jordan, the publisher of the *Bangor Daily News*, "beside herself with anger" when Erwin proposed cutting the budget for the Highway Safety Commission of which she was the chair.[31]

Reading the political coverage in the daily press, however, suggests to this analyst, at least, that while Erwin may be right about how many of the reporters really felt, their stories do not paint a very vivid picture of support for his belief that they made a big difference in the campaign. All reporters have favorites and biases but in the day-to-day reportage of 1970, those faults are not readily discernible to this writer.

Jim Brunelle, for example, wrote two quite uncomplimentary stories late in the campaign, one about Erwin's poor performance in the October debate and another one when he followed Erwin on a poorly advanced campaign swing through the Lewiston area. But one could well argue that it was the Erwin campaign that prompted the unflattering insights by displaying their ineptness.[32]

For example, what sensible campaign with a Republican candidate would ever take a reporter to Lewiston and Bates College unless that campaign had advanced the entire day and made sure it would be a success by packing the various venues? Given the Erwin camp's view of the press, it seems truly amazing that they failed to anticipate the pitfalls of a reporter-accompanied visit to this area.

Moreover, in any case, I would also analyze the press situation somewhat differently. Curtis was simply better at making news than Erwin. The press may have liked him better but even if they didn't, or were neutral in attitude, Curtis seemed to have had a natural flair on the campaign trail and as governor, he was in a position to make more news anyway and was much more accessible to the press on a regular basis.

Don Hansen, Phyllis Austin, Jim Brunelle, and others all undoubtedly had personal points of view but looking at their day-to-day coverage, it is hard to see firm expressions of their bias.

2. Better use of surrogates by Curtis. Curtis had much the better of allies and surrogates. The Democratic Party regulars helped out a lot.

Muskie was his friend and mentor as well as head of the Democratic Party. He helped Curtis out whenever and wherever he could. In contrast, Margaret Chase Smith did less and what she did, she did late in the contest when Curtis was gaining ground and had the momentum although Erwin credits her half-hour television appearance with him and his family as being the highlight of his campaign.

Curtis also had other surrogates who could attack with verve and effect. The prominent Franco American legislator Elmer Violette, for example, who served as campaign chairman, was very effective as was attorney Severin Beliveau, Democratic state party chair, and Representative and assistant House Democratic floor leader Joe Brennan.

It was Beliveau who was perhaps most critical in attacking Erwin over and over again on the question of his credibility, getting under Erwin's skin. How could Erwin cut 10 percent of the state government's budget? he asked. How could he cut taxes by 20 or even 30 percent?

Beliveau hammered away long and hard on these issues and was an effective asset in the campaign dynamics. Democrats focused on specifics and kept the focus on Erwin's claims and credibility from the beginning of the campaign to the end.

By contrast, the Republican state party chair, Cy Joly, and other prominent Republicans insisted on trying to tie both Curtis and Muskie to the sugar beet and potato processing plant fiasco in Aroostook County and the activities of Democratic fundraiser and entrepreneur Fred H. Vahlsing Jr.

While Republicans had an excellent issue in terms of the downgrading of the Prestile Stream itself, trying to tie Muskie, one of the fathers of the environmental movement, to the mess meant simply that they had to go against his popularity and the people's perception of him. Such an attack would have had to be mounted through the medium of TV. Attacking Muskie in the press to get at Curtis was a self-defeating strategy. Erwin was the Democrats' only target, while the Republicans scattered their firepower on a variety of targets.

Neil Bishop was never going to defeat Ed Muskie so that was a totally wasted effort that could have been useful in keeping the pressure on Curtis instead of being diffused across the whole spectrum of the Democratic ticket. One exception to this observation was Republican state senator Ben Katz who wrote some strong op-ed pieces strongly supporting Erwin and attacking Curtis.

So excited were the Republicans to have something with which to attack Muskie that they lost sight of the pointlessness of their effort in the context of winning the governorship. Their attack was diffused and ended up being dissipated.

Severin Beliveau, in particular, really seemed to get under Erwin's skin with his constant and effective attacks. Especially telling was Beliveau's charges that Erwin had inflated the crime statistics of Maine to produce an image of a state on the verge of a crime wave.

Writing in the *Bangor Daily News*, Beliveau laid out the evidence that Maine was actually one of the safest states in the Union (still true today!). Not only did Beliveau raise additional questions of Erwin's credibility, he goaded Erwin into a direct reply. It is one of the axioms of campaign dynamics that you never, ever let your candidate respond to the attacks of the other candidate's subordinates and yet here Erwin was, responding as if Beliveau, the party chair (read "hack" in campaign-speak), were worthy of an answer.

It is no wonder that when that happened, Beliveau went to Curtis and said, "We've got him."[33]

3. Important Republican leaders did not fully support Erwin. While one can debate the relative contributions of Cy Joly and Severin Beliveau to their respective gubernatorial candidates, one cannot debate that Joly was trying to help Erwin and wanted him to win and worked hard toward that goal.

The same could not be said for other prominent Republicans. There were three groups, some of which had overlapping membership. They were (1) the Republican leadership in the Maine Legislature, (2) some supporters of former Governor John Reed, and (3) some backers of Nelson Rockefeller. None found Jim Erwin much to their liking.

Let us look at the first, and in the eyes of Jim Erwin, the most important group of "under" or weak supporters. The Republican president of the Maine Senate, Joe Sewall, Speaker of the House David Kennedy, and House Majority Leader Harrison Richardson as well as Ken MacLeod all objected to Erwin's campaign strategy of attacking Curtis on the issue of the income tax. They had been instrumental in helping Curtis pass it and they took Erwin's position as an attack on them.

In the fall of 1969, they also tried to get Robert "Bob" Marden of Waterville, a previous Republican president of the Maine Senate, to run for governor to head off Erwin who had already run in 1966. As a group, they were not all moderates—it was difficult in 1970 to find a more conservative Republican than David Kennedy.

So it wasn't strictly ideological opposition although for decades afterwards Republicans of all ideologies often said it was. For some of the Legislative leadership, it was Erwin's attitude and style, not his politics that irritated.[34] Or it may simply have been that he was not a part of, nor interested in becoming a part of their "club."

In any case, at the time, it was not clear that the top Republican leadership in the House and Senate wanted Erwin to win. With the passage of over thirty years, it is still not clear whether they sat on their hands, offered minimal support, or offered major support and had it turned down. Certainly, they did not actively run around the state working hard for his candidacy. The same could be said of several Executive Council members such as Charlie Trumble and Ken Robinson, staunch Republicans who nevertheless liked Ken Curtis and liked working with the governor.

Setting aside these dimensions, by his own admission, Erwin was something of a "lone wolf" and ran his own campaign with his neophyte, 30-year-old campaign manager Robert "Bob" Fuller. Fuller maintains the Republican leadership "came to meetings and did whatever they were asked to do."[35]

Still, those moderate Republicans had worked with Curtis and liked him, said Beliveau, so the fact that they raised no money for Erwin and made few appearances for him sent a not-so-subtle reminder to some Republicans that they were not really supporting him.

Added to this group of Republican legislative leaders were other Republicans who were still smarting over Governor Reed's defeat four years earlier and who blamed Erwin for challenging Reed in the Republican primary.

Also, one could add the ongoing split in the Republican Party between the more moderate, even liberal Republicans who supported Nelson Rockefeller and the more conservative Republicans who supported Richard Nixon. Erwin supported Nixon and was loyal to him, without realizing or caring that significant elements of the Republican Party in Maine strongly supported Rockefeller for President in 1964 and 1968.

Of course, none of these "splits" would have mattered if Erwin had enough money for a full-fledged TV campaign and the polling data to show him how to direct its use. Had he run a modern, rationally focused campaign with up-to-date techniques, he would have won going away.

A modern campaign would have put Erwin in the driver's seat where he wouldn't have had to worry about other Republican people who didn't like his driving or where he'd been or whom he'd taken for rides previously.

This was one of the primary lessons Bill Cohen and his team drew from their analysis of this race when they launched their bid for Congress in 1972. Ironically at that time, Richardson, Sewall, MacLeod, and others were big and early supporters of Cohen, legitimizing him with skeptical Republican regulars so the Cohen campaign never had to face what Erwin perceived he faced.

As it was, however, there were Republican dimensions that hurt Erwin and in a close race, may have hurt him a lot. Certainly the postelection analysis of voting suggested that far more Republicans voted for Curtis than Democrats voted for Erwin. How much of that can be blamed on a half dozen party leaders in the Legislature remains conjecture.

It would be incorrect to blame these Republicans for the defeat but they certainly fit the mosaic of a losing effort. When a candidate loses by 55 percent to 45 percent, he or she can always wish they'd won but they don't usually obsess over a particular dimension of the campaign. When a candidate loses by less than 1 percent, however, it is perfectly understandable to think endlessly about the "might have beens" with regard to this particular dimension or another.

4. Erwin's negative public persona. Jim Erwin is a good man with a fine sense of humor. He can laugh at himself and is fair-minded toward others. But on the campaign trail, he could be rough and demanding and appear abrasive. Often he was too erudite for his audience.

When meeting people for the first time, he could also appear to be stiff and often seemed off-putting. He also had a lot of pride and it bothered him tremendously when voters responded negatively to him in person. "I like and respect Jim, but he was never meant to be a man of the street," said Gordon Smith, one of his strongest supporters even today, while Bob Fuller, his campaign manager says, "Jim was not a natural, easy campaigner."[36]

Erwin had an old-fashioned campaign style more suited for the 1940s of New Jersey (where his father had run unsuccessfully for governor) and the 1950s in Maine than the end of the 1960s. In fact, I would state categorically that had he run in Maine in either of those decades, he would have won and won rather easily.

Jim Erwin had an older view both of the role of government and the nature of political campaigns. When you got to know him, he was very appealing but on the stump, it was easy to mistake his brusque, no-nonsense manner for aloofness.

As Stan Tupper, the longtime, highly successful Republican congressman and astute observer of the Maine political scene, put it: "Jim Erwin? There is no finer man or better lawyer in Maine, but he was terrible on the campaign trail. He had no idea how to campaign."[37]

By contrast, Ken Curtis is still widely regarded as one of the nicest people in Maine politics. He has a very pleasing personality and equally important, he wants to be liked. He was pleasant and congenial on the campaign trail and he was personally well-liked even by people who despised his policies.

Warm and fuzzy, he was a sharp image contrast to the harsher, firmer, more intellectual and edgier Jim Erwin.

Much as the League of Women Voters would have us believe otherwise, political choices often come down to personality leanings. People "like" one candidate more than another and vote accordingly. Erwin started with a big lead and Curtis started in a big hole. In the end, Curtis narrowly won. Personality and ease of dealing with strangers was a factor in the outcome and, although it may not have been *the* independent variable, it did provide Curtis with a distinct advantage.

5. Better use of television by the Democrats. This was a huge difference between the campaigns, probably the biggest independent variable in the race. Until 1972, the major Republican candidates did not use television very much or very effectively. They simply didn't understand the medium let alone its political potential. This was true of the role models for Republicans as well as for aspiring candidates.

Margaret Chase Smith herself was to go down to stinging defeat that year without using a single 30-second TV commercial. Had she briefly aired even one commercial it is likely she would have defeated Bill Hathaway in 1972. She failed to see the importance of paid 30-second television commercials and she paid the price. Those who imitated her campaign style also missed the significance of that medium.

In 1970, the Democrats saw the 30-second ad as a key factor in all their races and acted accordingly, putting on an unprecedented effort and spending a disproportionate amount of their campaign funds on television. They believed in the medium and acted accordingly. It paid big dividends for them while the Republicans were two years away from moving to a television-based campaign.

There is supreme irony here. Erwin was courtly, polite, handsome and looked fit and energetic. He looked like he could take charge and handle any situation. He exuded right and righteousness. By today's standards, it's pretty clear that Erwin the candidate was made for TV. Yet he eschewed the 30-second commercial that was tailor-made for him and the positive image he could project. Even a fair TV effort would have won the day for him that year.

6. With hindsight, it is now possible to see this watershed election as not simply a contest between two gubernatorial candidates, but a de facto referendum. However it started, the election of 1970 turned out to be a referendum on the role of expanded government.

  Few may have liked the state income tax or even its concept, but many saw that expanded government brought goods, services, and opportunities that had been missing from the Maine scene and that quickly became desirable.

  Moreover, in the heady days of the late 1960s, the state income tax enabled state government to expand into many areas and even to stimulate economic development (as it is known today) both by priming the pump in terms of state goods and services but also in providing jobs for Maine people.

  The income tax started out as a millstone around Ken Curtis's neck. It ended up as a huge stone step on which he could haul himself up from the morass of defeat. Later (in 1971), the people of Maine would vote on the tax itself. In 1970, they could only vote on its surrogate. The surrogate narrowly won.

7. The overall weakness of the Republican ticket was in sharp contrast to the power of the Democratic slate led by Senator Muskie. Few previous observers have noted the importance of the weak Republican ticket in Erwin's decline. None of the other Republican candidates raised enough money to be even competitive and Erwin, for all his perceived faults (both during the campaign and retroactively), was by far the best candidate on the ticket.

  The Democrats had two strong incumbent congresspeople and the beloved Senator Ed Muskie at the top of the ticket and already being given serious consideration as a presidential candidate for 1972. Curtis had good company in his run for reelection. There is strength in numbers and having three strong Democratic candidates out waging vigorous campaigns helped Democratic turnout statewide.

  In addition, Muskie, who wanted to run for president in 1972, did not want to see his protégé Curtis lose and worked very hard for him during the fall of 1970. He undoubtedly helped raise more money for Curtis than his counterpart Senator Smith did for Erwin.

  Not just party leaders in Augusta, but Republicans all over the state failed to rally behind their slate in 1970.

8. Erwin's campaign made more mistakes than did that of Curtis. There was overconfidence in the Republican ranks—not necessarily always shared by Erwin—but Republicans made the mistake of assuming Curtis was doomed and acted accordingly. They did not assume they had to run a good campaign. They didn't, and lost. In

1970, many Republicans seem to have assumed they simply had to run a campaign for governor in order to be successful. This mind-set was pejorative to their actual chances.

9. Curtis ran a dogged campaign and did not let down when he was behind in the polls. His personal optimism carried over to his campaign and he never allowed his supporters to see his doubts, nor did he share the negative polling results with very many people.

It takes a great deal of courage and psychic energy to go out campaigning day after day knowing you are in a tremendous hole electorally. Given his personal tragedy in the summer, Curtis's performance seems heroic and the stuff of legends. Not many politicians ever come back from being 28 percent down to their challenger. Almost none overcome the personal and political hurdles Curtis faced.

Curtis ran for nine months well down in the polls—and knowing it—and never wavered, never quit. A lesser person would have thrown in the towel. Curtis was his own best asset.

10. Curtis had the advantages of a "modern" campaign. He had excellent, in-depth polling that enabled him to know where he was and how to react to his situation. He spent his campaign resources more effectively. His was a much more sophisticated campaign by today's standards. He was way ahead of Erwin in terms of the campaign qua campaign each waged.

Erwin's was much more a traditional Republican. "I'm running. Once you get to know me, and see who I am, you'll vote for me" was the Republican way in the Maine of 1970. Erwin was not a candidate who gave serious thought to any type of segmentation analysis of where the voters were going to come from with which to fashion a winning coalition.

Without focus groups or polling or any other scientific sampling techniques, Erwin was simply running blind while Curtis was not. But even beyond polling and TV, the Curtis campaign seemed better able to handle the challenges of the contest than did Erwin's. Certainly a focus group—any focus group—would have nudged the campaign away from the "rye grass" tactic!

11. Low Republican turnout in key areas hurt Erwin. In the 1970 elections, Republican turnout was lower than normal along the (then) rock-ribbed Republican coast. Only 325,000 people voted overall but Republican turnout was down compared with Democratic turnout. Erwin won the Republican vote and he won the Independent vote, but he did not energize his Republican base enough to overcome Curtis's bigger margin of victory among Democrats.

If each Republican precinct had only produced a few extra votes, Erwin would have won. The lower the turnout, the better the chance for the incumbent Curtis who could rally hard-core Democrats to "come home" at the end. He did.

Democrats had an unprecedented get out the vote effort with phone banks and voter identification programs and the heavy involvement of the AFL/CIO on the Democratic side. The Democrats were firing on all cylinders. The Republicans were not.

12. Finally, Plato Truman dropped out of the general election race. The fragility of the Curtis victory is still cast into sharp relief when one considers the Plato Truman factor. His getting into the race and attacking Curtis during the primary helped to keep Curtis's negatives high and Erwin's head-to-head standing high in the early phases of the game.

Had he stayed in, as Neil Rolde, Curtis's campaign manager, put it, "For Curtis, it would have been all over."[38] Rolde was correct.

To sum up: Jim Erwin was a good man who ran an old-fashioned campaign in an era when campaign techniques were changing significantly. Ken Curtis was a good man who ran a very effective campaign using modern campaign techniques. In the yin and the yang intertwined flow of electoral politics, the latter beat the former even though the former started out with a huge lead.

The election of 1970 is thus a priceless reminder of the causal efficacy of the campaign qua campaign in Maine politics. Had Erwin run a better campaign he would have won. Had Curtis run even a slightly worse campaign, he would have lost.

It was the campaign itself that turned out to be the true independent variable in the gubernatorial race of 1970.

WHAT IMPACT DID THIS
ELECTION HAVE ON MAINE POLITICS?

The election of 1970 was a true watershed election in the history of Maine politics and was to have momentous consequences for those politics.

1. The long-honored Republican tradition of grassroots activities and get out the vote efforts had been trumped by the increasingly effective use of television by the Democrats and by their own use of grassroots campaigning. Subsequent successful Republican candidates (such as Bill Cohen in 1972) would not make the same mistake by concentrating on this relatively outmoded campaign tactic.

2. The Democrats in 1970 enjoyed a significant advantage in their campaign methods. They had been practicing increasingly "modern" campaign tactics since the Muskie revolution of 1954 and in the gubernatorial race of 1970, Curtis simply had more modern aspects. His polling showed him where he was and how to shift gears, his media firm knew how to package and sell him to meet the image desires of the public, and Curtis was smart enough to follow both his instincts and his polling numbers.

3. The Maine personal income tax had come to stay. Curtis, almost defeated by the state income tax, was vindicated when in 1971 a move to repeal the state income tax failed by the huge margin of 3–1 (190,229 to 63,403). Senator Muskie, never at a loss for words, called Governor Curtis after the vote and indicated jokingly how much more popular the state income tax was than Curtis himself. Curtis took the comment with good humor.

The income tax was the engine that drove bureaucratic expansion in Maine. Curtis's survival went along with the survival of the income tax and the opportunity to change dramatically the nature and scope of state government. Under Curtis the desire for the state to provide more services for more people took active form and with the passage of the state income tax (and the failure of an attempted repeal referendum in 1971), the state had the resources to greatly expand its role.

4. The Big Box voting method would be eliminated. Even more significant from the point of view of the political process of Maine, the Curtis-Erwin contest of 1970 indicated to Republicans that the "Big Box," which allowed a voter to vote a straight party ticket, had become a significant threat to their party's fortunes now that Democratic registration figures approached their own.

The evidence came from, of all people, George Mitchell. Mitchell, a former aide to Senator Muskie and then a Portland lawyer, was one of those deeply involved in the recount of the 1970 gubernatorial election. He chose to publish his findings in an article in the *Maine Sunday Telegram* on January 10, 1971. "In Politics There Are Two Maines" showed with stunning clarity that there were two geographical markers that correlated with voting patterns.[39]

Mitchell found that Democrats were very strong in urban areas and Republican very strong in rural areas (hence the title "Two Maines"). Even more significantly, he found that Democrats were far more likely to vote a straight party ticket than were Republicans. Sixty-one percent of Curtis voters had used the Big Box and voted a straight party line compared with 48 percent of Erwin voters who voted a straight party ticket.

This was strong statistical evidence for what Republicans had long assumed and claimed—that Democrats were more likely to vote a straight party ticket no matter what the Republican opposition. While this pattern had little operational significance in the 1940s, in the 1950s when the Republicans had a huge enrollment advantage and as the parties got closer in terms of registration numbers, the straight party vote became much more important.

According to Mitchell, for example, in the 1970 race between Erwin and Curtis, it was the Big Box voters who provided the margin of victory. While Erwin got 52 percent of the ticket-splitter vote, he only got 48 percent of the straight party vote. In contrast, Curtis got 61 percent of the straight ticket but only 39 percent of the ticket splitter vote.

Overall, the statewide results showed that 48 percent of Erwin's votes were straight ticket votes compared to 61 percent of Curtis's votes. Urban areas provided Erwin with 44 percent of his vote via the straight ticket route compared with 51 percent in the rural areas.

Curtis, by contrast, received 55 percent of his votes via the Big Box in rural areas and 65 percent of his votes via the Big Box in urban areas. These urban areas, with their high percentage of Franco American and Irish American Democratic votes, thus provided Curtis with his margin of victory and pointed out the dichotomy between the rural Republican patterns and the urban Democratic ones. Curtis won 13 of the largest urban areas in Maine (losing only Presque Isle and Kittery).

In terms of the "two Maines," Curtis got 65 percent of the urban Big Box vote and only 35 percent of the ticket-splitter vote, while in the rural areas, he got 55 percent of the straight ticket and 45 percent of the ticket-splitter vote. For his part, Erwin got only 44 percent of the urban straight ticket vote and 56 percent of the urban ticket-splitter vote compared to 51 percent of the straight ticket vote in the rural areas and 49 percent of the rural ticket-splitter vote. Mitchell found this situation unhealthy and urged, "Thus, it is important to Maine's future that the Republican Party broaden its appeal to Maine's increasingly numerous urban voters, and that the Democratic Party do likewise in that half of the State which remains essentially rural."[40]

Mitchell rightly called the Curtis victory historic; it was the first time in Maine history a governor had been elected to two four-year terms. He also termed it "an affirmation of democratic process and of the basic decency and civility which characterize Maine people."[41]

Ironically enough, it was also a wake-up call to Republicans, for it showed in stark relief what a current advantage Democrats enjoyed from the Big Box ballot and Republicans who wanted to regain control over the state's political fortunes were not unmindful of the importance of these findings.

In any case, looking at the top of the ticket, Robert A. G. Monks, who wanted to become a U.S. senator from Maine, set about eliminating the Big Box and the handicap it now meant for Republican candidates.

This story, and the concomitant resurgence of the Republican fortunes in major elections after 1972 following the election to Congress of William S. Cohen, will be covered in the next chapter but it is both interesting and ironic that the calm, dispassionate article by Democratic activist—and soon to be candidate for governor—George Mitchell was to set the stage for remedial action on the part of the Republicans as they planned and executed their counterreformation.

But the elimination of the Big Box was by far the most significant campaign result of the 1970 election.

Mitchell then went on to call for the elimination of the Big Box because it would cause both parties to campaign more vigorously for all voters and this would be a step in the right, democratic direction. Mitchell believed that the Democrats, being the party that benefited the most (61 percent to 48 percent) from the Big Box, should take the lead in abolishing it.

Of course, Democrats did nothing of the sort as many party leaders were supremely uninterested in taking away their biggest electoral advantage. It was thus left to the Republican Party, led by the court challenge of Robert A. G. Monks, to be the catalyst for removing the Big Box in time for the fall 1972 election.

In this context, it is important to note two additional aspects of this situation. First, many Democrats wanted to keep the Big Box and assumed that Ed Muskie, if he were the presidential candidate in the next election cycle (1972), would help all Democrats, especially those at the top of the ticket.

At the same time, Democrats more interested in capturing the legislature assumed—rightly, it turned out—that elimination of the Big Box would help them win in rural areas with Republican majorities or pluralities. They were stunningly correct, for the Democrats captured the Maine House in 1974 and have never lost control of it since!

The removal of this impediment to democratic voting patterns led in turn to the possibility of Republican candidates making inroads especially in the Franco American urban populations. It thrust the Franco Americans into Maine's political spotlight as the key ethnic swing vote and the one most ready for a counterrevolution.

Thus Bill Cohen's 1972 counterrevolution was based on this simple progression, sparked by the man who would become the Democratic heir to Ed Muskie, both on the state and national scenes.

Irony is such a delicious part of politics in the Pine Tree State.

5. Finally, Republican recount forces were strengthened. Republicans felt they were outgunned in the recount and when a close race occurred again in 1974 in the First Congressional District contest between Congressman Peter Kyros and challenger David F. Emery, the Republicans, especially the law firm of Verrill & Dana, were ready.

As for the recount of 1970, Erwin and Beliveau both believe that had the Republicans challenged the results more vigorously, they could have won. The Democrats threw more people and more trained people in the process and by training their counters were able to challenge more Republican ballots and thus help keep a margin of victory.

When the Democratic machinery went into action following that historic race, they found the Republicans waiting and able to fend off their legal challenge. In the arcane world of political recounting, Emery's narrow victory was ensured by the narrow loss Republicans and Erwin had suffered only four years before.

5

The 1970s:

William S. Cohen vs. Elmer Violette

THE DECADE'S MATRIX

The 1970s began with Democratic dominance firmly in place, reaching a culmination that had begun with the Muskie revolution of 1954.

As covered in the previous chapter, in the race for governor, James "Jim" Erwin easily won the Republican primary, defeating Calvin Grass 89 percent to 11 percent while incumbent governor Kenneth "Ken" Curtis defeated Plato Truman 63 percent to 37 percent in the Democratic preliminary.

In the general election, Curtis overcame a huge deficit of 28 percent to narrowly defeat Erwin, 50.1 percent to 49.9 percent, in one of the closest elections since World War II.

In the race for U.S. Senate, Ed Muskie continued his successful electoral activity. Unopposed in the Democratic primary, he handily defeated (62 percent to 38 percent) Neil Bishop, a former Republican state legislator (1941–1949) and former Cony high school teacher who had, in 1954, led the very successful "Republicans for Muskie" effort. Bishop had earlier defeated Abbot Greene in the Republican primary 60 percent to 40 percent.

The races for Congress were all Democrat in outcome. In the 1st District Democratic primary, Peter Kyros, the incumbent, defeated John Rigazio 83 percent to 17 percent while Roland Speers took the Republican nomination with 60 percent compared to 20 percent for Robert Stuart and 20 percent for Robert Cramm. Kyros easily won reelection, 59 percent to 41 percent, over Speers with less than 1 percent going to Elwin Sharpe, a write-in candidate.

The 2nd District was even more firmly in Democratic hands as William Hathaway, the incumbent, easily turned aside the primary challenge of Albion Goodwin 89 percent to 11 percent and then won the general election by defeating Maynard Conners the Republican 64 percent to 36 percent.

Thus as the decade of the 1970s began in Maine, only Margaret Chase Smith held aloft the banner of the Republican Party and she was to go down to defeat in 1972. Democratic dominance seemed substantial and widespread as the Muskie revolution had achieved and even exceeded its goals in making Maine a competitive state for the Democratic Party.

In fact, by the end of the 1970 election cycle, it was the Republican Party that seemed headed for noncompetitive status. Only Margaret Chase Smith (born in 1897) represented the Republican Party in the Maine delegation and at 73, she was increasingly out of touch with the political dynamics and had never spent any time or effort building up the Republican Party save by example.

Within the next twenty-four months, however, there was to be a resurgence in Republican fortunes and eventually, a powerful counterrevolution to the Muskie efforts. In fact, 1972 was to prove every bit as important to subsequent Republican fortunes as 1954 had to Democratic development.

The inspiration for, and architect of, this transformation came from an unlikely source. Massachusetts native and Maine summer resident Robert A. G. Monks had looked over the Maine landscape and decided that he should become a senator from that state rather than from his "home" state of Massachusetts where he had served as Republican Party state chairman. He had previously begun to donate to Republican candidates (such as Denny Shute) in Maine and even an occasional Democrat (Bill Hathaway).

In the process, Bob Monks was to set in motion a profound sea change in Maine politics, every bit as important as that engineered by Ed Muskie 20 years before.

Monks saw in Maine some of the frontier aspects that were so appealing to so many since the state was formed. Weighing in on several commercial issues that had environmental and developmental import, Monks quickly made a name for himself.

His early polling showed the vulnerability of Senator Margaret Chase Smith (similar polling by Congressman Bill Hathaway pointed to the same conclusion). From both polls, it was clear that most Maine voters were unaware of Smith's age, 73.

In fact, Monks did not believe that Smith would even seek election and he sought not only to make himself the standard bearer but to encourage strong, centrist candidates to run for the 1st and 2nd Congressional Districts in order to strengthen the ticket which he would head. He had examined the election of 1970 in particular and noted the overall weakness of the Republican ticket and how it had dragged down the campaign of Jim Erwin.

Monks also sought to legitimize his overall efforts by enlisting the support of the principal Republican actors in the Legislature: State Senate

President Ken MacLeod, House Speaker Dave Kennedy, and Senate Appropriations Chair Joe Sewall.

For Monks, this combination of self-interest and concern for making the Republicans competitive again resulted ironically enough in the defeat of Margaret Chase Smith. But the concomitant election of William S. Cohen, the popular mayor of Bangor, was in turn to provide a model for subsequent Republican insurgence in the form of Congressman David Emery, Congresswoman Olympia Snowe, Governor John "Jock" McKernan, and eventually, Senator Snowe and Senator Susan Collins, both of whom had earlier worked or volunteered for and with Cohen when he was in Congress.

On the surface of election results, there is not much to distinguish Bob Monks. He belongs with Joe Brennan and Jim Erwin in having sustained three losses in major elections. His vote totals against Margaret Chase Smith in 1972 (33 percent to 67 percent), Ed Muskie in 1976 (40 percent to 60 percent), and in the Republican primary for U.S. Senate in 1996 (16 percent) are all unremarkable.

Yet Bob Monks is as responsible as anyone for bringing the Republican Party back from its nadir and reinvigorating it for the decades ahead. His impact, in terms of candidate recruitment, overarching strategy, financial support, and the introduction of modern campaign techniques into Maine, is nothing short of revolutionary and no scholarly study of postwar Maine politics would be complete or accurate without that recognition.

Stated simply, Bob Monks altered the way politics is done in the Pine Tree state and cast his shadow over the next thirty years of its politics.

For example, he led both the court and citizen initiative challenges to the "Big Box." Prior to 1972, partisans of either major party could vote a straight party ticket simply by checking off the "Big Box" on the top of the ticket. Officially called a "party column" system, this ballot was markedly different from the "office" style where voters had to mark a specific box for each office, not simply a straight vote for one party or the other.

As noted in the last chapter, this technique initially favored Republicans in the 1940s but by the late 1950s and early 1960s it was working to solidify Democratic predominance since Democratic voters, especially those in the urban Franco American wards of Lewiston and Biddeford, were more likely to use the Big Box than their counterparts in rural Republican areas.

Given the psychographic makeup of Franco American voters, this was a tremendous advantage to Democrats, an advantage undercut by the elimination of the Big Box and the campaigning dynamics of Bill Cohen, Dave Emery, Jock McKernan, and Olympia Snowe.

Putting the Franco American voters "in play" by eliminating the Big Box may well have been the most important aspect of the Monks legacy. Voters approved the switch from the "party column" to the "office form" by a margin of 63 percent to 37 percent in June of 1972.

The election cycle of 1972 saw Cohen emerging as the only successful Republican. He had beaten Abbott Greene in the Republican primary for Maine's 2nd CD 61 percent to 39 percent and then defeated Elmer Violette 54 percent to 46 percent, Violette having gotten the nomination over Lewis Maxwell by a margin of 79 percent to 21 percent.

In Maine's 1st CD, Robert Porteous defeated Clifton Young 78 percent to 22 percent in the Republican primary, only to lose to Peter Kyros 59 percent to 41 percent after Kyros had defeated Everett "Brownie" Carson 67 percent to 34 percent.

In the race for the U.S. Senate, Margaret Chase Smith defeated Bob Monks 67 percent to 33 percent for the Republican nomination while William "Bill" Hathaway was defeating Jack L. Smith 91 percent to 9 percent in the Democratic contest. In the general election, Hathaway pulled a major upset, defeating Smith 53 percent to 47 percent.

Two years later, 1974 saw Republican Jim Erwin narrowly capture the gubernatorial nomination with 39 percent of the vote with 38 percent for Harry Richardson and 19 percent for Wakine Tanous. George Mitchell took the Democratic nod with 38 percent of the vote compared with 26 percent for Joe Brennan, 24 percent for Peter Kelley, and 9 percent for Lloyd LaFountain.

The general election, however, saw the emergence of James B. Longley who, running as an Independent, captured 39 percent of the vote compared with 36 percent for Mitchell and 23 percent for Erwin. Other assorted Independents—Stanley Leen, William Hughes, and Leith Hartman—all received less than 1 percent of the vote. Longley's upset victory and his achievement as the first Independent governor in Maine's history will be covered in a later chapter.

David Emery was unopposed in the 1974 1st CD Republican primary while Peter Kyros defeated Jadine O'Brien 69 percent to 31 percent for the Democratic nomination. In the general, however, Emery upset three-term incumbent Kyros 50.2 percent to 49.8 percent.

In the 2nd CD, William S. Cohen was unopposed in the Republican primary while Markham "Mark" Gartley defeated Stewart Smith 66 percent to 34 percent in the Democratic effort. Cohen handily defeated Gartley in the general 71 percent to 29 percent.

Robert Monks defeat Plato Truman in 1976 in the Republican primary for U.S. Senate 84 percent to 16 percent while Ed Muskie was unopposed for the Democrat nomination. Muskie captured the general election 60 percent to 40 percent.

In the 1st CD, Dave Emery's narrow victory in 1974 stimulated a huge Democratic primary with Frederick "Rick" Barton (24 percent) outpolling James Mitchell (20 percent), Neil Rolde (18 percent), David Bustin (12 percent), Bruce Reeves (12 percent), Gilbert Boucher (9 percent), and Don Lowry (4 percent).

Emery won the general election of 1976 57 percent to 43 percent.

Cohen continued his dominance over the 2nd CD, defeating the Democratic nominee Leighton Cooney 77 percent to 20 percent with Jacqueline Kaye getting 3 percent as an Independent.

The 1978 cycle saw a vigorous race for the Republican nomination for governor with Linwood Palmer getting 49 percent to 38 percent for Portland attorney Charles Cragin and 13 percent for Jerrold "Jerry" Speers. On the Democratic side, Joseph Brennan received 52 percent compared with Philip Merrill's 36 percent and Richard "Spike" Carey's 12 percent.

In the general election, Brennan defeated Palmer 48 percent to 34 percent while Herman "Buddy" Frankland got 18 percent as an Independent even though he was endorsed by Governor James B. Longley and the *Bangor Daily News*.

Bill Cohen was unopposed in the Republican nomination for U.S. Senate as was Bill Hathaway in the Democratic contest. In the general, Cohen won with 57 percent to 34 percent for Hathaway while Independents Hayes Gahagan (8 percent), John Jannace (.6 percent), and Plato Truman (.2 percent) trailed.

In Maine's 1st CD, again Dave Emery was unopposed while four Democrats fought for the right to oppose him. John Quinn (31 percent) defeated Guy Marcotte (26 percent), Richard "Dick" Spencer (26 percent), and Louis "Sandy" Maisel, the Colby College professor of government (17 percent). Emery (62 percent) defeated Quinn (36 percent) and Independent Dave Madagan (3 percent) in the general.

The 2nd CD saw Olympia Snowe getting the Republican nomination unopposed while Secretary of State Mark Gartley defeated James "Jim" Henderson 64 percent to 36 percent in the Democratic primary. Snowe won the general election with 53 percent compared to 42 percent for Gartley and 5 percent for Frederick Whittaker.

SEMINAL ELECTION:
1972 2ND CD CONGRESSIONAL RACE

Bill Cohen did not set out to make a counterrevolution.

In fact, he had no grand design or plan except to win a congressional seat. But he was, in fact, to make a counterrevolution of enormous proportions, eventually providing a huge counterweight to the achievements of Ed Muskie.

The year 1972 was a true watershed in Maine politics all the more so because it is still largely unrecognized and indeed, seldom mentioned in the same breath as the momentous elections of 1948, 1954, and 1974.

It is hard to imagine now but by the election cycle of 1972, Republicans were on the Maine political ropes. There was only one major officeholder,

Senator Margaret Chase Smith, and she would go down to defeat in 1972. The Democrats had won eight of the last nine major elections (only Margaret Chase Smith won in 1966) and were gaining in enrollment numbers every year.

Robert "Bob" A. G. Monks of Cape Elizabeth was anxious to get to the United States Senate and he believed that Margaret Chase Smith would not run for reelection. He was convinced he should and would be on the ticket and wanted quality Republican candidates running for Congress alongside him. He urged former state senator Robert "Bob" Porteous of Portland to run in Maine's 1st CD as well as the mayor of Bangor, William S. "Bill" Cohen, to run in the 2nd.

Cohen initially held back. He was just paying off his law school bills and beginning his law practice in Bangor. His wife, Diane, was very happy in their new house and both were concerned about both the loss of privacy and the high cost of campaigning. Bob Monks promised—and later delivered—enough financial support to relieve Cohen's mind and make sure the campaign was financially viable.

Born in 1940, the son of Reuben Cohen, a baker of Russian Jewish extraction, and Clara Cohen, an Irish Protestant, Cohen graduated from Bangor High School (where he was an All-State basketball player) in 1958 and Bowdoin College (where he was the leading scorer on the basketball team and majored in Classics, graduating cum laude) in 1962 before going on to Boston University Law School where he received his L.L.B. degree in 1965.

Married to Diane Dunn in 1962, he returned to Bangor to practice law and participate in local politics, being elected to the school board and city council (1969–1972) before becoming mayor (1971–1972).

Monks not only provided Cohen with encouragement and peace of mind, he also got many of the Republican Party leaders—the same leaders who had not supported Erwin—to rally around Cohen. Ken MacLeod, president of the Maine Senate, was to be a major supporter along with Joe Sewall, Speaker of the House Dave Kennedy, Republican leaders Ben Katz, Richard Hughes, Harry Richardson, and others. All would give Cohen much needed legitimacy with party regulars, especially in his party primary.

For Cohen faced a tough primary battle with Abbott O. Greene, a TWA pilot who had run previously in Republican circles, losing to Neil Bishop in the 1970 Senate primary but then going on to serve as Bishop's campaign treasurer. In 1972, Greene felt it would be his turn. In the initial stages of the Cohen campaign, therefore, Republican Party leadership support was critical in making Cohen viable, and thus Greene wanted to stave off any leadership support for him.

But Monks's support for, and connections with, Cohen turned out to be a mixed blessing when Margaret Chase Smith decided to run for reelection. In fact, her first question to Cohen when he went to Washington to pay her a courtesy call on January 26, 1972, was "What's a Monks man doing here?"[1]

She and General Lewis continued to investigate Cohen's connections but did nothing to oppose him once it became clear that the Cohen campaign was going to stay neutral. For his part, Cohen had enough of a challenge with Greene and he did not want to alienate Senator Smith in addition.

Treading a narrow path between Monks and Smith during the primary was one of the chief problems for the Cohen campaign during the spring of 1972. Toward this end, James "Jim" Harrington, a University of Maine student and head of Youth for Margaret Chase Smith, played a key role, ending up irritating the Monks supporters by selling fundraising tickets for her out of the Cohen campaign headquarters.

He also brought with him another University of Maine recent graduate, George Smith. Smith had recently done work in New Hampshire on behalf of Pete McCloskey and was already active in Republican circles. Hired as a driver, Smith would later accompany Bill on his walk and become field man for Piscataquis, Somerset, and Franklin counties and would deliver them for Cohen in the general election. Subsequently, Smith became campaign manager for Dave Emery in 1974 and eventually ended up as one of the state's major power brokers in his capacity as executive director of the Sportsman's Alliance of Maine (SAM).

As campaign manager, it would be my responsibility to help juggle these competing forces and few things on the campaign trail that year would be as taxing. Prior to deciding to run, Cohen approached me to take "a hard-headed look" at the situation, saying: "If it looks good, you can be my campaign manager." I had returned to Bowdoin to begin teaching in the fall of 1970 after teaching at Dartmouth and Vassar.

Part of the appeal of my return was, of course, returning to my alma mater. Part of it was living in Maine and part of it was my interest in getting involved in politics. While teaching at Dartmouth College, I had worked on the campaigns of Gene McCarthy and Bobby Kennedy and had thick notebooks filled with ideas about running for office myself. Immodestly, I saw myself as a future governor of Maine!

Bill Cohen's campaign, I thought, would give me a chance to try out some of my ideas and get some on-the-job training as his campaign manager as well. Also, Bill and I were quite close, having been classmates and fraternity brothers at Bowdoin and after graduation, working that summer as police officers in Old Lyme, Conn. He and his wife, Diane, both had faith in my (then) somewhat ruthless cynicism and knew I would put their interests first, ahead of those of Monks, the Republican Party, and anybody else.

My initial overview of the situation soon led me to a number of conclusions:

First, the race was doable. The last few Republican candidates had lost not because the district had "gone Democratic" but because the candidates had run poor, underfunded campaigns. In fact, Republicans still had a roughly 106,000 to 92,000 registration advantage over Democrats but Republican candidates were not only failing to hold their Republican base, they were losing by huge margins among Democratic and especially Independent voters who made up 55,000 of the total. For example, 81 towns—such as Orono, Skowhegan, Auburn, and Caribou—with Republican pluralities had gone Democrat the last two cycles.

Second, it appeared to me that the Franco Americans were Democrats in name only; they basically believed in the Republican values of small business and less government interference and disapproved of governmental social engineering and they had not voted Republican because the Republicans hadn't bothered to campaign among them and share those values.

These voters were the key to the general election, I felt. For example, the normal Republican candidate came out of the heavily Franco American county of Androscoggin down 23,000 votes. The last three Republican congressional candidates—Foley (1966), Shute (1968), and Connors (1970)—had all gotten less than 30 percent of the Androscoggin County vote. In Lewiston, all had gotten less than 14 percent of the vote in the last three election cycles.

If Cohen could come out of Androscoggin County down by less than 10,000 votes, he should have a good chance to win. If he came out of Androscoggin county down by 6,000 or so votes, he would win. To do that, he would need to break 20 percent in Lewiston.

The Franco American vote was the key to both.

But to win the Franco American vote, Cohen would have to campaign long and hard among the Franco American voters and give them a chance to know him and learn of his views. Also, it was important that they learn he was not a child of privilege but that his father had worked fifteen hours a day in a bakery. The Republican stereotypical image of banker or utility executive had to be broken.

In this regard, the fact that Lewiston was less than a half hour away from the Bowdoin campus made student activity a big possibility as well. Cohen was very favorably received at his alma mater and initially over forty students showed up to listen to him and many subsequently joined the campaign.

Based on the Gene McCarthy model to which I had been exposed while teaching at Dartmouth during the 1968 New Hampshire presidential primary, students began passing out literature and campaigning with the candidate early in March.

Bowdoin students Cindy Watson, Jed Lyons, Bob Loeb, Mike Hastings, Rob Witsil, and others soon became staples on the Lewiston scene and they managed to recruit dozens of Edward Little and Lewiston high school volunteers. Eventually, the Cohen organization would not only canvass Lewiston and Auburn several times, they would also go door to door in Lisbon, Lisbon Falls, and other surrounding towns.

Third, given the geographic size of the district—the largest east of the Mississippi—it was important to have a scientific schedule based on where the ticket-splitter voters were. In other words, the district needed to be divided up by population in terms of campaign time but also, within those parameters, campaign visits while traveling were also based on swing voter locations.

Early on, we put down hard and fast rules that lunch breaks and pit stops and other campaign breaks had to take place in ticket-splitter locations. These were not popular with either the candidate or the driver and constant attention had to be paid to make sure the schedule and its guidelines were followed.

Fourth, along these same lines, I believed that the primary campaign was to be run as if it were a general election with heavy visits to Democratic areas and a media effort with heavy emphasis on TV and outreach efforts. This meant a lot of visits to plant gates and tours of factories where Republican voters were few and far between and where Republican candidates never came during primaries.

My thinking was that it was much better to lose in the primary than the general election and the Republican candidate would have to position himself early in order to overcome the "behavioral Democratic" nature of the district, i.e. people were used to voting Democrat and would do so again unless this initial inertia were overcome.

The validity of this approach was soon apparent when we visited mill gates and the workers responded favorably to Bill Cohen—until they saw the "Republican" on his campaign literature. That literature was then often thrown into the dirt and snow. The blue collar portion of the electorate simply had to see the candidate up close and personal and learn about him firsthand.

Fifth, and conversely, I believed that both the primary and general election required skillful use of television. The district was just too big and spread out to accomplish a victory solely on the ground. We had to have the best television and a lot of it. That TV had to be connected to the campaign on the ground.

Of the many contributions Bob Monks made to the 1972 campaign of Bill Cohen, among the most important was his underwriting the cost of hiring Mike Harkins of The Agency, a Delaware media consulting firm that specialized in moderate and liberal Republicans.

Selected by Monks's astute and insightful campaign manager, William "Bill" Webster, Harkins provided very valuable guidance and a much-needed frame of reference for campaign activities.

Soon nicknamed "The Littlest Gunslinger" for his combative nature, diminutive stature, and love for "beating the D's," Harkins came up with the early campaign slogan "Bill Cohen: The Man the People Found" and he made biweekly visits to Maine during the primary.

He knew when to send out direct mail and when to advertise in weekly newspapers. Weekly newspapers, he felt, gave you much better coverage for their cost as their issues would sit around for a whole week in the barber and beauty shops, fire stations, and doctors' offices. Also, he pointed out, there was a strong correlation between advertising in a weekly newspaper and getting that paper's eventual editorial endorsement. This could not be said for the daily newspapers who were much more ideologically driven.

Bill Webster too provided a great deal of help during the campaign despite his full-time activities on behalf of Monks. Both men helped the Republicans bridge the campaign knowledge gap that then separated Republican campaign operatives from their Democratic counterparts. Webster was always gracious and helpful when called up for help, even when it was clear that the Monks campaign was failing to arouse the widespread support for which he'd hoped.

In terms of issues and message, while Bill Cohen knew who he was and knew what message he wanted to convey and knew what overarching "game plan" ideas needed to be actualized, we were both neophytes as to day-to-day campaign specifics and both Harkins and Webster were invaluable, both becoming friends as well as professional associates. Mike Harkin's print and television commercials captured the essence of Bill Cohen and set his image in the minds of hundreds of thousands of Maine people.

A sixth important and key piece of the primary puzzle came from one of the first people we talked to about the race. Horace "Hoddy" Hildreth Jr. (himself a former GOP Congressional candidate) gave the very best advice about how to succeed in a contested primary. He stated it simply and for all time: "Stress familiar thoughts."

That was good advice then and it is good advice now. The majority of primary voters, whether Republican or Democrat, do not want to hear new ideas; they want to hear their own, old thoughts revalidated. Most campaigns by most candidates think they have to bring the primary voters something new in the way of concepts and ideology. The opposite is true. The people most anxious to hear new messages are those least likely to vote in the primary—Independents and those in other parties!

For his part, Cohen's opponent Abbot Greene was a no-nonsense, conservative candidate who rightly grasped the significance of the ties between Monks and Cohen and the importance of Monks's financial backing to the campaign of his opponent. Although he ran a largely and eventually losing negative campaign, he made it an uncomfortable one for Cohen, the most uncomfortable one he ever experienced.

Abbott Greene deeply resented what he took to be the unfair interference of the same party leaders who had failed to help Jim Erwin. Now they were more active than was desirable, endorsing his opponent in a primary. In terms of negative attacks, he would turn out to be the most formidable candidate qua candidate Cohen would ever face. He was not afraid to attack Cohen and did so readily and often, and he never backed down from the challenge.

By today's standards, the race got off to a late start. Cohen sent out a letter on February 4, 1972, and did not fly around the district kicking off his campaign until February 8, 1972. The first fly around the state was a new campaign tactic. Instead of announcing at one location—such as one's hometown—Cohen brought his message all across the district, starting in Auburn (for the Lewiston/Auburn media) where he enjoyed strong support from Republican Mayor Jack Linnell, then going on by air to Presque Isle and later Bangor and Orono.

I have written elsewhere (in *Just Do It!*) that initially Cohen was not a "natural" politician and his early forays into rural Washington and Hancock counties (Greene's base) were not always greeted by enthusiastic voters.[2] He was sometimes stiff and awkward, a fledgling candidate once he left the comfortable campaign confines of downtown Bangor.

But Cohen persisted and became much more able on the campaign trail. Quick-witted, highly intelligent and hardworking, he absorbed new information like a sponge. He pressed himself to understand a wide range of issues. He learned to listen carefully and intently to the people he encountered. He became a formidable candidate just the way he'd become a state championship basketball player and a cum laude graduate of Bowdoin College.

He made himself into an exceptional candidate by dint of hard work, intelligence, and sheer competitive drive. He ended up working 15- and 16-hour days, never letting up on himself as he sought to make himself into a formidable candidate. He focused on improving those aspects of his "game" at which he was weak and forced himself to do things he would have liked to avoid.

Cohen turned out to be the hardest working candidate I ever saw in action and one of the brightest. He studied briefing books and issues hour after hour. His competitive juices flowed when he was out on the campaign trail. He simply made himself into such a political force that at no time was he ever behind in any polls for any office.

Bill Cohen also had an affinity for television. From the very beginning, not only did he look great on TV, but his 30-second commercials captured the essence of this formidable, bright, competitive Mainer. Also, he was superb under the hot studio lights, never making a major mistake when the red light of the TV camera was on and the tape rolling. He had a presence on television that cannot be taught.

Bill Cohen also had what Hemingway called "grace under pressure." Others would say he was "inner directed." Whether facing hostile voters on the campaign trail, getting blasted by Greene and his supporters, facing discrimination as "a Jew" and "a half-breed," Cohen remained calm.

Even when the *Bangor Daily News* editorial board called him in during those early days to answer a ludicrous assertion that he had been accused of grave robbing, he kept his composure when he was grilled for several hours answering these ridiculous, hateful, and totally malicious charges.

Cohen himself very often alluded to his heritage of being an outsider: his father was Jewish and his mother Irish. Moreover, she was Irish Protestant, not Catholic. Cohen claimed never to fit with either religion and ended up, at least briefly, as a Unitarian. He maintained that this marginalized status helped him turn inward and know his own worth.

His background and his self-image as an outsider, while they may have denied him a sense of belonging, toughened him up spiritually and mentally and gave him a sense of inner worth. This sense of inner worth produced a solid core to which he could withdraw during times of stress. He was centered. He was grounded.

This psychological mix greatly enhanced his ability to withstand the pressures of the campaign trail. Later, of course, it would serve him in good stead in the firestorm in which he cast a crucial committee vote for the impeachment of Richard Nixon long before it was either fashionable or politically correct.

But in the spring of 1972, all of this lay in the future. The June 17 break-in of the Democratic National Committee headquarters was then a minor event for him. Much more pressing were the pressures of the campaign trail, the worries about money, the negative impacts on family and spouse, and the sense of doom hanging over him should he fail. Not by chance those closest to him chose "Bridge Over Troubled Waters" for the campaign theme song. Bill Cohen literally made himself into one of the best candidates in the postwar period in Maine and kept his inner peace while doing so.

Cohen's first poll came back on March 7, 1972. It showed Cohen with 12 percent of the vote and Greene with 10 percent, leaving over 70 percent of Republican primary voters undecided. This was very good news indeed and meant that Greene's previous run for political office had not left him with either a big name identification advantage or even a lead.

Of course, Cohen himself was virtually unknown outside of Bangor with only 18 percent of Republicans having heard of him, but relatively, he was in excellent shape and the campaign staff (myself, Tricia Baldwin the scheduler/receptionist, and Charlene Weatherbee and Diane Cohen who were in charge of volunteers) was quite enthusiastic.

Although we didn't know it at the time, this pattern was to persist throughout Cohen's entire political career. He was never behind any opponent real or potential, including Governor James B. Longley and, in the "election that never was" of 1975, Senator Ed Muskie. From 1972 on, Cohen always was in the lead in any polling we did.

Recognizing the need to get Cohen out into those areas where he was not known and leaving Lewiston/Auburn for the students to hold the fort, Cohen embarked on an extensive tour of Washington and Hancock counties. He got an excellent reception, especially in Eastport, Ellsworth (where he had the support of the popular state representative and later mayor Ruth Foster), and Calais in the heart of "Greene country."

The Republican convention (April 28–30) was another test. The Greene forces were well organized and with the keynote speaker that year in Augusta being Vice President Spiro Agnew, there were even more conservatives in attendance than usual.

But the Cohen forces more than held their own, getting a lot of support from Republican legislative leadership especially Republican majority leader in the state senate, Joe Sewall, and President Ken MacLeod and from students from all over the state. Jim Harrington continued doing an excellent job as liaison with the Smith forces. Cohen gave an uplifting speech with just enough raw meat for the party faithful and was quite popular with the rank and file, many of whom got to see him for the first time. Diane and Bill Cohen brought a good bit of glamour and charm to the Republican proceedings.

On May 8 he received the results of a new poll showing the progress he had made on the ground in the Republican primary. Cohen now had 22 percent of the vote compared to 12 percent for Greene. However, Greene was not finished and by the end of May, he was on the attack with a series of press releases and agitation by his campaign manager.

Cohen was upset by the charges—some wild, some right on the money—especially Greene's continuing linkage of Cohen to Monks who, it was clear by this time, was going down to defeat in the race for the senate nomination. Greene's strategy was simple: tie himself to Margaret Chase Smith and Cohen to Monks.

Then occurred one of those small campaign experiences that help to illustrate the ebb and flow of campaigns, a vignette that captures the campaign realities as they are unfolding.

The candidate's psyche often needs a tune-up.

In this case, as often happens, the candidate, tired and harried on the campaign trail, was overreacting to the personal attacks of his opponent and insisted on the campaign taking action. Cohen wanted some support out on the hustings.

As luck would have it, there was a candidates' forum in Lincoln, Maine, scheduled for the night of May 25. Lincoln was then, and still is, a rock-ribbed conservative place for Republicans and Cohen was apprehensive about the attack he thought Greene would undoubtedly launch there. Nothing would do but we had to mount a huge presence at the event.

Joe Sewall was pressed into service that night, as were state representatives Percy Porter and Walter Birt, along with the whole campaign staff and many volunteers recruited for this "crucial" meeting. I've always wondered what the seven Republicans who attended the Lincoln candidates' night thought of being outnumbered 2–1 by Cohen's entourage, let alone what to make of my long and impassioned speech for the "law and order" candidate Bill Cohen "who had been with me on the frontlines of fighting crime."

For that matter, it couldn't have been fun for Abbot Greene, being alone with his wife and having to listen to six or seven speeches on behalf of his opponent even before he got to speak. Ah, overkill! But as we drove back to Bangor that night, the candidate was once again at ease. We had demonstrated the muscle of our campaign and brought it to bear at a point where the candidate thought it mattered.

That meeting was also regarded by the staff as one of the turning points of the campaign because everybody got so excited about "roasting Rabbit" (Greene's nickname) that staff enthusiasm continued right up to the primary. Campaign workers always need little examples of one-upmanship to feel good about themselves.

Subsequently Greene appeared on a public television call-in show. Not only did Cohen staffers start his interview off with a negative "So you weren't actually born in Maine?" question but Cohen volunteers flooded the station with calls and got in every single question for Greene, delighting the staff but disturbing Cohen and the producers of the show. This was one of the last political call-in shows they did for many years as other campaigns took up our tactic.

Also, when Greene brought his "Greene Machine," a flatbed truck to Bangor, eager staff members chained it to a telephone poll so it couldn't be moved for hours.

Greene went down fighting, however, taking advantage of the Cohen campaign's failure to file a spending report properly to launch a last-minute attack on June 15th. Greene and his campaign manager, Peter Anderson, pressed hard, using the occasion to attack Cohen on a variety of issues and going as far as to accusing Cohen of accepting illegal funds from Monks.

As campaign manager, I had the task—and fun—of responding to the attacks: "I am not going to dignify this with a reply, except to say that we welcome any inquiry by federal authorities and have been in touch with them concerning our returns. They have assured us that our records are more than adequate."[3]

Cohen's finishing television burst was excellent, telling the story of "The Man the People Found" and providing the young mayor of Bangor with a most appealing public persona. Also Cohen worked extremely hard the last few weeks on the ground, putting in 16–18-hour days. I recall on more than one occasion he was literally asleep on his feet when those campaign days finished up at midnight.

June 19 was primary day. I went up to Lewiston and spent the day there with the Bowdoin and local volunteers, not leaving the city until 7:30 pm. By the time I got to Bangor, the returns were starting to come in and they were quite favorable with Cohen taking the major towns by a 2–1 or 3–1 margin and the entire district by a tally of 61 percent to 39 percent. But Lewiston was the jewel in the crown with Cohen beating Greene there by a 4–1 margin. Lewiston had delivered.

Overall, Cohen handily defeated Greene 61 percent to 39 percent and Greene faded from the Maine political scene. "Bangor Billy" was on his way.

Not so Robert A. G. Monks. He had lost to Margaret Chase Smith by a wide margin and we worried about his continuing commitment to Cohen and, if the truth be told, Bill and I also shared some survivor's guilt.

Consider for a moment, however, the mental state of Bob Monks on June 20, 1972. He had just spent $500,000, outspending his opponent 50–1 and losing 2–1. He would not be heading on to the fall competition. He would not be heading up a Republican slate. But Cohen would be going on. Other political figures might have abandoned the congressional candidate there and then especially when he considered the Cohen "neutrality" in the primary, but Monks did not.

He swallowed hard, kept his pledge to support Cohen's candidacy, and helped clean up Cohen's primary debts. To his credit, years later he admitted his run for the Senate was not based on issues or programs: "It was just sheer arrogance. I liked to think of myself as a senator."[4]

Monks has been such a larger than life figure on the Maine political scene, and his often hidden influence has gone unexamined for such a long time, that he deserves a much closer look by historians. So many of his contributions to the political life of the state lie beyond the scope of this book and warrant their own study by someone objective enough to overlook his three stinging electoral defeats.

In the meantime, state senator Elmer Violette of Van Buren had only faced light opposition in the Democratic primary. This was a very unusual situation because normally when a Franco American runs for major office in Maine, other elements in the Democratic Party, often strong candidates of Irish extraction, oppose them. But Violette had been a loyal party man and Ed Muskie believed in him and thought he should have a chance at the open seat after carrying on nobly against a much stronger Margaret Chase Smith in 1966.

Violette, then 51, had been born in Van Buren, Maine, in 1921. He was a very respected member of the Maine House and Senate and long a champion of such important environmental concerns as the Allagash Waterway. A decorated veteran, having served in the Army Air Corps during World War II, Violette was also a hunter and fly fisherman. A graduate of Ricker College with a law degree from Boston University (the same as Cohen), Violette enjoyed the out of doors, his family, and his religion as well as public service.

He had the experience of government and that would become a central theme of his campaign. "Elmer Violette: Put His Experience to Work for You" was his slogan and he personified a life of public service. As the *Portland Press Herald* put it, "He is at once a leader, a gentleman and a gentle man. There is no man better liked and respected in the Maine Legislature among both Republican and Democrats alike than Elmer Violette."[5]

Violette had served his party well and had been Senate minority leader. He had already run statewide, getting over 41 percent of the vote against Margaret Chase Smith in 1966. Violette knew the state and the issues it faced; he'd run statewide and knew how to spend his time effectively on the campaign trail.

He had Ed Muskie's strong support and endorsement and was well liked by those who knew him. Indeed Violette and some of his closest supporters such as Democratic House Leader John Martin felt he was entitled to take another shot at Margaret Chase Smith in 1972 but ultimately he deferred to Congressman Bill Hathaway and decided to run for Congress.

He had easily and gracefully won the Democratic primary, beating Lewis Maxwell, a poultry framer from Franklin County, 78 percent to 21 percent. He was a very nice man with a lot of experience, someone who didn't like controversy or negative campaigning.[6]

His candidacy worried me a lot.

If the Franco Americans were the key to the election, having to run against a Franco American was a major concern. It was one thing to "steal"

Lewiston from the distant Abbot Greene. It would be quite another to accomplish our purposes in Lewiston against a fellow Franco American. Not only was he a Franco American, over the years he'd dedicated himself to important legislation affecting that community and had been the driving force behind the law authorizing bilingual education in Maine.

Also, Violette's campaign manager was the savvy Neil Rolde who had successfully headed up Ken Curtis's reelection effort. I knew Rolde would be on top of the campaign from beginning to end and his experience would make for a steep learning curve for us during the general election.

Finally, despite Cohen's substantial victory in the primary, I had seen enough of the 2nd District to know that many people still have a very negative opinion of Republican candidates and the races they had run. Bill Cohen had driven over 26,000 miles throughout the sprawling 2nd District and had barely made a dent among the electorate, especially among the swing voters who considered themselves to be Democrat or Independent.

I felt we had to do something dramatic and important in order to change the basic "terms of trade" of the general election. I believed we had the summer to alter them and we had to use July and August to get in a position where we were strong enough by Labor Day to attract enough money to mount a successful TV campaign in the closing weeks. We couldn't afford to "go dark" at the end; we had to make Bill Cohen an attractive candidate for ticket-splitter Democrats and Independents.

THE WALK: CHANGING THE BASICS

Fortunately, at the time, I had a student named Bob Loeb. Bob was from Chicago and he'd watched a virtual unknown Dan Walker walk across the state to victory over the Daley machine in the 1972 Democratic primary. Walker had gotten the idea from Senator Lawton Chiles who had used the same technique in 1970 to walk across the state of Florida and into the U.S. Senate.

Bob offered his good idea to me one day after class and I immediately saw the genius of it as well as its perfect fit for what we wanted to accomplish. What better way to show a "new" kind of Republican, a "man of the people," than to have him show up, hot and sweaty on their doorstep? Later, after Labor Day, when I went back to teaching, Bob would become the day-to-day campaign manager. He had earned the position.

I thought his idea of the walk was pure genius.

First, we had a young, vigorous candidate, an all-state athlete who could easily (I thought) walk twenty miles a day. He would be hot and sweaty and not look like a stuffed shirt in a coat and tie as he came into people's backyards.

Second, although it is less true today, thirty years ago in politics, the summer was only used for light campaigning, a few fairs and speeches. The conventional wisdom was that people were not interested in "politics" before Labor Day and they would be turned off by excess campaigning. The walk, however, would seem natural and since it wouldn't be in the news all the time, many people wouldn't know it was going on even while it was accomplishing its purposes.

Third, I thought the Democrats would not see the walk for the revolution it truly was and they would continue to campaign "as usual" while we were changing the way people in Maine's 2nd CD viewed Republicans.

Fourth, since we didn't have enough money to be on TV during the summer and the fall, and we had a lot of volunteer help, help who got excited about the idea of a big adventure, we could combine a small budget with lots of enthusiasm and help.

Fifth, I was convinced the more people who met and saw Bill Cohen, the more people who would vote for him. I believed that he would learn a lot about the issues of the day even as the people were learning about him and he had the ability to absorb quickly all the new information as he went along.

When I broached the idea with the candidate and other members of the staff, there was significant opposition. Some thought it a waste of time. Some thought it would tire the candidate out for the fall. Bill himself was initially skeptical but on June 25, as we sat in a Brunswick park having lunch, he agreed, adding only, "Are you sure?"

As my memo of the time suggests, the goal of the Walk was to fix Cohen's image as:

a. A man who cares—"he cared enough to come, on foot."
b. A Congressman for all the people.
c. The candidate who understands rural problems and is concerned with them.
d. A hard worker—"My God, Emma, he walked to Houlton." [7]

I was very impressed with his commitment and so overjoyed with his decision that I offered to walk three days with him, "the first day, the last day, and one day in the middle."

Only after Bill agreed did the full weight of his decision hit me. We were really risking a lot. Once begun, the walk couldn't be stopped without making him a laughingstock. Six hundred miles, from Bethel to Ft. Kent, was a long way. Having the candidate's commitment, could we provide the logistical support to make it possible? Could the campaign do its part to keep the candidate in the field properly supplied and assisted?

The logistics of the walk were very daunting.

When most people think of "a walk" they think of something simple and easy. Most candidates walk around areas during their campaigns. They may do a neighborhood or a small town or a portion of a city. They may set aside a Saturday morning or even a whole day to "hit the bricks."

But a statewide walk is very different.

For one thing, it is not simple to pull off at all. You need considerable staff support to make it come out right. For example, you have to have one car trailing behind the candidate with a sign saying, as in this case, "Bill Cohen Ahead, Honk and Wave." You have to have one car going ahead with a similar sign so that people on both sides of the road and in the two streams of cars can see the candidate coming. Without this kind of identification, you don't have a candidate, you simply have a random person or bindle stiff walking along a road.

Also, although Cohen was to walk all across the district, and that turned out to be some 600 miles overall, there were a variety of routes that could be taken through various counties and towns. Therefore you had to have another team of advance people at least one week in advance scouting out the area for the best routes, where the most people were likely to see the walk and to make sure the candidate didn't miss any important locations.

This advance team lined up press contacts, provided for local radio and weekly newspaper coverage, and made sure that local opinion makers were included in the opportunity for interviews with the candidate.

The team was also responsible for making contact with the people with whom the candidate would spend the night. I believed that it was important for a "man of the people" to get into their homes for dinner and breakfast and the evening to find out what was really on their minds. It took a lot of time and effort to find the right family for each night's stay.

Once the walk began, it was clear that this overnight was among the most important selections the team could make. After a twenty-mile hike every day, the candidate was exhausted and really would have preferred to check into a hotel or motel and get some downtime. So landing in the wrong house for the night could be disastrous (and was in the beginning).

Finally, you had to have someone scouting one day ahead to make sure things had stayed the same, that the people were expecting the candidate and also to allow for any media coverage. Having the candidate arrive at a home or business where the people had forgotten he was coming was more than annoying, it was a missed opportunity and it also put the candidate in a poor state of mind.

The walk began on July 19th in Gilead, just west of Bethel, hard on the New Hampshire border.

The first day was not a great success on the ground. We started early and walked all day. Car after car whizzed by; some waved but most looked out at Cohen and the rest of us in bemused incomprehension.

It was nearly noon before Charles and Marlene Petersen, strong Cohen supporters in the primary and now his field people for Oxford and Androscoggin counties, recognized that most of the cars weren't from Maine at all but from Quebec, taking vacationers to Old Orchard Beach and other points south. This knowledge did not improve our mood.

Moreover, we had dramatically underestimated the time it would take to walk the 20 miles we'd allotted so Cohen had to walk until dark to cover 13 miles of the allotted route. Then, while the rest of us went home to hearth and libations, Cohen got to have dinner with two nice but talkative elderly ladies who kept him up well past midnight talking about social security.

The next day, Cohen had to be brought back to the campaign trail to start the process all over again. But by this time, his feet were a mess and he would end up in the hospital three times getting treatment for them while on the walk.

Only a person of considerable fortitude and with a strong fear of failure—to say nothing of intense rage at his supposed friend and campaign manager for having gotten him into such a mess—could have gotten through the next few days.

But from the first, press coverage was fantastic. In thirty years of following Maine politics, I have never seen a positive story that had such "legs" or staying power. While the AP did only a short story the first day of the walk, the story did contain a good quote from Cohen that set the theme for the effort:

> There is no doubt it will require quite an effort, but I have every reason to believe that the rewards will outweigh the hardships. In meeting people over the next 400 miles, I think I will have a big opportunity to gain a firm insight into the concerns of the people.[8]

The next day, the *Portland Press Herald* followed up with a huge story that featured a front-page headline, "Candidate Cohen Begins His Walk Across Maine." Written by John C. Day, a district correspondent for the *Herald* (not John S. Day, the political writer for the *Bangor Daily News*), the piece told "the story" of the walk, quoting Cohen: "This is an issue-oriented walk; people feel their representatives aren't listening to them so I am here meeting as many people as possible."[9]

Kent Ward of the *Bangor Daily News* also picked up on the central theme of the walk, which was to put Cohen in touch with "real people." In his "Cohen, GOP Get Boot Out of Walk," Ward said Cohen "is putting a little color and vitality back into a party that can stand huge doses of both."[10]

We could not have asked for a better public "launch" for the campaign. The initial coverage was huge and continuing.

And it set in motion a process by which the local and district reporters of the major daily papers covered the Cohen walk extensively as he entered their area. The resulting stories were picked up by other papers and bounced back and forth across the political landscape. Local media in the form of radio and weekly newspapers also came to cover him in action.

The walk took its toll, however, and Cohen's blisters got so bad that first week that he ended up in the Rumford hospital having them lanced. But Cohen persevered and by the end of the week, as he got to the Lewiston/ Auburn area, he was being recognized and enough media was coming out to make the effort seem worthwhile.

Logistical problems continued but day after day Cohen walked, his work boots and blue work shirt, his ready smile and wave, an increasingly well-known sight along the route. Within days, the workers who had thrown his campaign literature in the mud and snow stopped to offer him food, beer, and snacks. They saw him walking when they went to work in the morning and they saw him walking when they returned home. They were impressed.

Interestingly enough, the rigors of the walk itself were balanced by the incredible feeds people put on when he stayed with them. Cohen actually put on weight during the walk, saying only half in jest, "Every day was Thanksgiving." Interestingly enough the same pattern would prove true for Emery, McKernan, and Snowe during their walk: all gained, not lost weight.

The initial Democratic public response seemed to miss the potential of the walk. But while Elmer Violette was initially inclined to see the walk as something of a stunt, his campaign manager, the astute Neil Rolde, was struck immediately by its potential and the difficulty for the Violette campaign to find a counteraction.[11]

On the day the walk started, Violette challenged Cohen to a debate, saying, "Walking is fine but I think it is even more important that we begin talking so that voters know where we stand and what our records on the vital issues of the day have been."[12]

With the hubris of youth, we couldn't wait to debate Violette but, of course, put it off until the end of the walk. It was not until the middle of August that I sat down with Neil Rolde, Violette's campaign manager, to discuss terms, timing, and format for the fall debates. At the time, we were disconcerted about Violette's several calls for many debates and assumed that he and the Democrats knew something we did not and were prepared to embarrass or attack Cohen in some way we could not anticipate. Years later, Neil Rolde indicated that the whole thing was just a campaign tactic, "designed to give the impression Violette was strong and decisive."[13] It worked and made Cohen apprehensive prior to the first debate.

One big decision that summer which both camps had to make was whether or not to go to the party's national conventions. Most fledgling politicians like to go to these, thinking they will get visibility and exposure— and have some fun. In 1972, Nixon was the prohibitive favorite (or as his campaign slogan put it, "The One") and not a millstone until a year later! I though the candidate would like a break from the walk and should go but Bill insisted that he did not want to go to the convention.

We always thought Elmer Violette and the Democrats made a big mistake in the way they handled the 1972 Democratic convention. Bill Cohen was on his walk and tending to business in Maine while Violette was with Ed Muskie in Miami.

On television from the convention, Violette looked diminutive beside "Big Ed," "smaller than life" we said at the time, plus he was right there putting George McGovern and his left-leaning platform and poorly researched choice of vice president on the map. We thought Violette had made a scheduling error of considerable import. Only during the writing of this book did I learn that the reason Violette went to Miami was to help Muskie try to rally support for a long-shot effort to get the nomination away from McGovern!

Interestingly enough, when a possible (but amazingly artificial) alliance between the Muskie and Wallace forces fell though, several Maine Democrats took off for a break in the Bahamas. Chuck Cianchette rented a plane and took Violette, Rolde, and Fred Murray to the island of Eleuthera for lunch and a swim! On the way back, they nearly ran out of gas, stopping at Bimini and eventually coming back into the United States without checking in with the proper immigration authorities.[14] Imagine what we could have done with a picture of Violette lounging on a Caribbean beach while Cohen walked the state of Maine!

At base, Violette was a loyal party member and had once again put his own interests behind those of Ed Muskie and the Democratic Party by going to Miami.

This would happen repeatedly. Late in October, U.S. Senator Ted Kennedy came to Maine to campaign for Bill Hathaway in Biddeford. Ed Muskie asked Violette to come and help out, joining Ken Curtis, Representative Peter Kyros, Hathaway, and the two senators. He did so even at the expense of his own campaign in Lewiston and spent several days there.[15] He was so nice and self-effacing but he sometimes looked diminutive up on the stage with the larger than life Muskie and Kennedy.

On August 14, I met with Neil Rolde at Bowdoin to discuss debate formats. We both wanted a good number of debates so there were few disagreements.

There were also encouraging signs out of Lewiston during the summer. There were significant splits in the Franco American community and Cohen was getting the benefits of them. For example, and surprisingly enough, Representative Louis Jalbert, "Mr. Democrat," came to us early on, saying something to the effect that "Elmer Violette should not be the first Franco American congressman from this state. The first Franco American congressman should come from Lewiston."

It's still not clear today that Jalbert ever did anything to help Cohen—probably not—but his indication gave us a sense we could split the Franco American vote for sure and win the election. Interestingly enough, Violette's campaign manager Rolde remembers with some irritation coming down Lisbon Street and seeing Jalbert standing in front of the Cohen headquarters with Joe Sewall, the Republican head of the Appropriations Committee, at the opening of the office. He drove up onto the sidewalk and criticized Jalbert.

Properly chastised, Jalbert soon contacted him and reportedly offered Rolde, who is Jewish, the bizarre advice that Violette should attack Cohen for "not really being a Jew."[16] But Rolde indicated they never expected anything from Jalbert in any case, and in that, they were not disappointed.

At the very least, it showed us that Franco Americans in Lewiston were not solidly behind Violette, regardless of his ethnicity. The difference may have been pragmatic or it may have been subtle. Violette was Acadian French, from the St. John Valley and not Quebecois in origin like most of the people of Lewiston. As in all tribal politics, little differences mean a lot.

The Violette campaign became aware of the splits within the Franco American community whenever Violette was in Lewiston. His reception was strongest among those Acadians who had moved to Lewiston for work or family reasons and weakest among young Quebecois who saw ethnicity as a minor reason for political solidarity.[17]

As the walk continued, wherever Cohen went (such as Norridgewock and Skowhegan) he kept to the theme of reaching the people: "We are trying to touch the people excluded from the mainstream of political activity, the people who don't go to political rallies and teas."[18]

On August 10, Cohen reached Bangor, continuing to get great publicity. John Day, in the *Bangor Daily News*, portrayed him rather heroically, saying, "Cohen Strides into Bangor, Only 150 Miles Left To Go" as Cohen asserted, "I hope to refute the myth . . . which has reached gothic proportions . . . that there is only one party (the party of his opponent Sen. Elmer H. Violette) which has compassion for the people."[19] Often Cohen had to slow his walk for what he termed "the sick and infirm," i.e., the reporters.

Cohen's walk was thus well publicized and well covered by the time he reached central Aroostook County, as Cohen asserted that the "Walk Itself

Is An Issue."[20] Originally designed to stop at Houlton, the response to Cohen was so good we decided to extend it up to and through the Saint John Valley to end at Fort Kent. This added another 150 miles to the walk. He said, "This is probably the greatest experience that I have had."[21]

September 1 was the last day of the walk and Cohen was triumphant. He was joined by many staff members and local politicians for his entrance into Fort Kent. My main task that bright morning was to distract some of the local politicians in the group and make sure the TV cameras got Cohen going across the finish line and not just a shot of a mob. I was only modestly successful. Everyone wanted to be in the victory lap!

Following what was now The Walk, the Cohen campaign did a district-wide poll September 27–29. The 400-person sample showed that Cohen had moved into a discernable lead over Violette, 40 percent to 28 percent with 32 percent undecided.[22]

The walk had become "The Walk" and was now known to an astonishing 46 percent of the voting population. With this polling cohort, those who knew about "The Walk," Cohen's lead was an overwhelming 2–1. This was success beyond our wildest hopes. Moreover, Cohen was actually less well known among Republicans than the general public, especially those Republicans who lived in places such as Hancock and Washington counties where "The Walk" had not occurred.

The conclusion was obvious. Since "The Walk" was such a fine introduction to Cohen for people who did not know anything else about him, it made sense to take "The Walk" concept and bring it to those who had not yet heard about it via television and direct mail. "The Walk" became the central message for the general election as to who Cohen was and what he stood for.

In terms of an issue profile with all voters, Cohen did best with those concerned about controlling government spending, obtaining adequate medical and health services, controlling crime, and controlling drug abuse while Violette led with those concerned about creating more jobs. The bottom line? In the election of 1972 and considering the thousands of issues, there were not many wedge issues that divided Cohen and Violette. But the key would be to get the public to identify the most popular ones with the candidate and we looked to the debates as a chance to stake out some territory.

On September 7, I drove Bill to various newspapers and TV stations in Bangor to answer some charges of Violette.

The next day, Cohen had a debate with Violette on TV. I thought Violette won hands down, getting onto every issue and influence vector "lily pad" first. Cohen seemed oddly on the defensive, still anticipating some undefined attack from Violette. None came.

Violette had simply staked out a number of important positions, exhibiting his concern for rural Maine and veterans, consumer protection, tax reform, and full employment. Violette had clearly gotten the best out of the first debate and got a little momentum back.

All through the race, however, Cohen kept throwing out important cues to Democratic and Independent voters that Cohen was not simply a "conservative Republican." For example, October 4, Cohen came out in support of a national health insurance.[23] There was some Republican backlash towards this stance, but we knew those upset would eventually come home and not end up with the more liberal Violette.

During this time, Cohen's competitive juices really flowed and he improved both on the stump and especially on TV. He rallied from his poor performance in the first debate and I thought he handily won the October 10 TV debate on statewide public television. Kent Ward was less sure, stating, "Who got the edge over whom seemed unresolved at the end of the hour-long debate."[24]

In mid-October, Cohen forces sent out a direct mail piece to Republicans containing an October 16 endorsement from President Nixon, including the ironic closing paragraph, "I look forward to working with you in making the next four years among the best in America's history."[25]

Remember that at this moment, Watergate and the disaster that lay ahead for Richard Nixon had not occurred and he would easily carry the state of Maine. Our polling consistently showed Nixon with a huge (sometimes as high as 60 percent to 20 percent) lead over George McGovern. Having Nixon on the ticket was a net plus. McGovern was not playing well in Maine.

Other issues raised by Cohen during the fall election: 200-mile fishing limit, support for Nixon's plan to end the war in Vietnam, reduced burden of the property tax, expansion of health care programs, and concern about drug abuse. We felt these positions showed social concern and didn't give entire segments to the Democrats on the social issues. There were only a few major distinctions: Violette was in favor of the proposed public power Maine Power Authority and the Dickey Lincoln Dam. Cohen was not.

In fact, some rare sparks flew when Violette attacked Cohen for his stance on Dickey Lincoln in some of the harshest tones of the campaign, charging he "surrendered" when Cohen spoke at the University of Maine.[26] Since the entire Maine delegation was at the time supporting the project, this may have seemed like a statewide wedge issue but it was not.

Except for Aroostook County (which Cohen was going to lose in any case), the people of Maine were not in favor of the dam when they learned of its size and scope. Cohen was correct in predicting that "30–40 thousands of acres" of timberland would be flooded in the St. John's Valley but Violette was correct in asserting that "no part of the Allagash wilderness would be flooded."

I have long assumed that Violette was something of a prisoner to the big public works beliefs of Ed Muskie and other national Democrats, but Neil Rolde indicated that the reverse may well have been true: Elmer Violette may have believed more strongly in Dickey Lincoln than did Muskie!

We were very encouraged when tracking and voter identification polling in that Lewiston/Auburn area continued to show an upsurge in support for Cohen regardless of party affiliation. A late *Bangor Daily News* poll on October 28 showed a higher undecided vote (40 percent) than we were getting but still showed Violette trailing Cohen 35 percent to 25 percent.[27] This tracked very well with our internal key precinct analysis findings although the undecided cohort was larger in the BDN survey.

Cohen was determined to finish with a flourish.

We made a big final push in Androscoggin and Penobscot counties, mounting a big get out the vote effort. We organized Lewiston and Auburn (as well as Cohen's home base in the Bangor and Brewer area) in three shifts, 10 A.M. to 2 P.M., 2–5 P.M., and 5–8 P.M. with telephones, runners, and precinct polling place checkers. These workers were, of course, not just "Cohen" people but many were rank-and-file Republicans who were energized by his candidacy.

The Violette campaign also ended with mass mailings and leaflet drops to normal Democratic target groups: union members, teachers, farmers, and state workers. They made one mistake, however, at the end, running a radio ad in French to the Bangor community with its substantial Irish (and small Franco American) population.[28]

Violette had not totally ignored Lewiston, finally hiring French-speaking workers to register new voters and cutting radio commercials in French. But there was no door-to-door canvassing of the electorate in late October or early November in Lewiston, let alone in the surrounding towns such as Auburn, Lisbon, Lisbon Falls, Mechanic Falls, Leeds, Turner, and Durham.

His campaign manager, Neil Rolde, suggests that Violette simply did not like door-to-door campaigning and thought with his record and stature, he shouldn't have to and in any case, Violette had never had to campaign that way in the St. John Valley.[29]

In fact, Violette spent the end of October campaigning in the St. John Valley! To have Violette campaigning in his absolute base area during the end of the campaign was a huge plus for Cohen and gave us an open shot to the area in which we felt we had to do well in to cut down his margin.

By contrast, Cohen flew all over the sprawling 2nd District as the campaign ran down, stressing his major theme: "Government has drifted away from the people, and by keeping in constant touch with the citizens now and after the election, a Congressman can best represent the views of the people."[30]

Violette had simply not put in the time on the ground to counter the surge for Cohen in Androscoggin County. Some had tried to warn him about his need to campaign there but, when it came to the final stages of the campaign, he could be "very stubborn."[31] In the final stages of the campaign, he was ignoring the one area that could deliver him a victory in the election.

Looked at objectively, it had been a relatively low-key race, with few charges and countercharges, a positive campaign when all was said and done. Jim Brunelle ("Low Key Bout Has Nice Guy in Each Corner") rightly summed up the thoughts of many when he wrote that the race had not been based on mudslinging or negative attacks and that the candidates had not differed greatly on the issues. It was, he said, a race between two "nice guys."[32] John Day agreed, writing: "Two Nice Guys, But One Must Finish Last."[33]

I spent election day in Lewiston, then drove up to Bangor. Our key exit polling indicators flashed Cohen up by 10 percent wherever we looked. We knew we'd won by 6 P.M. Early returns on TV just after 8 o'clock had Cohen behind but we knew that wouldn't last. We were pleased to be able to say, "There aren't enough votes out there, Billy, to catch us."

Cohen won 54.4 to 45.6 percent.

It had been a close thing, however. Although Cohen won every county except Aroostook and Androscoggin, his overall margin was small and this was the closest race Cohen had run to date and it would turn out to be the closest race he would ever run.

Elmer Violette turned out to be the toughest electoral challenge Cohen would ever face.

Jim Brunelle at once figured out the Cohen strategy in his piece entitled: "Surprise Lewiston Vote Keyed Rep. Cohen's Win."[34] Instead of losing Lewiston 9–1, Cohen only lost it 2.5–1. He won Lisbon outright 1,331 to 1,111. Androscoggin County was not a net loss of 20,000 votes. Or 15,000. Or 10,000. Only 5,224 votes separated Cohen from Violette in this most Franco American and heretofore Democratic of counties.

REASONS WHY COHEN WON

Here are the reasons to be considered when asking: "Why did Bill Cohen emerge victorious in the 1972 2nd Congressional District race?"

1. "The Walk." Grueling, time-consuming, painful, it required a huge effort, but in the end, it was the single most important aspect of Cohen's successful campaign except for the candidate himself. All along the way, astonished—and later worried—Democrat insiders

came out to see him. For example, Auburn car dealer Shep Lee, Muskie's chief fundraiser and Democratic Party stalwart, came out on the campaign trail as Cohen approached Auburn and actually tried to convert him. But in the end, it was Cohen who converted the Democrats.

The 600-mile walk would be a test of fortitude and courage and would work out to a ratio of 11 miles for each percentage of the vote eventually garnered by Cohen.

As important as the walk was in and of itself, it was its use made by the Cohen campaign that promoted it and greatly enhanced its total impact. Footage of the walk was central to the TV commercials. The Cohen for Congress campaign brochure, which was distributed to several hundred thousand voters, was all about the walk, containing many candid shots of Cohen with Maine people all over the state. "This 600-mile walk was an honest attempt to learn what is on people's minds. I believe we succeeded in doing that," said the brochure.

2. Better television and modern campaign techniques. Gaining parity with Democrats, Cohen's commercials were better than Violette's and there were more of them. Simple, direct messages; images of Bill Cohen, a man of action and purpose; and the walk featured prominently in his list of accomplishments.

Mike Harkins's slogan, "Bill Cohen: The Man the People Found," captured the essence of his campaign and especially the 600-mile walk all across Maine. It was just the right antidote to the previous, often stodgy image of Republicans. Cohen had more television and better television as this Republican candidate was determined not to go the way of Burton Cross or Jim Erwin. The lessons of 1954 and 1970 had been learned by at least some Republicans.

Violette's TV was simply not in the same league. In fact, Violette ended up running an "old-fashioned" campaign reminiscent of Jim Erwin, while Cohen and his team brought to the Republicans the more "modern" campaign first pioneered by Ken Curtis!

3. Cohen was younger and more energetic. "If we'd only known to stop him then," said many Democrats years afterward. At the time, they thought he and his youthful followers were an aberration. Cohen's campaign attracted many youthful workers such as Jim Harrington, Jock McKernan, Gordon and George Smith, Mike Hastings, Jed Lyons, Rob Witsil, Cindy Watson. The able volunteer coordinators were Diane Cohen and Charlene Weatherbee. Violette himself attracted many young Democrats as well but their efforts were not concentrated in key areas but rather dispersed statewide.

4. Cohen was the hardest working Republican candidate since early Margaret Chase Smith. In 1972, 16-hour days were the norm. He worked and worked and worked. And he did so by a scientific schedule, always focusing on ticket-splitter towns and locations. It is true that Violette, too, worked hard but our perception always was that he took more time off the campaign trail and that his campaign days were not always scientifically programmed. There was no sense that his campaign schedule was driven either by polling or by swing voter/segmentation analysis.

5. Activities of Bob Monks. Without Bob Monks's encouragement and financial support, it is unlikely that Cohen would have entered the race, let alone had enough fundraising horsepower to run the media campaign which was so important. His support was a key variable in the Cohen for Congress campaign.

6. End of Big Box and the Francos in play. Lewiston and Androscoggin were the keys to Cohen's victory. He campaigned there much more than any previous Republican in modern times and his grassroots organization, manned and supplied by Bowdoin students but led by local prominent Franco American and Lewiston leaders such as Marcel Bilodeau and Lillian Caron, made the difference.

   An elaborate French version of the Cohen campaign brochure was distributed to the most Franco American sections of Lewiston and Auburn. Most towns in the county got at least one mailing and/or literature drop. Hard work, on the ground, block by block, were all features of Cohen's "surprise" showing in the area.

7. Cohen's affinity for television. It wasn't just Cohen's commercials that helped him. It was Cohen's style that was made for television. Having watched Maine politics for over thirty years, I believe there really are only two people, Bill Cohen and George Mitchell, who never made mistakes when the red light of TV was on in the heat of political battle. When it came to TV, Cohen was simply the best.

   Even with a fever of 104 degrees and a head so badly stuffed he couldn't hear during the tension of Nixon's impeachment, Cohen came through. He just wouldn't make a mistake when on TV. He might give the reporter an answer he or she couldn't use. He might give a seemingly trite metaphor: "On the one hand the glass is half full; on the other it is half empty." But he would never, ever shoot himself in the foot when the television camera was on him.

8. Grassroots support. Republicans generally overlook grassroots organization but this election it was possible to track the impact that organization had not only in crucial swing areas such as Lewiston, Presque Isle, and Bangor but in Republican base areas such as Brewer.

In Androscoggin County, for example, Mechanic Falls, Lisbon, Lisbon Falls, Durham, Leeds, and Turner were all blitzed with literature. On election day, over 100 Cohen volunteers were in action in Androscoggin County. Republican Party regulars were, of course, also out in force. The Cohen organization could never have turned out the vote it did without the ongoing assistance of these people in all the counties of the 2nd CD.

9. The dynamics of the election patterns that year also helped. Nixon running for president in 1972 was a big plus, in significant measure because his opponent, George McGovern, ran such a poor national campaign. With Nixon on the top of the ticket and winning handily and Bill Hathaway winning the senate seat against Margaret Chase Smith, many Republican and Independent ticket splitters "went back" to Cohen after having gone for a Democrat in between Nixon and the congressional line.

In this regard, it should be noted that the Hathaway race was the one that galvanized Democratic interest in 1972 and as Barry Hobbins points out, the building momentum of that race "sucked up a lot of money and a lot of operatives" that might have gone to Violette.[35]

WHAT IMPACT DID THIS ELECTION HAVE ON MAINE POLITICS?

1. As a Republican resurgence, the Cohen counterrevolution was a true revolution. Republicans began to use modern political techniques because they saw Cohen won with them: polling, focus groups, scientific schedules. Cohen was the mold—younger, more vigorous, more independent—that subsequent candidates imitated.

It was not that Cohen was a party builder in the way Muskie had been, but, rather, that Dave Emery, (George Smith, Emery's campaign manager in 1974, had been Cohen's driver and field man in 1972), Olympia Snowe, Jock McKernan, and Susan Collins all saw in Cohen the model for electoral success. Snowe and Collins both worked or volunteered for Cohen as well.

2. From the Cohen counterrevolution on, Maine's electorate can best be conceptualized as highly competitive. After the Cohen revolution, each of the voting groups had about one-third of the total in most outcomes. That is, in most general elections, one-third of the votes ended up being Republican (due to higher turnout), one-third Democrat, and one-third Independent (many of the 40 percent plus who are unenrolled do not vote).

It has become such a viable pattern that we hardly ever think about it. But what if Cohen—and later Emery, McKernan, and Snowe—hadn't won? Where would the Republicans be today? Certainly not as competitive as they are in 2003.

3. The walk became the campaign staple for an entire generation of Republicans. For the next twenty years, every successful Republican candidate for major office employed variations of the walk. Emery repeatedly walked across the 1st District, Snowe walked across the 2nd District, McKernan walked across the 1st District. For the next two decades, Republicans walked to victory, paying at least symbolic tribute to Bill Cohen and his first pioneering trek. Not all candidates who used the technique won their races, however; both Rollin Ives (1986) and Ted O'Meara (1988) walked in Maine's 1st District but lost.

    As late as 2002, Independent candidate Steve Kenny undertook a 500-mile walk on Route 1 from Fort Kent to Kittery and congressional candidate Dick Campbell biked across the 2nd District. Even Democratic Lori Handrahan had a trek across the District in her primary in 2002. All disappeared without a trace, finishing last in their respective races.

4. Better television by Republicans became the norm. Cohen's TV by Mike Harkins and The Agency was excellent, capturing his youth, his dynamism, and his leadership qualities. The 30-second ad became the staple for subsequent Republican candidates such as Dave Emery, Jock McKernan, Olympia Snowe, and Susan Collins.

    Increasingly, Republican candidates turned to national media firms to project their images onto the Maine political landscape, thereby matching—and in many cases, beating—the Democrats at the art form they pioneered.

5. Younger more energetic Republican candidates emerged. If Cohen could do it without paying his dues, why couldn't they? Although many were in the state legislature before running, all jumped over the hoop of playing a positive role in various election cycles for other, older, "It's my turn" Republicans. Emery in 1974, Snowe in 1978, McKernan in 1982 are all examples of this: they had served in the state legislature but had not run for major office beyond that body.

6. The end of Big Box put the Francos permanently in play. For the next thirty years, the number of Franco Americans who would vote Republican would grow tremendously and the number who would actually change their registration to become Republicans would rise dramatically.

    The Francos in play remains the single biggest independent variable in Maine politics, both candidate and ballot measure. Liberated by the removal of straight line party voting, Franco Americans in Maine became the most important swing vote in the Pine Tree State.

7. Expanding district offices served as political outposts. Cohen's efforts would push Muskie to do so as well. Emery would put one in Rockland, another in Augusta, a third in Biddeford, and a fourth in Portland. Now we take them for granted. Susan Collins has one in Biddeford. Cohen's first addition (beyond Bangor) was Lewiston; his second, Presque Isle. The district offices matched the political realities and needs. A presence equals a political opportunity. The federal government was paying; why not provide jobs for staffers, an opportunity to show the flag, a sense of citizen involvement and bring government closer to the people?

Only Congressman Tom Allen has bucked this trend, shrinking the number of congressional offices down to a single location in his hometown of Portland—a sad development for those without the means or inclination to drive several hours to visit his congressional office.

8. Citizen's Hours became major outreach efforts. First came Congressman Cohen who would hold "citizen's hours" in various places. The first was in Lisbon early in 1973. Then later, the staffers become surrogates for the Congressman. The Cohen operation decided that just because the election was over, the campaigning should not stop. We devised the notion that the congressperson could conduct congressional business with an eye toward political benefit as well as constituent service, using citizen's hours.

Congressman Cohen attending "citizen's hours" projected an aura of concern and caring and especially in some out of the way places, garnered long-term benefits from word of mouth: "He was here, Emma. I talked to him about social security."

After 1974, Dave Emery called them "Emery Town Meetings" and held them all over the district to enthusiastic crowds. Once this became an established tradition, it was only one step farther to have staffers hold the citizen's hours, freeing the congressperson up for other activities but keeping the grassroots flavor of the enterprise.

Since every member of the Maine delegation now does the same thing, it is hard to remember when none of them did this in a holistic, concerned manner. None of them did until 1973.

9. Citizen's Hours served as political advertising. This is quite different from (8). Going to a citizen's hour and meeting the congressman was one form of political interaction. But you didn't have to go to one to know they were there and they were a good idea. You saw the schedule advertised in the paper. You knew you could go if you

wanted. You felt the congressman or senator was reaching out to stay in touch.

Now every one in the Maine delegation has citizen's hours by officeholders and citizen's hours by staffers and we accept them as normal. They send out hundreds of thousands of postcards every year inviting citizens to come and visit them when they are in the area. In 1973, it was a major change and altered the political landscape because if other members of the Maine delegation were holding office hours, you couldn't afford not to.

10. The Republican Party qua party continued to decline in importance as Republican candidates do it on their own. The Margaret Chase Smith model had become the W. S. Cohen model as the party apparatus was increasingly bypassed. Only Dave Emery cared about building the party at the grassroots level. The Republican state committee became less and less relevant as time went on. The same thing was true for the Democratic Party. No money, little organization, always wanting to run campaigns too far to the right (if Republicans) or left (if Democrats), so why listen to them? Only in the election of 2002, with both national parties awash with "soft money," did the parties qua parties begin to regain some of their lost clout over candidates and their campaigns.

11. Finally, "The Election That Never Was" of 1975 took place. We are fortunate to have such a superb record of this development; otherwise hardly anybody would believe it happened, let alone in the way it actually did. Bernard Asbell was doing a book on the U.S. Senate and was profiling Ed Muskie during the entire time so we have a record of just what was going on from both sides of the "Election that Never Was."[36]

Cohen had won the election of 1972. When he got to Washington, he decided to go on the House Judiciary Committee, turning down some other more exciting assignments such as the Armed Services Committee. "I want to get my feet wet and stay in the background," he told me.

Within months, however, Cohen was thrust into the national spotlight of the Watergate hearings and America's huge constitutional crisis. Cohen would cast the deciding vote for impeachment long before it became popular. All of a sudden he was a national figure in the tradition of Margaret Chase Smith. He was on the cover of the July 29 issue of *Time* along with two other congressmen, Charles Wiggins of California and Robert McClory of Illinois.

He cruised to reelection, winning 71.4 percent of the vote versus Markham "Mark" Gartley's 28.6 percent, who himself had also been on the cover of *Time* as a returning prisoner of war during the

Vietnam war. Cohen was now a bright, shining, Republican national star.

Many Republicans in Maine and Washington wanted him to run for
Muskie's seat, up in 1976. In the beginning, virtually everyone in Cohen's
staff in Washington and most of their counterparts in Maine wanted him
to run. He had a new administrative assistant, Tom Daffron, who had
made his staff very professional and capable of taking on Muskie on that
level. National pundits, including newscasters, encouraged him to run.
Some Democrats and many Independents suggested that Muskie's time
had passed. Bill Cohen could become a senator by defeating one of the
most visible national Democratic figures.

It was a seductive prospect.

Thinking about the race from a consultant's point of view, it was exciting and to have knocked off Muskie would have put those of us on the
Cohen team in the national spotlight as well. I was also convinced even at
this early stage that we could come up with some smashing commercials,
especially two on the environment (outlined below), that would go to the
heart of Muskie's credibility.

So the 1976 senatorial race against Ed Muskie looked both exciting and
seductive.

But from the very first, I didn't feel comfortable with the situation. I had
a hard time making the assumption that when all was said and done,
enough Democrats would turn their back on the founder of their party to
give Cohen an edge with the ticket-splitters: "Moreover, when the chips
are down, I'm afraid I think the Muskie call for 'help me as I have helped
you and this party' is going to turn out more troops than 'the future is
now.'"[37]

I urged that we take the next six months and run a mock election. Let
Muskie do the best he could and we would do the best we could and then
see where we all were at the end of that period. "Let's have an election nobody knows about," I said, "and see how we do. Then we'll run—or not
run—in the real one."

Toward that end, on May 31, 1975, I met with Charlie Micoleau, Senator Muskie's administrative assistant and chief political guy. Charlie was
at Bowdoin (class of 1963) and we had a fair amount of mutual respect.
For different reasons, we didn't want the Cohen-Muskie matchup to take
place. I because I was afraid ultimately Cohen would lose. He because he
was afraid there was a real chance Muskie would lose. Neither of us
wanted to see our guy lose.

At the end of a long dinner and rambling political discussion with a lot
of mutual kidding and spinning, I made him an offer: "I don't know if
your guy or my guy would win but Maine would be the loser either way.

Why don't you take six months and see if you can make up the lost ground? If you can, I won't recommend that Bill make the race."

Charlie refused to admit that his man was behind and he may have been skeptical that I could turn the race off given all the momentum that he saw building toward Cohen's potential run in Washington and the state, but he quickly saw the advantage to everybody concerned. He vowed to redouble his efforts to get his man in the best possible position.

At that time, neither of us knew exactly where we were but our respective campaigns both took a benchmark poll in June of 1975.

Cohen's polling in June 1975, showed him in excellent field position. The head-to-head contest was very favorable to him. In the direct matchup, he led Muskie 49 percent to 41 percent with only 8 percent undecided.[38]

Moreover, Cohen had a 54 percent to 38 percent lead in his district, the 2nd. Remember that Cohen had yet to campaign in Maine's 1st District, so his being tied there, 44 percent to 44 percent, was a huge and meaningful indication that Cohen had a lot of upside potential.

These initial numbers said he could beat Muskie, no question about it.

Writing of the June 1975 situation, Asbell picked up the unexpected campaign dynamic as he followed Muskie through his routine:

> This is an election year. An election year? 1975? Yes, it is, a head start in Muskie's drive for reelection to the Senate in 1976. Before year's end, he will have spent one hundred days—virtually every weekend and recess day—in Maine, trampling out the impression that his heart and mind are too much in Washington on national affairs and too little on his home folk. That impression destroyed Maine's indestructible Margaret Chase Smith in 1972 and there are signs it is now hurting Muskie.[39]

He had already put his staff into "campaign mode." Muskie's private secretary, Dolores Stover, describes the change in policy for this election cycle: "The new policy is that when people from Maine come by and if you're in the office, this is until the election only, we'll try to give them a quick walk in."[40]

Muskie's polling was done by Pat Cadell, the Cambridge, Massachusetts, pollster who rose to prominence with George McGovern in 1972. His first major polling in Maine for Muskie was in June and showed results that disturbed Muskie and his staff.

Cadell had Muskie at 47 percent and Cohen at 40 percent, with the undecided cohort at 12 percent. Although the Muskie people did not know how bad the situation really was, these numbers were well down from Muskie's earlier 67 percent and 62 percent victories.[41] Incidentally, someone close to the Muskie campaign made sure we got his polling data and we had some fun with that. For example, I put an "op-ed" opinion piece into the *Bangor Daily News* using Muskie's own numbers.

Given the urban bias to many Democratic polls in Maine it is not surprising that the numbers were not exactly the same as Cohen's. But even
though Muskie looked better in his own poll, those findings were in and
of themselves quite a shock to the Muskie inner circle. They were worse
than they'd imagined.

Asbell put his finger of Muskie's problem:

> His more specific obstacle is a thirty-five-year old, blue-eyed, earnest, glam-
> orous Congressman from Bangor—Hathaway's successor from the Second
> District—named William S. Cohen, who has not yet announced his candi-
> dacy for the Senate as a Republican but is "assessing" his prospects with dis-
> quieting fervor. Everywhere you look, there's Cohen—especially around the
> First District where voters don't yet know him. Or do they?[42]

As "The Election that Never Was" progressed, Muskie got very testy
with all the talk about Cohen. On August 25, for example, he complained:

> This morning at a press conference, the other day on TV up north, every
> damned place I go, "he mutters," all they ask is about Billy Cohen. Do I think
> he's going to run? Do I think it's going to be tight? I just don't want to get
> into that with them. I'm not going to spend from now till November of next
> year helping them build up Billy Cohen. But they won't let me out of it.[43]

From Muskie's and Asbell's perspective, Cohen wasn't in Muskie's
league; he was just an upstart. He was young, dynamic, photogenic but not
a person of substance. He was just "Billy Cohen," "Bangor Billy," the style
guy. It was quite a shock to see him so close to Ed Muskie in his own poll.

Indeed, Muskie actually had more liabilities than Asbell—and probably
Muskie—knew. As the Cohen forces contemplated a possible run against
Muskie in 1976, his weaknesses seemed quite flagrant to us. We tried to
assess them objectively in June of 1975 and project which of them he could
correct by "game time," November 1976.

Tom Daffron and I identified at least five major problems that Muskie
would have to recognize and solve in order to reduce his vulnerability to
a challenge in 1976:

1. In his pursuit of the Democratic presidential nomination, Muskie's
   voting record had drifted far to the left of the political spectrum. In
   fact, Muskie's ADA (Americans for Democratic Action) rating was
   now higher than that of George McGovern. It was 100 percent! From
   Maine's more moderate, centrist position, Muskie's rating compared
   quite unfavorably to Cohen who stood at 56 percent.

   This may seem like inside baseball but the ADA rating is actually
   quite useful for positioning on a voting spectrum and was very en-

couraging to Cohen staffers in Washington. Could Muskie counter this situation? Yes, he could begin casting more highly identifiable "conservative votes." He did so all fall long.

2. Not only did many Maine people identify Muskie as "too liberal," but also they found him to have become "a big spender." Muskie was now for big government and this was an era of high taxes and high inflation. He wanted to spend too much. He was for expensive public works and welfare projects. He wanted things Maine people didn't think they could afford. He was wasting their money down there in Washington.

    Could Muskie counter? Yes, and he did, most skillfully. He went out and created a new Senate Budget Committee that he then chaired. Muskie began talking about prudent fiscal policy! He sounded like that old Yankee skinflint who had gotten elected governor in 1954! In fact, he did this switch in routine and emphasis so well that by the fall of 1975, even the conservative *Bangor Daily News* would applaud him for moving to the center on fiscal matters. The ease with which Muskie had conned the BDN into accepting him back into the fiscally responsible fold was very disheartening to us.

3. In 1974, Muskie had few district offices and his constituent service languished behind the more aggressive Cohen staff. Cohen already had three district offices in his CD, one in Bangor, one in Lewiston, and one in Presque Isle. Muskie only had three for the whole state. One in Portland (which was positioned so that any constituent seeking the Muskie office needed to pass by the office of Congressman Emery), one in Bangor, and one, surprisingly enough, not in Lewiston but Waterville.

    Tom Daffron, Bill Cohen's talented and energetic administrative assistant, had made Cohen's constituent service the best in the state and the most visible. Daffron himself was a very big asset and would have helped enormously in many ways had Cohen ultimately decided to run against Muskie. He had a lot of political skill and he routinely worked 16-hour days, often seven days a week.

    Could Muskie counter? Yes, he could and he would, opening more offices and having his staff go all out to get involved in local situations that showed how much Muskie cared. As Tom Daffron put it, the Muskie operation opened district offices "in carload lots," adding Lewiston and Augusta and Biddeford.[44]

    Both staffs engaged in exciting races with each other to help local communities with arcane projects. For example, both staffs devoted huge amounts of time to keeping the post office open in Witipitlock! Saco Defense got a lot of motion from both for their machine guns! Tiny hamlets found themselves visited by both Cohen and Muskie.

Both staffs churned out press releases dealing with local, state, and national issues trying to "round out" their candidate's profile. It was a war! Unrecognized and underreported but a war nevertheless.

4. Muskie had spent a lot of time on the national campaign trail and was perceived by many as being more interested in other places. As Asbell put it: because Muskie has been "pursuing the presidency for the past seven years, he's lost touch with the people. They resent that fact. They'd prefer to have the type of Senator who's kept much closer contact with his constituents and serviced them better."[45]

Could Muskie counter and repair this image damage? Yes, now he would have to come back to Maine more often. According to Asbell, this would mean coming back every single weekend and running like it was 1954 all over again. Muskie, by coming back every weekend, substantially reduced his vulnerability. He was no longer the remote presidential candidate; he was "Ed," home to mend fences. People knew he was mending them and they appreciated the effort.

5. Previously known as "Mr. Environment" and in the minds of his staff still "Mr. Environment," Muskie did have significant liabilities here. He was no longer "Mr. Clean" in any absolute sense. Not that he had changed so much—although he'd had to compromise to get some of his landmark legislation through Congress—but the environmental movement in Maine had become more demanding and Muskie was on the wrong side of several important issues.

I always thought that ironically enough, this issue was Muskie's Achilles heel and if Cohen had run, two mistakes would have been central to the campaign. These two major issues where Muskie was truly out of touch with Maine voters were quite substantial and, I thought, tailor made for 30-second commercials.

The first was Muskie's continuing advocacy of the Dickey Lincoln Dam, a huge WPA type project that would have erected a dam as high as the Empire State building and flooded a big portion of the St. John Valley in northern Aroostook County. This had been a mainstay of Democratic thinking for many years but had now become unpopular in Maine.

Among Democratic public works projects, this was among Muskie's favorite. Voters did not want it in 1975 and they would not want it in 1978 when it became a millstone around Bill Hathaway's neck in that election. Muskie was now on the wrong side of a major, wedge issue and knowing his stubbornness, we were convinced he would not change his position.

I could imagine a powerfully gripping TV spot showing the lovely St. John Valley filling up with a tidal wave of water, one which not only destroyed the Valley but the Franco American Acadian culture as well. This would be powerful stuff, I thought, and a searing body blow to Muskie among those 1st District ticket splitters who would cast their vote on environmental stances alone.

Also, Muskie's perceived connivance in the 1965 downgrading of the Prestile Stream in Aroostook County to help Muskie's well-known fundraiser Freddie Vahlsing could also be made into a devastating TV commercial.

The Vahlsing's potato processing plant had gone bust but not until after the Prestile Stream had been degraded to accommodate the new, highly polluting plant. As soon as the plant went on line, fish died by the carloads and the Prestile stream became an open sewer. There were even reports of eels going blind and trying to get out of the water! Canadian authorities complained bitterly about the pollution flowing into their country.

It was a nightmare for "Mr. Clean." We would bring the nightmare back to life.

People of Aroostook County were still angry and I thought this issue would hurt Democrats in two of their bases, not just with environmentalists but also in Aroostook itself, especially in the St. John's Valley, normally a Democratic stronghold. In most elections, Democrats need to carry Aroostook in order to win statewide.

I had already constructed the Prestile commercial in my mind: images of sightless eels "swimming on the grass" to escape the stream. This would be a powerful, high emotion, high impact 30-second spot that would curl the voters' hair. During this period, I often woke up in the middle of the night excited about bringing these striking images to the voting public!

We had some other moments of fun during "The Election that Never Was" as well. For example, on September 9, Asbell captures the delicious sound of Muskie's own poll numbers being used by us.[46]

On November 4, 1975, the Cohen forces also got a huge break when Lillian Caron became the first woman mayor in Lewiston history as Bowdoin students joined forces with local reform elements to upset the Democratic old guard in that city. Caron was a strong Cohen supporter and kept Muskie waiting for over an hour on election night when he came to pay his respects but saw (or called) Cohen right away. She and many others in this key precinct wanted Cohen to run and promised to deliver Lewiston for him if he did.

But it was not to be.

On December 15, Cohen did a second poll. In this one, Muskie had closed the gap. Cohen now led only by a razor-thin margin. Cohen's lead had shrunk to two percentage points, 47 percent to 45 percent with still only 8 percent undecided.[47]

This deterioration in the head-to-head situation was bad enough but it masked even worse news within. It was the internal cross tabulation changes that really told the story: (1) Cohen had lost 5 percent in his own district, while Muskie had gained 5 percent and (2) in the 1st CD, Muskie had picked up 4 percent, while Cohen, despite a lot of campaigning there on his own, stayed the same.

We clearly saw a momentum shift.

With Democrats, Cohen had lost 3 percent (but still held an unrealistic 20 percent) while Muskie picked up 9 percent of Democrats. In my judgment, Cohen was still being held up artificially by his continued strong support among Democrats and union members. I did not believe he could count on these in November 1976.

In our judgment Muskie had repaired enough damage and gotten enough voters back to make the race a real crap shoot, a toss-up. While Cohen was still ahead, Muskie had made enough inroads—and the right inroads—to look far tougher than he had just six months ago.

Overall, the perceptional aspects had changed markedly. Muskie had identified his weaknesses and had moved smartly to correct them. Most tellingly, for example, he had completely fooled the *Bangor Daily News*, the most important print base of Cohen support, into accepting him back as a fiscal conservative. If he'd been able to fool them this easily in 1975 on such a core issue, imagine what he could do to them in 1976, we thought.

We believed Muskie would go on working to correct his situation and in the end, the Democratic Party would rally to their founder. Of that there could no longer be any doubt. The Republican Party simply did not have the institutional commitment to make the same kind of effort on behalf of Congressman Cohen.

Seeing the December polling, I was both relieved and deflated; the race would have been great theatre and we might have won and we might have lost but it just didn't feel right to me or ultimately, to Cohen and those closest to him.

But we quickly saw a silver lining. There was much promise in the other matchups we had put into the poll looking at Maine's junior senator. Here lay the true wave of the future. By contrast with his small lead over Muskie, Cohen had a discernible and firm lead of over 20 percent over Maine's other senator, Bill Hathaway.

Even if James B. Longley, Maine's first and popular Independent governor, were to jump into that senate race in 1978, making it a three-way contest, Cohen would still win handily.

I urged that Cohen not run and my memo of the time speaks to both the issues I feared and to the promise of 1978, concluding, "Patience is not my strong suit, but I think you should look toward Hathaway."[48]

Cohen really did not want to back away from the challenge and until the very last moment kept getting a drumbeat of encouragement to run especially in Washington from national Republican figures.

On January 2, however, Cohen called Muskie to say he was not going to run. Muskie was very relieved, as well he should have been. Win, lose, or draw, Cohen would have certainly given Ed Muskie a run for his money and with Muskie's well-documented short fuse on the campaign trail, who knows what might have happened?

Cohen's public announcement was brief and statesmanlike:

> While the polls showed that it would be possible to win a Senate race, it was clear that the contest would be very close. A Senate campaign might well become a bitter and divisive one, thereby dissolving the cohesiveness and effectiveness of the entire Maine delegation that has for the past three years worked in a non-partisan manner, for the benefit of all Maine citizens.[49]

When Cohen announced his decision on January 3, 1976, there were many disappointed Cohen staffers and supporters. There were many relieved Muskie staffers and supporters. But there was one truly miserable individual, Senator Bill Hathaway. Bill Hathaway could see the future and the future was not his.

He knew, in the most profound terms, what Cohen's decision not to run against Muskie would mean to him. It would mean Cohen would challenge him in 1978. Cohen did, easily defeating Maine's junior senator.[50]

Ironically, the obscure 1975 "Election That Never Was" would count him as its victim, perhaps its only victim.

6

The 1980s:

The Maine Yankee Referendum

THE DECADE'S MATRIX

The 1980s saw the continuing rejuvenation of the Republican Party and its increasing success at the ballot box. The decade also saw the soaring popularity of the citizen initiative with dozens of ballot measures (as opposed to bond issues).

The election of 1980, for example, saw the Republicans in control of both congressional districts and their two incumbents, David Emery in the 1st and Olympia Snowe in the 2nd, easily won reelection.

Dave Emery bested Harold "Hal" Pachios 69 percent to 31 percent and Olympia Snowe defeated her Democratic opponent, Harold Silverman, 79 percent to 21 percent.

The Year 1980 also saw the first major league campaign for a referendum issue. The measure to prohibit generation of electric power by nuclear fission was defeated 59 percent to 41 percent but not without the largest opposition campaign launched in the history of the state, dwarfing earlier efforts such as the 1973 effort to create a public power authority in Maine. We shall be returning to this issue as the case study for this chapter.

Utilities were also the subject of the 1981 referendum to create the Maine Energy Commission, another ballot measure that was defeated by modern campaign techniques 62 percent to 38 percent.

The next year, 1982, saw the reelection bid for Governor Joseph "Joe" Brennan. Opposed in the Democratic primary, Brennan defeated Georgette Berube 77 percent to 23 percent and then went on to overcome Charles Cragin in the general 61 percent to 38 percent after Cragin had carried his Republican primary with 38 percent of the vote to 33 percent for Sherry Huber and 29 percent for Richard Pierce.

The 1982 Senate race was widely heralded as a close contest between the popular 1st CD Congressman Dave Emery and the appointed Senator

George Mitchell. Mitchell had run such a poor campaign in the 1974 gubernatorial race (see chapter 7) that many observers predicted that either
Emery or Congresswoman Olympia Snowe would easily defeat Mitchell,
but Mitchell proved to be a very resilient candidate and effective campaigner as he rolled up an impressive 61 percent to 39 percent margin
against Emery in 1982.

Republicans maintained their control over both of Maine's congressional districts in 1982. In the 1st CD, John "Jock" McKernan defeated
Oram Lowry in the Republican primary 77 percent to 23 percent while
John Kerry overcame his Democratic opposition with 39 percent of the
vote to John O'Leary's 37 percent, Philip Merrill's 21 percent, and Plato
Truman's 4 percent. In the very close general election, McKernan received
50.3 percent to 47.9 percent for Kerry.

In the 2nd CD, James Dunleavy won the Democratic primary 51 percent
to 49 percent only to be overcome by Olympia Snowe 67 percent to 33 percent in the general election.

In 1983, the effort to repeal the moose hunt was defeated 61 percent to
39 percent as the mainstay of Maine rural politics, sportsmen and women,
rallied.

The 1984 cycle saw incumbent U.S. Senator William S. Cohen easily defeating Elizabeth Mitchell 73 percent to 26 percent while in the 1st CD
Barry Hobbins lost to Jock McKernan 62 percent to 36 percent with Independent Plato Truman (who had previously run as a Democrat and as a
Republican) getting 2 percent. In the Democratic primary, Hobbins had
defeated Ralph Conant 63 percent to 37 percent.

Olympia Snowe was once again easily reelected, garnering 76 percent
of the vote versus Democrat Chipman Bull's 23 percent and Independent
Kenneth Stoddard's 2 percent.

The effort to pass an Equal Rights Amendment in Maine was defeated
63 percent to 37 percent.

The Maine Green Party was founded in January 1984 after several
years of what its co-founder and Bowdoin professor John Rensenbrink
called "movement building." Rensenbrink describes the tension between those who wanted a political party and those who wanted a
movement and indicates that it was not until 1990 that the Greens
moved into "serious statewide organizing."[1] Rensenbrink would later
run for the U.S. Senate on the Independent–Green ticket in 1998.

As Rensenbrink put it: "In the mid-1980s, we formed a group called
the Merrymeeting Greens in mid-coastal Maine where five rivers con-
verge before flowing out to the sea, hence the word merry-meeting. We
had been meeting for a year of study of Green values. More and more,
we realized that an in-depth comprehensive understanding of present
problems demanded by an ecological analysis was a challenging under-

taking indeed. More than that our study make us keenly aware that a new 'definition of the situation,' a new reality, was beginning to enliven us."[2]

Electoral success came later, when the Greens received 8.8 percent in Jonathan Carter's 1992 bid for Congress in Maine's 2nd CD and 5 percent in his 1994 bid for governor. Other Green efforts included 7 percent in Pat LaMarche's bid for governor in 1998 and 4 percent for John Rensenbrink that year in his run for U.S. Senate.

The ongoing role of the Green Party and its impact on the two-party system in Maine continues to be hotly debated. Some see it as a new movement bringing new people and new ideas into politics in the Pine Tree State, challenging both major political parties. Others see it in terms of its impact at the ballot box as an electoral offshoot of the Democratic Party and thus a creation that assists Republicans and Independents by splitting the Democratic vote.

We will be examining these hypotheses in the coming chapters as we look at the election for Congress in Maine's Second District in 1992 and especially the effect of the Green candidate in the 1994 gubernatorial election. In both instances, Democratic regulars insist that the Green candidate, by siphoning off left-leaning Democrats, cost that party both elections. The Greens argue that they draw from all segments of the population.

There is some evidence, for example, that upscale Republicans often find the Green positions attractive. For example in 1980, the polling for the Maine Yankee Shutdown referendum showed that the economic issue was the strongest motivator for keeping the plant open and that this was true of Republicans, Democrats, and Independents. However, such key Republican bellwethers as Sebago, Camden, Bar Harbor, and Kennebunk showed that upscale Republicans were not as persuaded by the economic argument, perhaps feeling that saving $250 a year was not worthwhile. These "rich Republicans with sailboats" became a new psychographic group for that election and the Green Party was to do quite well in some of these precincts as time went on and Ralph Nader was also to run above his statewide average in these towns. His statewide total was 5.7 percent, but in Sebago he received 6.5 percent, in Camden 10.7 percent, and in Bar Harbor 13.8 percent.

In 1986, Congressman Jock McKernan ran for governor and got elected, in effect switching positions with Joe Brennan. After dispatching Porter Leighton in the Republican primary, McKernan (40 percent) defeated James Tierney the Democrat (30 percent) and two Independents, Sherry Huber (15 percent) and John Menario (15 percent). Earlier, in the Democratic primary, Tierney gathered 37 percent of the vote compared with 24 percent for Severin Beliveau, 21 percent for William Diamond, and 15 percent for David Redmond.

Temporarily term limited out from running for governor, Joe Brennan defeated H. Rollins Ives 53 percent to 47 percent to capture the 1st District CD, while in the 2nd, Olympia Snowe again proved very difficult to challenge, getting 77 percent of the vote against Richard Charette who had earlier defeated Ernest Gallant in the Democratic primary 58 percent to 42 percent.

There were a number of ballot measures in 1986, an effort to limit "obscene" material failed 72 percent to 28 percent, and local "measured" telephone service was likewise defeated 58 percent to 42 percent.

In 1988, Senator George Mitchell was reelected, handily outpolling Republican Jasper Wyman 81 percent to 19 percent. Mitchell's margin was the largest in postwar Maine history.

Joe Brennan was easily reelected in Maine's 1st CD, getting 63 percent of the vote over Ted O'Meara who had earlier defeated Linda Bean-Jones in the Republican primary 52 percent to 48 percent.

In Maine's 2nd CD, Olympia Snowe continued her winning ways, defeating Democrat Kenneth Hayes 66 percent to 34 percent.

SEMINAL ELECTION:
THE 1980 REFERENDUM ON MAINE YANKEE

Since 1909, Maine has been one of the 26 states in the United States that permits citizen initiatives in ballot measure contests. From 1940 until 1980, there had been only a few truly important referenda in Maine, most of them low budget affairs. The decade of the 1970s saw a quickening of the pace of ballot measures but virtually all of them were relatively small in scale in terms of the cost and size of the campaigns.

In 1971, for example, there was an attempt to eliminate the state income tax, a measure that did not pass. The next year, the "Big Box" or straight party box was eliminated. In 1973, the proposed public authority of Maine was defeated and in 1976 the Bigelow preserve was established. 1977 saw the repeal of the uniform state property tax and in 1979, the returnable container law was upheld.

The preservation of Bigelow mountain was a forerunner of the 1980 antinuclear referendum in that grassroots activists discovered that by circulating petitions on election day, it was possible to get 25,000 signatures in one day and more if wanted. Lance Tapley led that total effort and changed the nature of politics in Maine by showing how it could be done. In fact, he, along with Joe Steinberger, was among the earliest models for Ray Shaddis and his shutdown referendum in 1980.

In 1980, the political landscape of Maine changed dramatically and substantially. From that point on referendum politics in Maine would never be the same. The state's referendum on the Maine Yankee nuclear plant altered the way ballot measure politics were to be conducted in Maine for the next several decades. The campaign ushered in twenty years of highly contentious, very expensive, "national" issue races with groups and organizations and individuals from all over the United States coming to Maine to participate in major contests virtually every electoral cycle after that.

After 1980, voters would be asked to vote on the Maine Yankee plant two more times (1982 and 1987), to repeal the moose hunt (1983), to pass the Equal Rights Amendment (1984), to vote on radioactive waste storage (1985), to ban cruise missile testing (1989), to allow large stores to be open on Sundays (1990), to widen the Maine Turnpike (1991 and 1997), to establish term limits (1993), to limit human/gay rights (1995), to affirm gay rights (1996 and 1998), to establish forest practices and pass a Forest Compact (1996 and 1997), to establish the so-called Clean Elections Act (1996), to ban clear cutting in Maine's forests (2000), and to approve assisted suicide (2000) to name but some of the most prominent.

Highly contentious races such as the 1995 vote on human/gay rights, the 1991 vote to ban the widening of the Maine Turnpike, and the 1987 vote to close Maine Yankee all topped 40 percent in voter turnout, running up higher totals than for many nonpresidential year efforts.

Money poured into many races, coming from all over the United States. In fact, in the 2000 vote on assisted suicide, more money came from outside the state to support the measure than came from within the state!

Ray Shaddis and his wife, Patricia, moved to Edgecomb where he was a potter, sculptor, and farmer. His concern about nuclear power grew after the Three Mile Island nuclear accident in Pennsylvania in 1979. As he put it: "All we have between us and disaster is the competence of the plant's designers and operators, which we have no faith in anymore, and the odds, which aren't too great if you look at them."[3]

As Shaddis saw it: "We had a choice of running or fighting."[4] He started his effort in January 1979, when an initial meeting drew hundreds of people to the Edgecomb Town Hall. They decided to collect signatures in an effort to shut down the Maine Yankee facility. The group got a tremendous boost from the earthquake that struck Maine on April 17, 1979. Measuring 4.0 on the modified Mercalli scale, the quake raised many fears about what could have happened to the nuclear plant if the quake had been worse or the plant was operating. Ironically, it was shut down for repairs at the time.

The antinuclear forces turned in 55,834 signatures in December 1979. The legislature could have voted on the measure at its next session but legislators didn't want to have to make that decision, so they put it out to the voters.

Oddly enough, the Maine Yankee nuclear plant didn't seem to be in difficulty. It had operated without major incident since it began in 1972, and in July 1978, it set a new world's record for continuous days (372) of operation.

From the first, the nuclear referendum attracted nationwide interest and wild claims and hyperbole. For example, former Congressman Stan Tupper claimed that if anything were to happen at Maine Yankee, 100,000 tourists would have to be evacuated by the U.S. Navy if it "happened to have some ships in the vicinity."[5] This was clearly an issue where people not only felt strongly, but also raced to worst-case scenarios!

While there had been a 1978 vote in Montana prohibiting the construction of nuclear power plants, the 1980 effort would have been the first to shut down an operating plant. The effort was national news from beginning to end. Such well-known entertainers as Peter, Paul and Mary, Marshall Dodge of "Bert and I" fame, and Dan Fogleburg supported the proposed shutdown, donating money and concert time. There was thus a lot of pop culture support for the shutdown.

Because of the "inherent and unreasonable risk of economic, physical and mental harm," the shutdown referendum would prohibit all generation of electric power by the simple statement: "Shall an act to prohibit the generation of electric power by means of nuclear fission become law?"

The Maine Yankee plant had itself been closed in 1979 so the Nuclear Regulatory Commission could study whether it could withstand the effects of an earthquake!

Between the Three Mile Island accident and the earthquake in Maine, Ray Shaddis and the antinuclear activists had a huge head of steam. They rallied many people and organized several important marches, first to the plant itself and then to the capitol in Augusta.

My experience with ballot measure campaigns and referenda had been very limited through the 1970s. In those days, consultants who dealt with politicians tended to ignore or look down on "issue" consultants. Elected, candidate politics was where the action was and where the financial and prestige payoffs were located.

Moreover, I had little background in the politics of energy generation. Having grown up in Niantic, Connecticut, with its four nuclear generating plants in nearby Waterford, and nuclear submarines routinely based in New London, I took nuclear power for granted. We never thought much about it, often skin diving in the very waters where nuclear plants and submarines were located.

When antinuclear attacks began to appear in the local papers in Maine during the late 1970s, I had the temerity to write a short article for the

Brunswick *Times Record* entitled "The 'Safest' Forms of Energy," which tried to put nuclear power into perspective with coal and oil on a "continuum of relative danger."[6]

To me, my conclusion seemed straightforward and balanced:

> Let us face the dangerous facts together and rationally assess which way we are to go. Let us argue about ways to make all fuel cycles safer. Let us cut down on our use of all forms of energy so as to minimize the additional risks that would be added by future use. But let us not proceed in an atmosphere of hysterical frenzy, going from idealizing nuclear power as a cost free benevolent genie to condemning it out of hand as a doomsday monster out of control. It was and is neither.[7]

Nothing prepared me for the firestorm of criticism that followed the publication of this article. The local *Times Record* that published the piece was inundated with hostile letters to the editor. One wag called it "at best inane." I was called at home and at work with threatening messages, day and night. I was labeled a "bad parent" for even considering nuclear power. The attacks continued for several weeks, especially after I followed up the initial article with a rebuttal entitled "Thinking about the Thinkable"![8]

At the time, I thought writing about nuclear power had been a huge mistake. Who needs people calling you up in the middle of the night and saying bad things about you, or hanging up after cursing you? But the following year, when antinuclear activists attempted to shut down the Maine Yankee atomic power plant in Wiscasset by banning the generation of nuclear power in the state after January 1, 1981, it brought me to the attention of Skip Thurlow, president of Central Maine Power, the parent company of Maine Yankee.

On, April 1, 1980, I met with Skip Thurlow, Norm "Storming Norman" Temple, and Robert "Bob" Leason, all of Central Maine Power, the principal owner of the Maine Yankee nuclear plant. There were a few tense moments when I stated how significant the challenge was. I said, "You can't do it alone. You need help. This is not the public power referendum. You have new adversaries. They are tough and hard-nosed. They will show you no quarter; this is not just a political agenda for some other purpose such as getting Peter Kelley elected governor in the 1973 public power authority struggle. They mean business."

I also pointed out that this would be a full-time campaign, requiring experts, and Skip Thurlow couldn't expect to run the company and the campaign at the same time.

On April 9, Thurlow formed a small working group that would become the Save Maine Yankee inner circle: Skip; John Menario, former Portland city manager; Michael Healy, partner of the law firm Verrill & Dana; and myself. Skip Thurlow was an outstanding man and manager. He knew how to delegate, putting his best talent—Robert "Bob" Leason, Charlie Frizzle, Don Vigue, John Randazza, and Norm "Storming Norman" Temple on the task, adding Pat Lydon when the time came to get out the vote. Annette Steven and Peter Thompson were to do excellent jobs in their roles as spokespeople for the company. Bob Leason was superb, carrying out the directions of Thurlow while at the same time keeping the campaign team happy. He was a critical player.

Picking a topflight manager was crucial. We needed managerial experience but someone who understood the nature of politics. There would be a huge budget to administer and a lot of strategic direction to take. John Menario was an ideal choice. Savvy and streetwise, he could also cast a spell over the myriad of corporate players the referendum needed.

Menario turned out to be an excellent public campaign manager: feisty, quick on the uptake, and disciplined. He represented Save Maine Yankee at many, many functions without a misstep. He also came up with the basic campaign slogan, "Give Maine People the Power to Compete." Mike Healy of Verrill & Dana provided wise counsel and a steady hand, orchestrating the many legal issues that swirled around during the campaign.

There was another positive aspect to Thurlow's leadership: he trusted Maine talent. The national nuclear industry took the vote very seriously and argued that it had profound implications nationwide. As Kirk Williamson of the Edison Electric Institute put it, "If it passes, we're going to see a flurry of antinuclear activity."[9] So the big Fortune 500 companies with nuclear interests, such as Westinghouse or Stone and Webster, naturally wanted to run the show and not let "local yokels" mess up the future of their $100 billion industry. But Thurlow insisted that the Save Maine Yankee working group control the agenda and the program.

As the campaign developed, there were regular representatives from the Edison Institute (Fred Webber), Westinghouse Electric (Joe Keegan), and Maine's paper companies, the state's largest users of electricity, (Robert "Bob" Turner). They were very helpful, especially Turner, but the basic campaign decisions were made by the working group and Chuck Winner when he joined the team as media and ballot measure guru.

Menario also added Democratic Representative Sharon Benoit of South Portland to coordinate volunteers. Later other key people joined the Save Maine Yankee operating group: Pam Hughes and Professor Richard Morgan from Bowdoin; George Smith, the current executive director of the Sportsman's Alliance of Maine and my personal friend and comrade from the political campaigns of Bill Cohen and Dave Emery (he had been Emery's campaign manager in 1974); and Lil Caron, Maine's first woman mayor from Lewiston.

I saw as the top priority the choosing of the right media firm but I wanted one with experience in nuclear power issues and one that would fit in with the working group. I felt we needed to make the absolute right decision early on or we would have a most difficult time.

One firm I desperately did not want was Smith and Haroff of Washington (an offshoot of the old Mike Harkins's firm, The Agency, that had been so helpful in the 1972 Cohen election). Smith and Haroff were then doing work for the Edison Electric Institute and were thus familiar to Westinghouse and other nuclear suppliers. But as the election of Cohen to the U.S. Senate in 1978 had proven to me, Smith and Haroff could do good commercials but they tended to respond to the candidate and to his administrative assistant, Tom Daffron, rather than me (whose game plan we were following) or the day-to-day campaign manager, Dick Pierce.

For the Maine Yankee effort, I felt we needed a campaign where the messages and operations were tightly controlled from the top and where the media firm responded to the needs of the campaign, not the needs of the head of the utility or national nuclear interests. I wanted them to respond to Menario and me, not the corporate interests of the nuclear industry.

On April 17, we interviewed Tom Chellis of Portland and Jay Smith of Smith and Haroff and a week later, we talked to Bob Sann from Syracuse. As I feared, Jay Smith of Smith and Haroff put on a full-court press at their presentation, fawning over Thurlow and Keegan but ignoring Menario and me. Both Keegan and the CMP team were very impressed with Jay. But I remained adamant, insisting we interview the California firm of Winner/Wagoner. Thurlow, in particular, was very concerned we were even interviewing a California-based firm. It offended his engineer's sense of order and propinquity.

But once he saw Chuck Winner in action May 2, the choice became an easy one. Chuck came from California to pitch the account. He sat on the table with his Italian designer clothes and his big leather purse and just talked about the referendum. Cool, calm, with no notes, no brochures, no fancy or flattering pitch—just a rational presentation that reeked of pure genius. Chuck knew ballot measures inside and out. I could see he knew exactly what we needed and how ballot measures were so different from candidate situations. He was a heavy hitter nationally, with clients ranging from the space shuttle to major league baseball.

In addition, he knew the nuclear industry—and as importantly, they knew him and trusted his judgment. This would be important because the first $1 million campaign in Maine history required nuclear suppliers from all over the country to send in huge amounts of money—and to keep sending it. Menario and I knew it would cost a ton of TV airtime to overcome the horrendously bad publicity of Three Mile Island.

As I have written in *An Insider's Guide to Maine Politics*, Chuck Winner had "the face of an angel, the teeth of a shark."[10] He was calm and cool and self-possessed. His smile could light up a room; I found him positively endearing. But his annoyance with mistakes and follow-through failures became legendary. He knew exactly how a ballot measure campaign should be run but he wanted all the local input he could get to fit into his basic template (which had enabled his firm to win 9 out of 10 ballot measures all across the country).

After seeing Chuck's performance and hearing Menario's and my ringing endorsement, Joe Keegan, who had been adamant for Smith and Haroff, turned to Thurlow and said: "Skip, Westinghouse would be happy to work with Chuck Winner."

Chuck took control of the campaign from day one and taught us many lessons. One occurred at the very beginning. Taking a page from our political careers, Menario and I had planned a fly around the state, announcing his heading up the committee and getting the campaign off to a flying start with press conferences in Presque Isle, Bangor, Portland, Lewiston, and Biddeford. We were dumbfounded when on May 22, Chuck canceled Menario's fly around. He did so without a second thought.

Although we objected at the time, we soon saw the wisdom of Winner's thinking. In a ballot measure you want to control the flow of information as much as you can, so you don't want wide-open press conferences where you have no control over the questions asked or the answers subsequently used by the print and electronic media. Above all, you don't want your opponents to get equal airtime.

Candidates always want the spotlight. Ballot measures on controversial issues don't. We would take our message to the people in 30- and 60-second ads, not press conferences. We would live by the first rule of ballot measures: "Maintain control at all costs."

Meanwhile, Ray Shaddis had taken complete charge of the Yes side. Bright, hard-driving, and sure of himself and the righteousness of his cause, Shaddis took control of the disparate antinuclear committees and didn't brook any rivals. As John Rensenbrink, Bowdoin professor and founder of the Maine Green Party and one of the leaders of the nuclear referendum committee later put it, Ray Shaddis was "imperious" and as a result there was little coordination among all the nuclear activists due to his being a "total autocrat."[11] As matters turned out, the antinuclear forces could have used the diverse talents of Rensenbrink (who had run for the state senate and understood the world of the Franco Americans) and Lance Tapley (who until Chuck Winner showed up had led the way in ballot measure principles).

Ray saw himself as central to the movement; having all that public attention was heady stuff. At least at one press conference, the working press gave him a standing ovation as he entered the room. It was no wonder he liked the limelight and the David versus Goliath image the media gave him. Shaddis and the antinuclear movement had a lot going for them. In the spring of 1980, they had considerable momentum and some very real advantages.

The basics of the entire campaign appeared stark and clear at the very beginning. The early polling data showed a number of interesting and defining aspects. There was a large undecided vote and there were two major "drivers" of public opinion. The first was a cluster of issues we termed "health and safety." The second was "economics."[12]

From the very first, it was clear that these two issue clusters would dominate the debate and how each side handled the other's strong points would determine the outcome. The second rule of ballot measures is "stick with your best argument(s) and avoid your opponent's." Remember that most referenda are won with a single theme or two. The public can only absorb so much information so you need focus and repetition.

The antinuclear activists had by far the best arguments. Questions about radiation, leukemia and birth defects, and accidents all drove voters away from support of the plant. They were extremely difficult, if not impossible, to counter. Regardless of the "facts" of the health and safety issue, the emotional power was all on the side of the shutdown forces. The axiom of "fear drives out favor" was all on their side and their powerful issues. The more the antinuclear forces focused on these issues, the harder it was to combat them.

Indeed, it was very dangerous to even discuss them. Many supporters of the plant, those prepared to vote No initially, would drift away from that support the more health and safety was discussed. It didn't matter what we said about those issues; nobody wanted to hear about radiation rates and leukemia and birth defects. No matter what you could or would like to say about these issues, if you talked about them—even if you had the right "answers"—your supporters drifted away from you.

Of course, the most ardent proponents of nuclear power wanted to talk about these subjects. Many of the antis' claims were simply not factually true. But in ballot measures, "your friends will cause you more damage than your opponents" and you could not let your well-meaning supporters get you away from your best influence vectors and onto your worse ones.

On the other hand, the economic arguments—the cost of replacement power, the alternative energy supplies and the damage they would do to the environment, the costs of a shutdown—all drove voters away from a Yes vote. All of these moved people from Yes to No. The more economics were discussed, the stronger Maine people became for keeping the plant open.

Thus from the very first polling, the entire campaign was clearly seen in the resulting cognitive map. If the voters went to the polls voting on health and safety issues, the plant would be shut down. If the voters went to the polls voting on economic arguments, the plant would be kept open.

Then there was the lesson of authority figures. There was a wide range of credibility quotients when various people and organizations spoke out on this issue. Some people had much more credibility than others. Some organizations had more credibility than others. And it depended on what messages they were sending. The No side therefore carefully tested authority figures, the people who would be bringing the messages. One of the interesting dimensions we discovered was not only did "a scientist" test well as an authority figure on this issue, but "a foreign scientist" tested best of all!

We therefore identified Professor Will Hughes of Bowdoin's physics department as a very powerful figure. He was a respected scientist and with a dark beard and a Germanic aura of authority, he appeared somewhat "foreign."

He and Professor of Environmental Studies Richard "Dick" Hill of the University of Maine became the chief authority figures for the campaign. They were to prove "tougher" and more credible than anyone the Yes side could produce.

In preparation for the referendum, I asked Peter Burr to modify the grid-outcome system of regression analysis (first developed by David Emery in his successful bid for Congress in 1974) using key precincts that had proven so effective in measuring candidate races. Using the same demographic and psychographic models, Command Research provided some very interesting initial parameters for the election. The subsequent weekly tracking assessments became the yardstick against which we measured our progress.

The baseline matchup had approximately 40 percent against the shutdown, 30 percent for the shutdown, and a huge 30 percent undecided. There was a great deal of antinuclear strength in Lincoln, Knox, and Sagadahoc counties with Waldo on the brink. We thought the Yes side had considerable upside potential in their base. Should the antinuclear sentiment spread out from this core area, the No side would be in significant trouble.

There was also worse news in the demographics. While those of English or Scotch background (32 percent of the electorate) were against the shutdown, there were pockets of what we termed "rich Republicans with sailboats" in places like Kennebunk, Sebago, and Bar Harbor who were not persuaded by the economic arguments. Also, the Irish Americans (17 percent) were definitely for the shutdown.

The key would be the Franco Americans who made up 18 percent of the total voting population. Just as they had been the key swing vote in Maine candidate elections since 1972, now they became the key swing vote in the Maine Yankee referendum. They would determine the outcome. They were, fortunately for the No side, the demographic group most likely to be influenced by the economic argument, our best.

But however you looked at it, this election was up for grabs!

Given the high numbers of undecided, the grassroots strength of the opposition, and the need to frame the debate and get the campaign revolving around our issue, economics, we decided to go on TV early, right in the middle of the summer. At the time, this was very unusual for Maine politics. Normally, television advertising had been used only in the fall, often only during the last two or three weeks of a campaign. But Save Maine Yankee was going up early, "in the clear" to set the stage.

It turned out to be a very wise move.

The production of the Save Maine Yankee commercials was amusing and illustrative of the cross-currents of deep emotion abroad that summer. On July 2, Winner/Wagoner began filming a commercial at Bowdoin. It featured a 60-second commercial with Professor Hughes walking across the campus, talking directly to the audience and framing the debate. We were used to normal Maine production activities with a director and a single cameraperson so we thought we could go onto the campus and get the shot in the can before the shoot became a huge incident.

We were wrong.

The shoot turned into a big "Hollywood" production. Chuck brought a huge crew of a dozen people, special lighting trucks, and miles of cables, guarded by key grips, etc. It looked like *Gone With the Wind* was being reshot. Antinuclear activists—who undoubtedly considered Bowdoin their personal sanctuary—were enraged. "Our beloved campus is being used," they cried. Various college administrators were called as the filming went on for several hours until at last, the cry "That's a wrap" was heard.

The filming of the Hughes commercial caused a huge flap. Dozens of students and antinuclear faculty members then flocked to the Dean to complain over a period of several days, called numerous administrative figures at home and the office, and alerted the local newspapers. Members of the Bath-Brunswick Area Concerned Citizens for Safe Energy, led by Professor John Rensenbrink, expressed great concern and insisted that any commercial *not* show the Bowdoin campus in any recognizable way and that the same commercial carry a disclaimer that clearly stated that the physics professor in it, Dr. Will Hughes, was not speaking for the College.

Professor Hughes ridiculed their assertions, insisting, "The opinion of every professor is his own. I can't imagine that anyone would be naïve enough to believe that one professor's opinion reflects the position of the entire institution."[13]

The antinuclear forces were right to try to stop the commercial. It was an extremely powerful one. The commercial would turn out to be the most important turning point in the campaign and one of the most effective ballot measure spots ever put on the air in Maine. Professor Hughes, in his long, authoritative, and powerful one-minute commercial, walking slowly and decisively from the signature building on campus, Hubbard Hall, stated: "Remember, the referendum does not mean new nuclear power plants can't be built. It means closing Maine Yankee, which provides safe, clean energy for all of us. The referendum must be defeated."[14] Hughes's delivery had punch and power and believability.

Dean Fuchs made several attempts to address the concerns of the antinuclear stalwarts but the Save Maine Yankee Committee refused to even consider them and the College was faced with having to get a new law firm to represent them since the College counsel, Verrill & Dana, had already contributed to the Maine Yankee effort and one of its partners, Mike Healy, was already serving as the Save Maine Yankee counsel and treasurer.

Also, to his credit, Dean Fuchs came down on the side of First Amendment rights of free speech: "I don't see anything unethical about faculty members taking a position on controversial issues."[15]

The Hughes commercial was decisive. It changed the minds of 90,000 Maine voters and dominated the airways and the debate for much of the summer and locked in the No vote at high enough levels to win the race if that vote turned out on the special election day, September 23.

Meanwhile, the Yes forces scored some points of their own. On July 14, the shutdown forces received a significant boost when the Natural Resources Council of Maine voted to shut down the plant. Claiming to be the largest environmental organization (with 2,500 members and 75 affiliated organizations claimed), the NRCM stated that it was "the environmental issue of the century."[16]

In the *Press Herald* article, Ray Shaddis said the endorsement "adds stature to our position" while Annette Stevens, president of Maine Citizens for Maine Yankee, said, "It's just beyond belief that they'd do this. The NRC has so much concern for the state of Maine and I'm amazed they'd support closing down a plant that provides one-third of the state's electricity."

But SMY was ready with a counterattack. The creation of "Maine Citizens for Maine Yankee" was the inspiration of Chuck Winner. He had the Save Maine Yankee committee mail all licensed drivers in Maine, sending them postcards enabling them to join the committee. We would end up with a huge "organization" that would have instant credibility on the ground and a bigger grassroots operation than the antinuclear activists, even though the mind-changing aspects of the campaign would be on television.

By early August, the committee had over 30,000 people signed up to join and it was a powerful tool to counter the other side's grassroots efforts. On August 13, the Committee to Save Maine Yankee announced that it now had 30,000 members, making it the largest citizens' committee in Maine history.

The next day, August 14, Common Cause attacked the "Committee to Save Maine Yankee," calling it "not a committee at all" but "a thinly veiled front for the Central Maine Power Company," as wrote Nancy Grape in her "Common Cause Tags Me. Yankee Committee Front for the CMP."[17]

Joseph Steinberger, executive director of Common Cause in Maine, said Save Maine Yankee spent $79,000 on its direct mail campaign to get 30,000 signatures. He claimed that the Nuclear Referendum Committee had 60,000 names since that was the number of voters who had signed petitions to shut down the plant. Moreover, Common Cause claimed that "their polling" showed the state "about equally divided on the referendum" and objected to being "bombarded by a massive media campaign using soap selling tactics."[18]

For his part, chair John Menario replied that the committee was legitimate and faulted Common Cause for pretending to be neutral: "It's pretty traditional with that group not to fully understand what they say before they say it."[19]

Actually, both parties were correct. More voters had signed the shutdown petitions, but Save Maine Yankee, with over 30,000 people who had signed cards to specifically join that organization, was a Maine record at the time. It remains one today. No organization for a ballot measure has ever signed up more members.

Also, although the main purpose of the Save Maine Yankee Committee was to create a "counterweight" to the antinuclear movement in the minds of the public, it ended up having substantial grassroots activism in its own right. "Grassroots versus media" campaigns is the way the 1980 referendum is characterized.

In reality, it was not that simple a bifurcation. This is a simplification: many firms, especially those dependent on low-cost energy, were adamantly against the referendum and took grassroots actions on their own. Also, there were some within the antinuclear movement who wanted to wage their campaign on TV.

L.L. Bean and many other Maine companies opposed the referendum. Bath Iron Works, for example, stated that it would add up to $1 million to that company's energy bills and added, "When armchair authorities say that energy costs increase won't affect Maine, they just don't know what they're talking about."[20]

Maine's paper companies, the largest users of electricity in the state, also urged their workers to vote against the shutdown referendum and

donated considerable sums of money to the Save Maine Yankee Committee. They were joined by hundred of small businesses as well. The economic message prevailed in company after company and was carried to
their own workers, giving the Save Maine Yankee effort a grassroots
power that was unexpected when the referendum began.

Lance Tapley is quite right in pointing out that conceptually there is
something of a difference between the "true" grassroots of ordinary citizens acting on their own and what he calls "Astro-turf" grassroots organized and energized from the top down by corporations.

But the net political impact is exactly the same.

One of the things that concerned us a lot was that the data showed
many people didn't like nuclear power and didn't like CMP and didn't
like high electrical rates. We were afraid a movement might get started
along the lines of "It'll be illegal to shut down the nuclear plant so that
won't happen. Why don't we vote to shut it down to send a message that
we don't like things?"

This notion of a protest vote was worrying. This was especially true
when Bob Cummings of the *Maine Sunday Telegram* wrote a prominent
front-page piece entitled "Voters May be Powerless to Shut Maine Yankee."[21] We really worried about this aspect, a cost-free "protest vote."
Why not cast a vote against nuclear power for health and safety reasons
and for the mental stress of Three Mile Island? Why not send a message?

The *Portland Press Herald* had it right when they said:

> One of the more troubling aspects of the September referendum is the
> prospect that some voters may mistakenly perceive the ballot as sort of an ab-
> stract exercise rather than as a concrete proposal. Its intent is to close Maine
> Yankee. Anyone who wants to send any other message ought to use another
> method.[22]

Fortunately, the Yes side never did latch onto what would have been a
very effective strategy combining fear over nuclear power with dislike of
the electrical utility CMP. It isn't clear whether the antinuclear forces ever
seriously considered this as an option. In any case, the various antinuclear committees were not always in sync. This provided a very substantial contrast between the Yes and No forces. The No forces were highly
centralized but with a very democratic decision-making apparatus at the
top.

After early July, when the Save Maine Yankee team was in place, I cannot recall a single decision that was not hashed out by the committee and
decided by it. Skip Thurlow, CMP, and Maine Yankee, to say nothing of
the nuclear industry, never insisted on a decision going one way or another. Skip Thurlow had established a campaign structure and style that

promoted diverse opinions and strategies. It was one of the most democratic decision-making processes I've ever been involved with during 30 years of political activity.

By contrast, the antinuclear Yes side was highly fragmented and localized overall but the campaign decision making was highly centralized in the hands of Ray Shaddis. This is a very important and overlooked dimension in Maine politics. The "one man band" aspect is reflected not only in the Shaddis operation but also in Bruce Reeves's effort in the 1981 Elected PUC referendum and the various campaigns of Jonathan Carter regarding Maine forest practices.

It's true there were such wide variety of entities opposed to Maine Yankee that one automatically thought of Mao's dictum "Let a thousand flowers bloom." So too did Ray Shaddis. He also believed, "I took a page out of Chairman Mao's book . . . we had many other committees and they had to go their own way."[23]

There was the Maine Yankee Nuclear Referendum Committee, Greater Portland Nuclear Referendum Committee, Bath/Brunswick Nuclear Referendum Committee, Harpswell Concerned Citizens, Biddeford Nuclear Referendum Committee, Professionals for Safe Alternatives, and many others. All told, there were eight or nine different Yes bumper strips (my personal favorite being "No Nuke of the North) and many different press releases and points of view expressed publicly.

But, according to John Rensenbrink, there was no "serious strategy council on an ongoing basis, only Shaddis and a few supporters."[24] Shaddis was the heart and soul of the major portion of the campaign and he stayed in charge from beginning to end.

This campaign style was one thing, the strategy of the Yes side another. At Save Maine Yankee, we worried most about them staying "on message" on the health and safety issues and adding to that, the "send a protest" dimension. Had they stayed on health and safety and added the "send a protest" dimension, the referendum could have gone the other way.

But the antinuclear movement felt they had to answer the economic argument and they made the fatal mistake of trying to argue the various dimensions of that position without realizing that it played right into the Save Maine Yankee hands. Also, while they had credible spokespeople on the health and safety issues—nurses and doctors—they did not have credible spokespeople on the economic issues.

Put bluntly, if Ray Shaddis as a potter and a farmer didn't want to use nuclear power, that was fine but what standing did he have in talking seriously about economic issues for companies that employed thousands of Maine people? The answer was: he and other antinuclear activists were simply not credible when arrayed against professors and businesspeople.

Shaddis could say that the power produced by the 400-megawatt plant could easily be replaced by cogeneration and conservation. And he could actually be correct. But few undecided voters would believe him on this issue.

Certainly not compared to the authority figures on the No side who said, consistently and constantly, that the shutdown would cost $140 million a year and would result in a 30 percent increase in power bills. However you ultimately came down on the issue of nuclear power in Maine, you were more inclined to believe business leaders than antinuclear activists when it came to judging the economic effects of the shutdown.

Shaddis argued that the shutdown would cost the average family $88 a year or 10 cents a day while the Save Maine Yankee committee said it would cost $250 per family per year.[25] At that time, the average Maine family income was $7,000 a year and with the cost of fuel and heating oil thrown in, Maine had one of the lowest percapita incomes in the nation. Losing one-third of its cheapest energy simply had to be disturbing to most families. Some voters were willing to pay that price; others were not.

In addition, in some sense in this referendum, it didn't really matter which figure was used; the fact that both sides were arguing about the economics, not the health, of nuclear power was a huge plus for the No side. The more you argued about the economics, the more people solidified against the referendum. The more the Nuclear Referendum Committee talked about the economic specifics, the less they could talk about health and safety, their winning issues. Companies helped by raising the specter of lost jobs. Once the Yes side felt obliged to refute the economic arguments, we knew we had won. It was now just a matter of execution. As John Menario puts it: "We controlled the message by controlling the messenger," and in one very important TV debate with Shaddis, Menario kept the topic on economics for virtually the entire time.[26]

Interestingly enough, the Yes side soon struck what they took to be a crucial blow. On August 20, all across the state, news stories broke about the funding of the referendum. The Committee to Save Maine Yankee (CSMY) had received over $500,000 compared with $63,000 for Maine Nuclear Referendum Committee (MNRC), the principal opponents of the plant. Some of the donations (such as $50,000 each from Westinghouse and Central Maine Power) looked huge and to some, out of place.

The Yes side made a lot out of the amount of money. They also pointed out that most of the Yes money had come from inside the state while most CSMY money had come from outside the state.

The Yes side thought they had a good and telling issue. So, too, did some of the state's most prominent politicians. Governor Joe Brennan, for example, in what the No side took to be a highly irritating and gratuitous remark at a special press conference on August 22, said he was "not overly pleased" by the thousands of out-of-state dollars being spent.[27] The next day, Local 385 of the United Food and Commercial Worker's Union joined in and urged a Yes vote.

Did these charges matter? Columnists, pundits, and many politicians as well as many Yes supporters thought they did. But the nightly polling was crystal clear. They didn't matter at all. There was nothing in the data, hard or soft, which said the money issues—either the amounts or the sources— mattered at all! All the disclosures and indignation didn't budge the numbers at all when the report came out.

Those who were in favor of the shutdown gave the massive spending by opponents as another reason to vote to shut down the plant. Those who opposed the shutdown accepted the fact that it took a lot of money to inform the public about the potential damage the shutdown would cause. The funding issue did not seem to affect those who were undecided.

By this point in the campaign, there was a pretty solid front of political opposition to the shutdown vote. Opposition included Senator William Cohen, Senator George Mitchell, Congressman Dave Emery, Congresswoman Olympia Snowe, and their electoral opponents. Brennan would finally oppose the shutdown later in September, irritating Shaddis but doing nothing to change the numbers already favoring the No side. We, of course, would have welcomed Brennan's endorsement during the summer. By fall it was irrelevant to the campaign dynamics.

The Yes side had a good deal of support as well. Particularly prominent was John Newell, former president of Bath Iron Works and former member of the Atomic Industrial Forum. In a long op-ed piece in the *Maine Sunday Telegram* entitled "Nuclear Power is Neither Cheap Nor Necessary," he stated: "The accident at the Three Mile Island nuclear power plant was a warning of the awesome potential for disaster that a nuclear power plant can create."[28]

Shaddis himself upped the ante by declaring "the Wiscasset nuclear reactor presents a health risk unparalleled in Maine history" while Dr. Rosalie Bertell weighed in citing the dangers of leukemia and other genetic maladies.[29]

On September 16, responding to reports some broadcasters were angry that the antinuclear campaign was getting lots of free airtime (under the then-operative "Fairness Doctrine") but then putting their campaign funds into print ads in the statewide newspapers, Polly Campbell, cochair of the Greater Portland Nuclear Referendum Committee and a board member of the Maine Nuclear Referendum Committee, indicated their group was going to buy airtime and they did. Under the Fairness Doctrine, the Federal Communications Commission required stations to provide free airtime to opposing viewpoints. Some stations such as WABI had been giving the antinuclear movement one free spot for every four the No side had bought.

During the last week, the shutdown was endorsed by the Maine State Nurses' Association, Maine Women for a Nuclear-Free Future, and the Lincoln County Democratic committee. Shaddis predicted victory because "most Maine people have grave reservations about nuclear power. The people simply have a right to choose and should not be forced to take a risk on behalf of a commercial enterprise."[30]

Maine Information Radio Network, on September 19, showed the No vote at 49 percent and Yes at 27 percent. On September 20, the *Bangor Daily News* put it at 59–38 percent, again for the No, the News having already opposed the shutdown in its editorial of September 13 ("The News votes 'No'"). Governor Brennan, who had earlier hedged his bets, weighed in on the No side the next day.

The coming vote was national news. *The New York Times*, *Washington Post*, *Wall Street Journal*, *Barvon's*, *Time*, and *Newsweek* all did prominent stories on the event.[31]

Both sides had massive get out the vote efforts. There was a huge turnout. 390,541 voters showed up for a September off-year election. This was the fourth highest turnout of Maine voters in all of its history, exceeded only by the presidential elections of 1960, 1972, and 1976. It was the highest turnout for any referendum standing alone.

The early returns on election night caused a minor panic. Chuck Winner, who had flown in from California to participate in what he thought would be a victory celebration, was heard to demand somewhat incredulously when the Yes vote was initially ahead: "Where are those votes coming from?"

The answer was the early returns were coming from the small coastal towns, the best locations for the antinuclear activists. By contrast, all day, our exit polling in key precincts all over the state were unanimously signaling a victory of 10+ points or better. Once the Franco American centers such as Lewiston and Biddeford, Waterville, Saco, the Saint John Valley, and Westbrook came in, the No side pulled ahead to stay.

The actual outcome was 58 percent to 42 percent, with the No tallies running 2–1 everywhere except Waldo, Lincoln, Knox, and Sagadahoc counties. The polling data had been astonishingly accurate right down to the county level.

It was a crushing victory for Maine Yankee. And on one level it was a stinging defeat for Ray Shaddis and the antinuclear movement.[32] Still, the antinuclear movement had established itself as a major player on the Maine political scene.

Also, to be fair, the very last laugh belonged to Ray Shaddis as the antinuclear movement he had led in 1980 eventually persisted through two more defeats (in 1982, losing 61 percent to 39 percent; and 1987, losing 59 percent to 41 percent). But in the end, Ray Shaddis got to be on the decommissioning panel when Maine Yankee was finally shut down in 1997. Shaddis not only had the satisfaction of achieving his goal, but when the shutdown actually came, there was neither widespread nor local economic devastation, just as he had predicted.[33]

As reported in the *Portland Press Herald* of December 26, 1980, the nuclear shutdown referendum turned out to be the Associated Press top story of the year for all of New England.

REASONS WHY THE NO SIDE WON

1. The No side ran a more modern, professional campaign. Chuck Winner of Winner/Wagner brought modern, national political forms and processes to the Save Maine Yankee campaign. He thus revolutionized the way ballot measures were conducted in the state. Many aspects were copied from day one and translated to the Save Maine Yankee II and Save Maine Yankee III efforts as well as to a host of other later campaigns. The 1980 nuclear shutdown referendum was a seminal event. It changed the way ballot measures were done for the next twenty years.

   Shaddis, like Bruce Reeves and Jonathan Carter who would follow him on the ballot measure trail, seemed to disdain professional help. Polling, media firms, public relations organizations, consultants of every type—all were to be avoided. It was as if they thought "amateur" was a holier title than "professional" and they acted accordingly.

2. The Yes side was fragmented and diffuse, with multiple power centers and multiple messages. The Yes side was fragmented in terms of decision making by various committees while the No side was highly disciplined and focused on the economic issue to the exclusion of all others.

   There were so many antinuclear committees, often saying different things, that the voters were often confused and there was no central control over message, timing, or tactics. At the height of the referendum, there were at least 12 different committees.

   At the same time, and I did not realize this until researching this chapter, both the primacy and decision-making style of Ray Shaddis and the Maine Nuclear Referendum Committee made it unlikely that the collective wisdom in the antinuclear movement could be brought to bear in the context of the ongoing campaign. Thus the Yes side had the disadvantages of multiple power centers

but without the positive interaction such multiplicity could provide. There was probably more collective wisdom on the total Yes
side than came to the surface in the campaign.

As a result, there were many missed opportunities as the Yes side
failed to take advantage of tactical and strategic mistakes the No
side made.

For example, I woke up one morning that summer to a stunning
news story on TV. Maine Yankee had bought and was bringing to
Maine a generator from Three Mile Island! There it was on a huge
truck, trundling right up the Maine Turnpike. I jumped out of
bed and immediately called Skip Thurlow at home. His calm and
engineer-based reply was: "We got a very good buy on it; it's from
the non-damaged side of the plant"!

Oh my goodness!

Strangely—and to my great relief—the anti-forces did nothing to
capitalize on the incident. I thought at the time, "What a golden opportunity to get the debate back on their issue!" To this day, I believe that had the antinuclear side stuck to the safety issue, the outcome would have been much closer if not in their favor. In terms of
the final results, the closer you were to the plant, the less likely you
were to support it. Health and safety issues did matter.[34]

3. The No side had greater resources. The Save Maine Yankee Committee had much greater resources at its disposal and used those resources to great effect, changing the minds of Maine voters. Although one could argue this was necessary in light of the incredibly
powerful images and events the Yes side had at its disposal after the
accident at Three Mile Island in 1976, nevertheless, the material advantage was huge.

It should also be noted, however, that in Maine ballot measure
campaigns, having more resources than your opponent is not a
guarantor of victory. Having more money than your opponents
in a ballot measure situation in Maine is simply not in and of itself enough for victory. It is not the independent variable it's
cracked up to be.

The side with the most money has lost a host of important ballot
measures in Maine: the Bottle Bill (1976), Widening of Maine Turnpike (1991), Local Measured Service (1986), and Forest Compact I
(1997) and Forest Compact II (1998) as well as Assisted Suicide
(2000).

This has also been the case in a number of candidate races as
well. For example, in the 1974 election for governor, Mitchell spent
$158,000, Erwin spend $126,000, and Longley spent $73,000. Long-
ley finished first, Mitchell second, and Erwin a distant third!

4. The Yes side had a flawed strategy. The Yes side had the best driver issues in terms of health and safety but they didn't stay on that single message. They didn't believe in polls so they didn't know which were their best issues and which were not.

They tried to engage the issues raised by the SMY campaign. But the more one argued about the economics, the more people solidified against the referendum. The more the Nuclear Referendum Committee talked about the economic specifics, the less they could talk about health and safety, their winning issues.

Also, the Yes side made a serious mistake in going after the economic argument, which they could not win. They simply didn't make enough use of fear generated by the Three Mile Island incident. This huge advantage in terms of the climate of opinion was thrown away when they responded to the Save Maine Yankee game plan and conceptually played into its hands.

For example, in our nightly tracking, whenever the other side raised health and safety concerns, numbers jumped up in the locality. On August 16, John Newell, former president of BIW said, "Milk in the Wiscasset area contains 389 percent of the national average for strontium 90, a cancer-causing isotope."[35] Whether true or untrue, meaningful or not, this kind of information drove even our supporters away from a No vote whenever the other side used it.

5. The No side stayed on message and didn't follow the advice of some of its friends in the industry. This was a huge challenge, one of the biggest of the campaign. In ballot measures, your friends will do you more harm than your enemies and keeping those who liked nuclear power—and wanted it expanded, with more plants built— had to be kept at bay. At one point, for example, the Citizens for Fusion showed up ranting and raving. On September 12, the "Fusion Energy Foundation" and the "Independent Commission to Investigate Media Corruption and Unfairness" attacked Shaddis as "immoral."[36] This was just what the No side didn't want, an attack to get Shaddis sympathy.

It was a remarkable example of the referendum rule: "your friends will cause you more problems than your enemies." Chuck Winner had been right again. He'd warned us before the campaign ever started that we would see our "friends" causing us major problems while trying to "help" us.

6. Nightly tracking of TV began for the first time. The ability to track the efficacy of specific ads with specific audiences became the key to controlling the symbolic flow of the campaign. The melding of the DMA data to the key precincts' history amounted to a true polling revolution (see below).

7. Voting turnout was heavy. The 1980 referendum was a watershed event and the resulting controversy made many voters turn out to vote. With the exception of three presidential elections, this special election had the highest turnout of any special election in Maine political history. This worked to the advantage of the No vote because the more people who voted on nuclear power, the more who supported it. The farther you moved away from the "true believer" cohort of antinuclear voters, the better the plant did. So getting a higher than normal turnout was important to the No side.

44.4 percent voted. By Maine standards, this was a large turnout for a referendum. For example, the turnout was considerably higher than the 20 percent who had voted on nuclear waste storage (1985), the 26 percent who voted to ban cruise missile testing (1989), the 36 percent who voted to keep the Maine moose hunt (1983), the 29 percent who voted to repeal the uniform property tax (1977), the 25 percent who voted to pass term limits (1993), even the 44 percent who voted to limit human (gay) rights (1995).

WHAT IMPACT DID THIS
ELECTION HAVE ON MAINE POLITICS?

1. The Maine political scene was never the same after 1980. In terms of ballot measures, there were more and they were more expensive and national in scope. Here was a West Coast advertising firm that fought and won a referendum all the way across the nation. Each facet deserves its own analysis but taken together, the total impact of the first Maine Yankee Nuclear referendum was more than substantial. It represented a true sea change in Maine politics.

2. Citizen-initiated ballot measures became more common. After 1980, most election cycles had at least one major ballot measure that had been put there by citizen initiative. Often there were several. 1982, for example, saw votes on tax indexing, repeal of the setting of milk prices, and Maine Yankee II. 1989 saw a vote on the public financing of gubernatorial elections and cruise missile testing! In the period from 1960 to 1980, there were only a half-dozen citizen-generated referenda; from 1980 to 2000, there were nearly 30.

3. Ballot measures became more expensive. The Save Maine Yankee campaign was the most expensive ballot measure effort in the history of Maine politics to that point. Although its expenditures would be greatly exceeded in the two "Forest Compact" or "Ban Clear-Cutting" elections of 1996 and 1997, it was the Maine Yankee

effort that raised the bar financially. The Committee to Save Maine Yankee and the various antinuclear referendum committees spent over $1 million. The previous most expensive referendum was the 1976 Bottle Bill with $400,000 while the 1973 public authority referendum cost $243,000.

4. Ballot measures became more "national" in scope. Maine was to attract a great number of "cause" people from all over the country, culminating in the Physician Assisted Suicide campaign of 2000 in which not only did most of the money come from out of state, so too did the national organization, polling, and media efforts.

   Maine became a playing field, a venue as well as a target. This was due in part to the relatively small cost of running a ballot measure campaign ($1 million) compared with other, larger states. Also, of the 50 states, only 23 permit citizen initiatives so opportunities elsewhere were limited and national cause people could only go so many places. Plus there is still the mystique of the state's slogan and reputation of (however undeserved) "As Maine Goes. . . . So Goes the Nation."

5. Ballot measures became longer in duration. Many ballot measure campaigns became year-round efforts. Shaddis extended the time frame dramatically—to 18 months—but many other causes would follow and the long lead time required to initiate a petition drive well ahead of the proper legislative session would ensure that campaigns became much longer. Shaddis had brought a new level of commitment to the process and those who followed would appreciate the degree of his dedication.

6. Ballot measures became a gold mine for consultants especially in "off" years. The 1980 referendum changed my life as a consultant and that of many others as well. No longer were candidate campaigns the only place for professionals to make money. No longer were candidate campaigns the only financial game in town. There were many, many opportunities to make money and have fun in electoral politics now that ballot measures had become lucrative and ubiquitous.

7. Ballot measure rules became apparent. For my part, I saw the Maine Yankee effort as a true watershed with rules for successful campaigns. Over the years I have refined a few of them but here are the basics that came out of the 1980 campaign. Some of these include:

   a. The need for control over the wording of the ballot measure,
   b. Extensive research opportunities at the front of the election cycle,
   c. Tight control over spokespeople,
   d. Sufficient control over the umbrella committee,

    e. Absolute and complete control over all aspects of the paid media effort,

    f. Sufficient financial resources to give reasonable hope that the paid media effort can overcome any free media handicaps,

    g. Sufficient time to develop the proper themes,

    h. Ability to frame the debate and keep the campaign on message,

    i. Representation by aggressive, tenacious legal counsel,

    j. Control over the time and content of all free media efforts.[37]

8. The emergence of key swing voters as perpetual targets: Franco Americans, women in the home, and "cruel yuppies." Party affiliation, which is still an important diagnostic tool, gave way to other categories of analysis both demographic and psychographic.

    We will be looking at "cruel yuppies" a bit later, but here it should be noted that for ballot measures in the 20 years after the Maine Yankee shutdown referendum, Franco Americans (of all parities and in all locations) became vital to understanding how ballot measures would come out.

    The same was true with the category of women who worked at home. "Women in the home" became a key independent variable in looking at referenda issues. For example, they defeated the Forest Compact in two votes a year apart (1996 and 1997) and then, in the Forest Practices Referendum of 2000, voted in overwhelming numbers to defeat the proposal that had come from the very forces who had opposed the earlier Compact!

9. New revolutionary polling, which melded candidate key precincts with ballot measure correlations, proved extremely important. Peter Burr set up and translated partisan election outcome key precincts to ballot measures. For the first time in Maine political history, nightly polling was undertaken every day TV ads were on. This methodology proved to be amazingly effective in subsequent ballot measure campaigns such as the second effort to widen the Maine Turnpike, the first Gay Rights referendum, as well as the Assisted Suicide and Forestry referenda of 2000.

    Using the grid-outcome system, untrained volunteers could quickly and easily (to say nothing of cheaply) be harnessed to make sense out of a smattering of polling information. Using 60 million grid-outcomes matched against each other in regression analysis made it possible to override any sampling errors.

10. Psychographics emerged to blend with and at times supercede demographics.

    We have used the example of the "rich Republicans with sailboats" as a way of showing some psychographic categories that helped to explain referendum voting patterns. After the Save Maine Yankee effort, subsequent ballot measures were to focus increasingly on psychographic categories as ways to explain voter behavior.

In the 1991 and 1997 votes on widening the Maine turnpike, for example, upper income voters in the suburban arc around Portland were the deciding swing group. In 1991, these "cruel yuppies" decided that the highway drainage ditches were "sacred wetlands" and could not be sacrificed. In 1996, however, enough cruel yuppies had been caught in traffic jams on their way to Boston—or simply between Wells and Portland—that they voted 2–1 to widen the turnpike, their fondness for "sacred wetlands" long forgotten.

This psychographic grouping, which transcended party lines, also played a role in the 1994 1st CD congressional race, voting Republican Jim Longley Jr. into office over Biddeford Democrat Duke Dutremble but then, in the next election cycle, voting Longley out and Democrat Tom Allen in.

After 1980, psychographics became a very valuable political tool.

11. Maine Yankee was shut down by its owners. Antinuclear referenda lost in 1980 and again in 1982 and 1987. The grassroots forces arrayed against the plant tried hard and often but they could not convince a majority of Maine voters to shut down the plant. Tired of fighting battles with antinuclear activists and convinced costs of continuing to run the plant outweighed the benefits, the owners threw in the towel. Skip Thurlow had planned to keep the plant running until at least 2010 but he was no longer around, having been forced into retirement.

The Save Maine Yankee ballot measure of 1980 was the most important referendum of Maine's postwar period, not only because of its specific outcome, but also in terms of its size and scope and degree of national interest, and because of its long-term impact on the process of ballot measure politics in the Pine Tree State.

7

The 1990s:

Angus King vs. Joseph E. Brennan vs. Susan Collins

THE DECADE'S MATRIX

The 1990s witnessed some of the most important and contentious and costly ballot measure campaigns in Maine's political history. By the year 2000, the cost and scope of such campaigns had reached truly unprecedented levels.

The 1990s also saw the most evenly balanced records by Republicans and Democrats of any of the decades under review, thanks in at least some part to the emergence of the Green Party, which in several important races helped to provide the margin of victory for Republicans. Although the Green Party drew its strength from Democrats, Independents, and Republicans, behavioral Democrats provided most of its operational base, a base that was to materially detract from the chances of the Democratic candidates in the 2nd CD race of 1992 and the 1994 governor's race.

The gubernatorial race of 1990, however, was decided by the draining off of Democratic votes by an Independent, Andrew Adam. We shall be covering this most interesting of races in the concluding section of this chapter, but suffice it to say here that the reelection of Jock McKernan was quite an accomplishment, coming as it did with the incumbent down 17 percent as late as mid-September to his Democratic challenger, former governor Joe Brennan. McKernan was narrowly reelected 46.7 percent to 44 percent with 9.3 percent going to Adam.

While Adam's vote total was not as large as many previous independent totals, a disproportionate percentage of his total vote came out of Democratic strongholds such as Lewiston and prevented Brennan from attaining the normal winning percentage among registered Democrats in key precincts during that election.

In the U.S. Senate race, Bill Cohen easily won reelection, getting 61 percent of the vote over Neil Rolde with 39 percent of the vote.

The 2nd CD saw incumbent Olympia Snowe narrowly reelected 51 percent to 49 percent over Patrick McGowan.

In the 1st CD, there was a wild scramble in both parties for the nomination since it was an open seat, Brennan having moved into the gubernatorial sweepstakes.

On the Republican side, Dave Emery won the nomination as he outpolled John McCormick in the primary 62 percent to 38 percent. In the Democratic primary, Tom Andrews received 36 percent of the vote compared with Jim Tierney's 34 percent, Elizabeth Mitchell's 17 percent, Linda Abramson's 11 percent, and Ralph Conant's 2 percent.

The general election showed the Democrats maintaining their hold on the 1st CD, with Andrews outpacing Emery 60 percent to 40 percent.

In 1990 a ballot measure was passed (63 percent to 47 percent) to allow for retail stores to be open on Sundays. This was followed in 1991 by a referendum to stop the widening of the Maine turnpike that passed 59 percent to 41 percent and in 1992 by a ballot measure dedicating revenues from hunting and fishing licenses that passed 74 percent to 26 percent, showing the strength of an alliance between the Sportsman's Alliance of Maine (which ran the campaign) and the Maine Audubon Society (which supported the effort).

There were no elections for governor or U.S. Senate in 1992 but both congressional races proved interesting. Tom Andrews, the incumbent, was unopposed in the 1st CD Democratic primary but the Republicans had a scrappy primary among Linda Bean, Anthony Payne (33 percent) and John Purcell (21 percent), won by Linda Bean with 46 percent of the vote. The general election saw Andrews easily reelected 65 percent to 35 percent.

Maine's 2nd CD witnessed a competitive three-way race, won by Olympia Snowe with 49 percent of the vote over Democrat Pat McGowan (42 percent) and a strong Green Party candidate, Jonathan Carter (9 percent). Just as Andrew Adams had sapped traditional Democratic support in the Brennan/McKernan race of 1990, so Carter took more votes from McGowan than from Snowe.

The decision of George Mitchell not to seek reelection opened up a U.S. Senate and two congressional seats in 1994 and set off a variety of changes in the political landscape; that, coupled with an open gubernatorial position due to McKernan being term limited, resulted in a record number of candidates for those four positions with 16 people vying for the governorship alone while 8 sought the 1st District seat and 11 the 2nd.

In the Republican primary, Susan Collins captured the nomination with 21.5 percent of the vote, followed by Sumner Lipman's 19.9 percent, Jasper Wyman's 15.9 percent, Judith Foss's 13 percent, Paul Young's 11.2 percent, Mary Adams's 8.7 percent, Charles Webster's 6.9 percent, and Pam Cahill's 5.8 percent.

On the Democratic side, Joe Brennan coasted to a substantial victory 56 percent to 24 percent over Thomas Allen while Richard Barringer (9 percent), Robert Woodbury (8 percent), and Donnell Carroll (3 percent) also contested.

In the general election, however, it was Independent Angus King duplicating the feat of 20 years previous by James B. Longley as he narrowly defeated Joe Brennan 35.4 percent to 33.8 percent as Republican Susan Collins got 23 percent and Green candidate Jonathan Carter got 6.4 percent of the vote. Mark Finks, a Republican conservative, also drew write-ins. Carter's vote was significant as it was the first time the Greens had qualified in a gubernatorial race and was of considerable assistance in helping to elect Angus King. Ralph Coffman was also a write-in candidate.

Mitchell's abrupt departure thrust Tom Andrews into a U.S. Senate race for which he was more than a little unprepared, while Olympia Snowe was ready to go. She easily defeated Andrews 60.2 percent to 36.4 percent with Plato Truman running as an Independent getting 3.4 percent.

Maine's 1st CD saw a spirited contest for both Republican and Democratic nominations. Jim Longley Jr. received 43 percent of the vote in the Republican primary, besting Charles Summers (25 percent), Kevin Keogh (18 percent), and Theodore Rand (14 percent). On the Democratic side, Dennis Dutremble (33 percent) defeated Bonnie Titcomb (24 percent), William Diamond (24 percent), and William Troubh (19 percent). Longley won the general election 52 percent to 48 percent.

The 2nd CD had Richard Bennett taking the Republican nomination with 29 percent of the vote to Stephen Zirnkilton's 26 percent, Glenn MacNaughton's 25 percent, and Hollis Greenlaw's 19 percent. John Baldacci won the Democratic nomination with 27 percent of the vote, besting James F. Mitchell (23 percent), Janet Mills (18 percent), James Howaniec (14 percent), Mary Cathcart (13 percent), Jean Hay (5 percent), and Shawn Hallisey (1 percent). Baldacci won the general election 46 percent to 41 percent over Bennett with Independents John Michael (9 percent) and Charles Fitzgerald (5 percent) also contesting.

Term limits passed 63 percent to 37 percent in 1994, Gay Rights in 1995 (53 percent to 47 percent).

Bill Cohen's decision not to seek reelection in 1996 likewise stirred the political pot as Susan Collins (56 percent), John Hathaway (31 percent), and Robert A. G. Monks (13 percent) contested the Republican primary. On the Democratic side, Joe Brennan (55 percent) defeated Sean Faircloth (26 percent), Richard Spencer (13 percent), Jean Hay (5 percent), and Jerald Leonard (1 percent).

The general election again saw Collins triumphant with 49 percent of the vote compared to 44 percent for Brennan, 4 percent for Green candidate John Rensenbrink, and 3 percent for Taxpayer Party William Clarke.

In the 1st CD, Jim Longley Jr., running unopposed in the Republican primary, was defeated (46 percent to 54 percent) by Tom Allen who had earlier defeated Dale McCormick by a thin margin of 50.1 to 49.9 percent.

In the 2nd, John Baldacci was reelected over Paul Young 72 percent to 23 percent while Aldric Saucier, the Independent, got 5 percent.

In 1996 and 1997 the proposed Forest Compact was defeated for the second time 52 percent to 48 percent.

The year 1998 closed out the election cycles for this century and a major record was set. Angus King, the incumbent Independent governor, was reelected with the highest vote percentage in Maine history for a three-way race, eclipsing the earlier record set by Joshua Chamberlain in September 1870.

King received 59 percent of the vote compared to 19 percent for the Republican nominee, Jim Longley Jr., 12 percent for Tom Connolly, the Democrat, 7 percent for Pat LaMarche, the Independent/Green candidate, and 3 percent for Bill Clarke of the Taxpayers Party. Earlier, Jim Longley Jr. had won the Republican nomination with 66 percent compared with 20 percent for Henry Joy and 14 percent for Leo Martin. On the Democratic side, Tom Connolly had defeated Joseph Ricci 82 percent to 18 percent to earn his spot on the fall ballot.

What is not often appreciated in the King record setting was the role played by well-known hunter and outdoorsman, Ezra Smith of Winthrop. His late commercial comparing King to an L.L. Bean shoe, "more comfortable now that it's been worn," added 5 percent to the King running total, thereby putting him into record territory.

In the 1st CD, Tom Allen received 60 percent of the vote compared with 36 percent for Ross Connelly and 4 percent for Eric Greiner, an Independent. Ross Connelly had earlier defeated David Ott for the Republican nomination.

The 2nd CD saw John Baldacci returned to office with 76 percent to 24 percent for his Republican challenger, Jonathan Reisman. Neither man had been opposed in his respective primary.

SEMINAL ELECTION:
THE 1994 GUBERNATORIAL RACE

The Election of Maine's Second Independent Governor

Any analysis of post–World War II Maine politics must contain a section on the election of Maine's first Independent governor, James B. Longley. The 1974 election campaign that put him in the Blaine House deserves our attention. But I believe that if Longley had been the only elected Independent during this period, his achievement, while still important, could not be considered as seminal for the process of politics in Maine. At the same time, as Sandy Maisel and Doug Hodgkin have pointed out, his victory in and of itself spawned a number of subsequent Independent candidates.

But while this would have affected the Maine political scene in terms of additional candidates, it would not have in and of itself changed the outcome side of the ledger. It is only through a second election of an Independent candidate that we can see a true change in the overall process, taking it beyond a single important but idiosyncratic event. A single event is not a pattern in terms of outcomes.

That is why the 1994 election of Angus King is so important, for it validates that true political history was made in 1974, an historical event which would have an impact on the course of politics in the Pine Tree State beyond itself.

But until now, virtually no observers have figured out what that pattern was and none have chronicled it in the context of the postwar period. Yet the pattern is identical. Longley and King won by putting together the same political coalition! Exactly the same.

In this chapter, we shall be examining that coalition and its workings in some detail but in order to place that coalition in the proper context, we need to briefly examine the Longley election of 1974.

To the party faithful, the governorship is the Holy Grail. It has visibility and patronage and a bully pulpit. It provides a standard around which to rally the partisan troops and gives the party in power a tremendous opportunity to enhance its position statewide, both at the grassroots level and in terms of policy formation. It makes partisans feel good about themselves and their missions.

Therefore, to Republicans in 1973, Bill Cohen seemed the likely candidate to lead the party. With the defeat of Senator Margaret Chase Smith in 1972, he was the only major elected Republican. He was young, dynamic, and photogenic. He had proven himself to be a very formidable campaigner and he was undefeated.

A number of party officials as well as many of his closest supporters wanted him to run. Many Republicans thought the Democratic standard bearer would be Representative Peter Kyros from Maine's 1st CD. With Cohen in the 2nd and Kyros in the 1st, it looked like a natural matchup, and a number of Kyros's closest supporters also saw merit in his candidacy. Even by mid-1973, there was no love lost between the Cohen and Kyros staffs and both relished the idea of knocking off the other congressman. "Better to take him out now rather than waiting until he is stronger" was the theme of the day.

Thus, well over a year before the crucial 1974 elections, the parties had two strong, proven candidates who, it could reasonably be expected, would make excellent gubernatorial standard bearers. They were in the next generation after the Muskies and Smiths and Hathaways and they were proven commodities on the campaign trail.

As strange as it may seem, I believe James B. Longley was able to become Maine's first independent governor in 1974 precisely because this "dream" matchup between Republican and Democratic congressmen did not take place. Had Cohen decided to challenge Kyros—or Mitchell if he had entered and won a primary against Kyros—the political history of Maine would have been quite different for I remain a firm believer in historical malleability.

But there was one huge obstacle for either Kyros or Cohen that ultimately prevented them from even seriously considering the governorship and that was their basic political mind-set.

In my experience, although there are a few prominent exceptions, there are basically two kinds of Maine politicians, those who want to go to Washington (Cohen, Kyros, Emery, Mitchell, Allen, Snowe) and those who want to be governor (Brennan, Baldacci, King, Longley).

Jock McKernan, however, is one figure who was relatively happy doing either job. I am grateful to Governor McKernan for not only substantiating my bifurcation, but also for raising the issue of Ed Muskie who seemed at home in both positions as well (although Muskie took the train out of Augusta the very first chance he had and never looked back). McKernan and Muskie certainly were unusual in being totally at home in both Washington and Augusta.

So Bill Cohen decided not to run for governor in 1974 and thus left a wide open field for both the Republicans and the Democrats. I have no doubt that had he run, he would have beaten any possible primary opponents and our polling showed he would have easily disposed of any possible Democratic candidates (such a Peter Kyros, Joe Brennan, or George Mitchell).

I honestly believe that James B. Longley never would have been elected in 1974 had Cohen carried the Republican banner. Even after Longley became a very popular governor, our polling showed he would have been trounced by Cohen had Longley challenged him for the U.S. Senate in 1978. Also, Longley was successful in large part because of voter disillusion with the Watergate scandal but Cohen's star never shone brighter with Democrats and Independents than after he voted to impeach Richard Nixon in July of 1974. He would have been virtually impossible to beat in the fall of 1974. But Cohen did not run and the governor's race of 1974 belonged to Longley. He would set both a precedent and a pattern.

1974: THE ELECTION OF MAINE'S
FIRST INDEPENDENT GOVERNOR

So the stage was set for James B. Longley's improbable and ultimately successful run for the governorship. With Cohen out of the way, the Republican field was wide open. State senator Harrison "Harry" Richardson of Cumberland was soon in the race and he was initially opposed only by state senator Bennett Katz of Augusta who appeared ready to make a run but then dropped out, eventually endorsing Jim Erwin.

Some conservatives in the party, however, led by former party chair Charles Moreshead, the then current party chair, Harold Jones, and the party's executive director, Alex Ray, encouraged—indeed insisted— former attorney general Jim Erwin run as well. Erwin and Richardson were eventually joined by Millinocket state senator Wakine Tanous and Bath's senator Tarpy Shulten (although he would eventually drop out).

On the Democratic side, it was to be a spirited race among state senators Peter Kelley (Aroostook), Joe Brennan (Portland), Lloyd P. LaFountain (Biddeford) as well as George Mitchell (Waterville), a close confidant of Senator Muskie. Longley, who had been appointed to a cost containment commission by then governor Ken Curtis, made early noise about running but no one in the political establishment of either party took him very seriously.

Early on, many political insiders thought the fall 1974 race would come down to a battle between dynamic and charismatic Richardson and a more epigonic and intellectual Mitchell. Few even mentioned Longley. Mitchell did his part to fulfill that prophecy, winning the Democratic primary with 37.5 percent of the vote to 26.4 percent for Brennan, 24.1 percent for Kelley, and 9 percent for LaFountain.

But Jim Erwin won the Republican primary 39 percent to 38 percent for Richardson and 19 percent for Tanous. Having already run twice for governor and lost, Erwin was not highly regarded by many insiders, even after he won the primary. Moreover, his 1974 campaign, like his earlier 1970 one, was based on grassroots and traditional campaigning for Erwin did not seem to have much of a strategy for television.

Also, he had difficulty raising money and his campaign never really seemed to get off the ground. Indeed, as the campaign wore on, there seemed to be a disconnect between what was really happening and what the Erwin camp thought was happening. His campaign slogan, "Erwin This Time," is regarded as one of the worst in modern times, tying him to his earlier, disastrous loss to Ken Curtis in 1970.

I remember late in the campaign at the end of October going up to Erwin headquarters in Augusta on some mission for Cohen and politely standing there as Paul Hawthorne, Erwin's campaign manager, proudly pointed to a huge chart-map of the state with many, brightly colored pins showing the Erwin organization and what they were doing. The exercise reminded me of Adolf Hitler at the end of World War II deep in his Wolf's Lair bunker, moving around German formations on the Eastern Front, formations that had ceased to exist some time before.

For his part, Mitchell started out with many advantages. George Mitchell was born in Waterville on August 20, 1933. When his mother died, he was placed in a Lebanese family. He went to Waterville High and then to Bowdoin where he graduated cum laude in history. He was also in ROTC and emerged as the leading officer and went to Germany to work in intelligence.

After his army service, Mitchell went to Washington and joined the staff of Senator Ed Muskie. A strong bond developed between the two men and Muskie would be Mitchell's patron for the remainder of his life. Working on Muskie's 1968 vice presidential and 1972 presidential campaigns gave Mitchell a desire to enter the political fray himself. He returned to Maine and practiced law (having attended Georgetown Law School at night while serving as a Muskie staffer).

The year 1974 should have been a banner year for his general election campaign. President Nixon was under a huge cloud from the Watergate affair and he would resign on August 9 of that year. Mitchell should have been well positioned to take advantage of the situation but his years in Washington allowed others to paint him with an "insider" politician label.

Worse, in the minds of some, he had been a lobbyist, which some clients regarded as unsavory. In this regard, not only Republicans but also Longley's Independent supporters made much of his involvement in the abortive Vahlsing potato-processing plant that so polluted the Prestile stream in Aroostook County.

Also, the Mitchell campaign overspent the (then) advertising spending cap of $162,000 by over $23,000 or 14 percent. As the campaign wore on, Mitchell seemed more and more part of "the problem" in politics, not its solution. Mitchell's humble beginnings and his meritorious rise were lost in the image of a political insider who had been involved in the Washington mess.

Mitchell's lack of charisma was also something of a detriment. He often sounded boring on the campaign trail and he made a number of mistakes. For example, although Mitchell is now known for his environmental stances, in 1974, he was still tied to the increasingly unpopular Dickey Lincoln public works project. And he blundered badly in buying up all the billboard space in Maine at the very time the environmental movement was trying to get all billboards removed from the Maine landscape.

On April 18, 1974, Longley resigned from the Longley Commission (having been appointed by Governor Ken Curtis to see if there were ways state government could become more efficient) to explore an Independent bid for governor. Despite having told Curtis he would not run, Longley announced on June 7 that he would seek the governorship. This upset Curtis and the Democrats very much.[1]

Longley was intense, charismatic, and driven. He soon established himself as a force on the campaign trail, working long hours with almost manic energy. He positioned himself as an outsider, cleverly linking problems in Washington with "professional politicians" and the situation in Maine. He said he was someone with no axes to grind, no political debts to pay. He shrewdly positioned himself as the underdog, but the underdog who knew the score. He called himself the "fiscally responsible" candidate who was beholden to no one.

The voting registration figures gave Longley some upside potential. In 1974, 40 percent of Maine voters were Independent or "unenrolled" while 38 percent were Republicans and 37 percent were Democrats. The Independent cohort, however, contained a much higher percentage of non-voters than did either the Republican or Democrat groups.

Looking back on the press accounts of the 1974 race, I am struck with how successful Longley was in getting coverage. In fact, in 30 years of following Maine politics, I've never seen a candidate for higher office who had such a knack for getting the Associated Press (AP), United Press International (UPI), and the daily newspapers to publish his laundry slips. Much of the credit for this feat must rest with Longley's intrepid press secretary, James "Jim" McGregor. The results were truly stupendous.

Take, for example, the coverage of a single week in July. On July 17, Longley called on candidates to report their expenditures on a monthly basis, calling it a way to restore confidence in government. This got considerable coverage in the *Portland Press Herald*. Then, the next day, when George Mitchell had received the endorsement of the Maine Building Trades Council, Longley immediately cried foul, claiming their backing was "unfair."[2] How would he know, one might fairly ask? Longley's charges ended up getting as much coverage as the initial endorsement!

A few days later, Longley called for a second chance for Mainers to vote on the existing lottery even though that call was less than clarion: "There perhaps should be a re-examination of the lottery in any event." The *Portland Press Herald*, on July 22, 1974, carried this fragment of a thought as if it were hard news. Three days later, he was back in the *Herald*, denying having said that "partisan politicians" were "less than honorable."[3]

On July 25, Longley again trumped Mitchell in the news, this time complaining about the AFL-CIO's Committee on Political Education (COPE) endorsement of George Mitchell. He called their action "discrimination" in the *Portland Press Herald* of July 25, 1974.

Thus Mitchell had received some important endorsements (much more important in 1974 than today) but Longley had reaped most of the press coverage from them! He had also raised some very valid points such as how could the AFL/CIO and the Maine Teacher's Association, those most "Democratic" of interest groups not be "democratic" in their assessment of candidates? By refusing to let Longley even address their members, they were shown to be undemocratic.

"I came from the South," says McGregor, "where politics is a way of life. I told Jim, 'We've got to get out of the last paragraph (where third party candidates were normally assigned) or you don't have a chance.'"[4] He succeeded with a vengeance. This was big league press activity by any measure.

Even from a distance of thirty-five years it is still possible to feel Mitchell's justified frustration. On September 5, for example—and I'm not making this up—McGregor got Longley significant coverage in the *Bangor Daily News* for attacking a statement Mitchell made on the radio saying Longley was more likely to take votes away from Erwin than himself!

Longley even got coverage in the *Press Herald* when he told the Holy Cross Men's Club of South Portland to "vote or stop complaining." Imagine a regular party candidate trying to get press coverage for such a civic banality today. Not to be outdone, the *Bangor Daily News* gave space to Longley's pedestrian assertion that there were many lawyers in government and that although he had a law degree, he was not a lawyer but a businessman![5] Even rereading these articles several times, it is hard to believe they are real and not a political spoof. McGregor was earning his pay and the state's newspapers were bending over backwards to accommodate Longley.

From the Mitchell perspective, Longley's rising visibility and press attention should have been an early warning sign. Mitchell should have been preparing negative ads for use in the fall in the event the Longley phenomenon continued. But he did not, seemingly like a rabbit fascinated by the snake and unable to move away before he became its dinner.

In terms of his issues, Mitchell tried to stick to normal Democratic standards: he was against the rise in the cost of living, he was for more and better jobs, he was concerned about "the serious plight of our elderly" and "the need for quality health care."[6] Incidentally, these issues are identical to those central in the 2002 gubernatorial election!

But at the time, Mitchell himself became the issue on several fronts. On August 17, headlines in the *Portland Press Herald* blared: "Panel to Probe Law on Mitchell, Tanous Ads." Mitchell claimed that the law on advertising limits was not meant to apply to bumper stickers, pamphlets, and other traditional forms of campaign material. In the hothouse of the Watergate era of 1974, that sounded like politics as usual to undecided and Independent voters.

Republican Attorney General Jon Lund pursued the matter while Longley called for an independent audit "to remove any cloud of suspicion that might surround the election process in Maine."[7] The two major candidates played right into Longley's hand—they attacked each other but not him. Both parties had not yet learned the lessons of Watergate.

Longley exuded confidence. On September 10, at the opening of his Portland headquarters, Longley stated flatly: "I think I'm going to win. I think the people of the state of Maine are ready for a good businessman."[8] Indeed, by mid-September, many Republican insiders (including former state party chair and major power broker Jack Linnell) had already consigned Erwin to third place. But virtually no one in the Republican or Democratic hierarchies saw Longley as the next governor. For years, many students of Maine politics tried to make sense out of his dramatic, last-minute victory.

Still Mitchell didn't pay much attention to Longley; he was busy charging that Erwin was trying to "squirm his way out of a debate."[9] As late as October 29, Nancy Chandler of Mitchell's political organization said, "We're not attacking Longley," and Mitchell believed that Longley "has no actual chance of winning the election."[10] These assumptions and tactics would prove to be huge mistakes.

For his part, Erwin claimed that he did not want to debate candidates individually but would debate all the candidates (including the three Independents, James B. Longley, Stanley Leen, and William Hughes). He said it would be the "height of inconsideration" to exclude the Independent candidates from a debate.[11] The six eventually did have an inconclusive and somewhat frustrating debate on Maine Public Broadcasting Network on October 16. In Maine, debates seldom accomplish much and this case was not an exception.

On October 6, 1974, Erwin released a Northeast Markets poll that showed him with 36.7 percent to 26.5 percent for Mitchell. No mention was made of Longley's position. Jim Brunelle, writing in the *Herald* on October 6, said "A Voter Would Do Well to Eye Polls Skeptically." For his part, Brunelle appears to have missed the significance of nearly 40 percent of voters being undecided. This was an ominous sign for both of the two major parities!

Why, after running for governor before and losing narrowly, would Erwin have such a low vote total? And why would he publish such terrible numbers? Because the *Bangor Daily News* had also recently (October 5) released a poll showing Erwin with 21.8 percent of the vote and Mitchell 21.6 percent. Now that was even worse news—for both the major party candidates.

Next came the *Bangor Daily News* poll of October 18. Conducted by the Social Science Research Institute of the University of Maine, it showed Mitchell getting 27.5 percent of the vote, Erwin 20.5 percent, and James B. Longley 10.7 percent. By contrast, Bill Cohen was getting 71 percent of the vote in Maine's 2nd CD and Mark Gartley was getting 17.4.

Late in October, Erwin, however, really thought he had the jugular of Mitchell and attacked his Vahlsing connection. Erwin repeatedly linked Mitchell to environmental degradation and claimed Mitchell was trying to lower water quality while Erwin, as attorney general, was trying to enforce it. Erwin was on the attack.[12]

Mitchell responded the next day, calling the charges "a smear" and focusing on what he said were the realities of the lawyer-client relationship: "I represent hundreds of clients . . . if I defend a burglar and he is found guilty, does that make me a burglar? Of course not."[13]

Erwin then put ads in the major newspapers after Mitchell accused him of "mudslinging." Mitchell, he said, had been a member of the Board of Directors and an officer of Maine Sugar Industries. He had also been a director of both Vahlsing, Inc. and New York Sugar Industries.

Maine Sugar Industries defaulted on $10 million worth of its State of Maine loans as well as the $3 million in interest while Mitchell was a stockholder, buying in 1965 and selling in 1971. Mitchell was also a paid lobbyist during the 104th session of the Maine Legislature where he opposed legislation "to reduce the pollution of the Prestile Stream, which had become an open sewer," and Erwin said, "George Mitchell accuses me of 'smearing' him with the truth about his Vahlsing sugar beet connection." Mitchell's defense that "We directors were largely window dressing, rubber stamps, I suppose" gave Erwin a chance to ask in the same ad, "If George Mitchell were to become governor, whose rubber stamp would he be?"[14]

Mitchell then called in Ed Muskie to defend him and Muskie let off a broadside on October 26, terming Erwin's charges "a political football that has been kicked around during every election."[15]

Whatever the realities of the situation and Erwin's handling of the political opportunity it presented, writing twenty-five years later, the liberal *Boston Globe Magazine* remained troubled by the Mitchell–Vahlsing connection.[16]

Ignoring Longley's challenge, both Mitchell and Erwin continued to slug it out in print. Erwin, in particular, relied on print and speaking engagements to get this message out, not the 30-second commercial, which would have been a much better medium for these types of attacks.

Donald Hansen, political reporter and editor for the *Portland Press Herald*, wrote a story on October 29, 1974, that carried the headline "Longley to Spoil Someone's Nov. 5, Likely Erwin's," stating, "It is probable that

James B. Longley will elect the next governor of Maine. The only unanswered question now seems to be: who will Jim Longley elect." But John Day, writing in the *Bangor Daily News* on October 28, saw a "3-Way Race Developing." He was the only major print reporter to see the dramatic upsurge for Longley.

On October 31, 1974, Northeast Markets published a survey in the *Maine Sunday Telegram*. Its methodology was a bit hazy: "based on data collected by Northeast Markets for a number of clients." It showed that Erwin had been leading in July with Mitchell a strong second and Longley a distant third with less than 10 percent of the vote.

In this poll however, Erwin was down to 25 percent. Mitchell was supposedly rising up to 38 percent but Longley had made the biggest move, doubling his vote total from 10 percent to over 20 percent. Erwin continued to rely on his own internal numbers generated at the grassroots. Mitchell thought the election would be close but that he would win. Longley was convinced he would win.

According to Willis Johnson, one of the reasons Longley thought he would win was that the University of Maine's Social Science Research Institute, led by Dr. Bruce Pulton, continued to poll right through the weekend prior to the election and sent the numbers on to Longley and the BDN.[17] John Day of the BDN saw those numbers over the weekend and was convinced Longley was going to win but his editors wouldn't let him run with the story.[18]

On October 31, the *Bangor Daily News* endorsed Longley with a strong editorial, calling him "the best choice" and harboring "a hunch that candidate Longley's potential to grow in the governor's office is greater than either of his principal gubernatorial opponents. Think about it."

This mounting excitement set the stage for Jack Havey, Longley's media guru, to come up with a dynamite ad that captured Longely's intensity as he ended the campaign with a new slogan: "You Never Waste Your Vote When You Vote for the Best Candidate." Using radio and TV, the Longley campaign dominated the airwaves the final few days with a fresh, exciting commercial.[19] In those days it was possible to get a new commercial into the television rotation over the weekend. Today, however, all changes have to be made by Friday noon.

McGregor says Havey provided the final finishing kick, telling them to "get off their asses and get up to Bangor" where he shot a new powerful set of radio and TV spots.[20] Havey had already been responsible for Longley's basic campaign slogan, "Longley for Governor: Think About It!"

The endorsement of the *Bangor Daily News* (which conferred great legitimacy to a third party candidate) and the weekend blitz of the airwaves put Longley over the top despite the *Portland Press Herald's* claim on November 3: "Mitchell Is Seen Easy Winner Over Erwin In Poll" and indicating Mitchell would outpoll Erwin by 9 percent and Longley by 19 percent!

Election Night 1974 was a nightmare for both major parties.

Mitchell was very disappointed: press photos show he and his wife watching the very discouraging returns with an equally glum Senator Bill Hathaway. His recent big lead had withered away to nothing. He would, however, eventually rise out of the ashes of defeat when appointed to the U.S. Senate by Governor Joe Brennan. Mitchell would go on to great glory, winning reelection to the Senate in his own right in 1982 and setting a percentage record in 1988, getting 81 percent of the vote against Jasper Wyman.

Longley had gotten 40 percent of the vote while Mitchell polled 37 percent and Erwin 23 percent. For Erwin, it was a bitter night as well; his only consolation probably was that he had helped bring Mitchell down, too. For him, it was the end of an era.

Longley, however, was like a skyrocket shooting up into the midnight sky. He had triumphed over all odds. He had made himself governor despite the efforts of the two parties. His supporters were ecstatic. A new era was going to dawn in Maine politics. "The people of Maine have dared to be first," Longley said in the *Portland Press Herald* of November 6, 1974. He was correct. Maine had become the first state in the nation to have an Independent governor.

WHAT FACTORS ENABLED LONGLEY TO TRIUMPH?

1. Erwin's poor campaign never got off the ground. None of the mistakes of 1970 had been rectified. For example, his campaign buttons simply said, "Erwin This Time" or "Erwin," as if his name were enough. Mitchell's at least said, "George Mitchell for Governor." But only Longley's had a spark. His said, "Longley for Governor: Think About It!" This slogan is regarded by many insiders as the best slogan of the postwar period.

2. Mitchell's cerebral and lackluster campaign lacked a meaningful and winning segmentation strategy. He got ahead on name recognition and choice and tried to ride out the Longley charge. He also made many campaign mistakes. For example, his scheduling seemed to have him constantly at places such as Bowdoin College rather than on the streets of Lewiston and he bought up most of the billboard space in the state to promote his candidacy—while running as a candidate who cared about the environment!

   In this race, he often seemed shy and diffident, a far cry from the campaign powerhouse he turned into in the 1990 U.S. Senate race.

At one point in the race he had to insist to John Day: "They say I'm a plastic man, a dull campaigner. I don't believe I am." *Bangor Daily News*, October 14, 1974.

3. The temper of the times put Erwin as a Republican and Mitchell as an insider on the defensive. The post-Watergate mood of the country abetted a strategy of "throw out the rascals." Longley seemed like a breath of fresh air, his "outsider" status and his stern charisma different from the politicians of the day.

   He made a lot out of his outsider status and constantly drew the distinction that he was what the times needed to clean things up and throwing the rascals out was a big part of the flavor of that era. Sometimes voters seem reassured by "the rascals" and we then call them "successful incumbents" but in 1974, voters wanted a change for its own sake.

4. Longley's intensity and drive was a huge factor. He had, according to his media guru, Jack Havey, "no plan, no strategy" but he was a "super campaigner who loved the campaign trail where he would get excited and 'close the sale'" with individual voters; he was "a very, very good insurance salesman."[21]

   Both Mitchell and Erwin seemed bland and dull and epigonic by comparison and although Mitchell later (1980) made himself into a good campaigner, in this election he was almost as poor a candidate as Erwin. Longley worked harder than many candidates and confronted voters with an intensity rarely seen in Maine politics.

   McGregor also points to another Longley attribute that served him well. He could marshal up "righteous indignation" at the drop of a hat and could make people feel very guilty if they wouldn't do what he wanted.[22]

5. Thanks to Jack Havey, Longley's message was simple, direct, and effective. Jack Havey of Ad Media was the person who came up with Longley's slogan "Think About It!" as well as his last weekend advertisement: "You Never Waste Your Vote When You Vote for the Best Candidate." Havey, one of the most talented artists and advertising figures in Maine history, was at the top of his game.

   In the cynical aftermath of the breaking of the Watergate scandals, Longley appeared not only to be a new voice, he was also direct and a breath of fresh air into a stale political room. He positioned himself as the perfect outsider. He was the underdog. He got coverage in the daily newspapers for virtually everything he said, no matter how irrelevant or self-serving.

   Jack Havey deserves a lot of credit for translating that reality into images and word pictures to which the voters could relate. His brilliant media strategy included a husbanding of Longley's scarce resources until the end when the bulk of his \$23,753 TV and radio budget was spent during the last week of the campaign, especially the last weekend.[23]

Considering this was Havey's first political effort, an appreciation of the importance of his contribution to the Longley triumph needs to be underscored. It was not a bad effort the first time out!

6. James "Jim" McGregor, Longley's aide, confidant, and press spokesperson, also deserves considerable credit. He helped make Longley credible to Maine's reporters and he knew what buttons to press to both get their attention and to smooth over Longley's inevitable overstatements and gaffes. Young and devoted, McGregor had spent two years in Maine (he was originally from Alabama) serving as UPI's bureau chief. McGregor had won a Pulitzer Prize for his writing and knew his craft inside and out.

He served as driver, confidant, and all around factotum as well as press secretary, keeping up as frantic a pace as Longley. He also, given Longley's propensity to shoot from the hip and to be a tad loose with the facts, served him well by retracing Longley's steps and trying to "set the record straight." Previous accounts have tended to stress McGregor's contributions in terms of this overall "body man" combination but in fact, his press achievements were stellar. It is doubtful Longley would have succeeded without his contributions.

Thus in keeping with one of the main themes of this book, the contribution of staffers and campaign workers to the eventual success of various politicians, Longley was very well served by both McGregor and Havey. There would obviously have been no Longley without the candidate himself; his drive, his charisma, and his intensity all helped put him over the top. But without the talents of Jack Havey and Jim McGregor, Longley would have been a footnote in Maine political history, not the focus of half a chapter.

7. The failure of the two parties to take him seriously until it was too late gave Longley time to build up a head of steam. There was much wishful thinking in the two parties. They simply did not believe Longley could win because no one had ever won that way. They did not believe that something that had never happened before could happen.

The press, of course, although they gave him good coverage and liked his great quotes, had also dismissed Longley until very late in the game. On October 28, however, John S. Day of the *Bangor Daily News* saw Longley as viable and noted that Longley had been attacking both other candidates while they had been ignoring him.[24] For the most part though, both the parties and the press had missed the threat of Longley until the very end of the campaign.

8. The failure of either major candidate to "go negative" against Longley on TV allowed him an open path. He got a free ride in the sense that neither major candidate attacked his positions or promises, enabling him to say the most incredible things and make the most incredible claims all in a vacuum. Longley sailed along unchallenged during the entire campaign. The press loved him for his somewhat crazed antics and he was always good copy. They didn't think he could win but they enjoyed the way he was sticking it to the other candidates, needling them and making wild claims.

9. But Erwin and Mitchell did go negative on each other. Erwin's attacks on Mitchell for the sugar beet fiasco led to Mitchell attacking Erwin for mudslinging that in turn led Erwin to attack Mitchell for "smearing" him. Whatever the merits of either man's case, neither delivered a knock-out blow against the other and positioned Longley as being above the fray. Neither Erwin or Mitchell ran campaigns that took into account Longley's upside potential.

10. The Democrats' misreading of the Franco American vote is now legendary. The elimination of the so-called "Big Box"(discussed in chapter 5) set in motion a process by which the Franco American community reduced its direct ties to the Democratic Party. Although Cohen had won the congressional election of 1972 with their help, Democrats did not yet see the full significance of their political emancipation.

Therefore, the Mitchell for Governor campaign mounted the biggest get out the vote ever assembled in Lewiston. By midday, it was clear that that effort was taking hundred and hundreds of Longely voters to the polls. Although Mitchell was to narrowly carry the aggregate of all Franco American communities in Maine, Longley's impressive margin in Lewiston and Auburn was more than enough to put him over the top and the Mitchell campaign made sure that every possible Longley voter got to the polls that day. When the dust settled on election night, Longley had received 66 percent of the vote in Lewiston and 73 percent in Auburn.

THE GUBERNATORIAL ELECTION OF 1994

Political observers and insiders were stunned by Longley's 1974 victory. Many predicted that the Longley victory would lead to a sea change in Maine politics. But remarkably, nothing changed for twenty years in terms of major election outcomes!

For two decades, the Longley victory looked more and more like a fluke, not a viable process-changing event in the political life of Maine.

Numerous candidates ran as Independents and all received less than 20 percent of the vote, most less than 15 percent. There had not been a sea change in the political life of Maine. Many who ran after 1974, many talented, well-financed candidates, all lost. Why?

As it turns out, there was only one way to be elected governor as an Independent and a candidated needed five variables, all of which had to be present to make victory possible. Those five variables were: (1) the Republicans had to nominate a poor candidate or a good candidate who ran a poor campaign, (2) the Democrats had to nominate a poor candidate or a good candidate who ran a poor campaign, (3) there was only a single credible Independent candidate, (4) that candidate had to peel away urban Democrats (Franco Americans), and (5) that candidate had to peel away small-town Republicans.

Only in the election of 1994 did a candidate find a parallel seam in the political universe and saw the true demographic and political reasons behind Longley's seemingly unique victory.

Angus King did not set out to make Maine political history. His early foray in politics was diffident at best, deciding to run for Congress in Maine's 1st CD, only to withdraw the moment Joe Brennan announced he was seeking the seat. He simply didn't want to lose to a better known and more popular figure in the Democratic primary.

Although a lifelong Democrat and a staffer for Senator Bill Hathaway, he decided to run as an Independent in 1994, willing to take his chances on defeating Joe Brennan in the general election, not in a primary where he was afraid the odds were stacked prohibitively against him.

King wanted to be governor.

Born March 31, 1944, in Alexandria, Virginia, and a 1966 graduate of Dartmouth College, with a 1969 law degree from the University of Virginia, he was an early staffer for Pine Tree Legal Assistance and Senator Bill Hathaway (becoming chief counsel to the U.S. Senate Subcommittee on Alcoholism and Narcotics in 1972). In 1983, he became vice president and general counsel of Swift River/Hafslund. In 1989, he founded and was president of Northeast Energy Management Inc. which promoted statewide conservation for large and midsize companies. He eventually sold the company to Swift River/Hafslund for a reported $12 million.

My own initial reaction to his candidacy was quite ambiguous. My wife and I were good friends with him and Mary Herman, his second wife. And I thought he could win, the early exploratory polling showed Joe Brennan under 50 percent (always a good benchmark when 95 percent of the voting population know who a candidate is).

It also showed that contrary to popular opinion, few knew King even though he'd been on the PBS *MaineWatch* program for over a decade. But among the much smaller number of people who knew both King and

Brennan, King actually led Brennan. To me, that meant that if everybody got to know both candidates equally, King would win.

So King's upside potential wasn't the issue for me. Rather it was the anxiety that a candidate campaign can cause. As indicated in the last chapter, ballot measure campaigns are so much easier to direct and control than candidate campaigns. I have never mastered the art of doing day-to-day candidate efforts. I get too wrapped up in them and take all the responsibility onto my shoulders even if the candidate doesn't want it. I got the only ulcer of my life in 1972, managing Cohen for Congress.

After 14 years of ballot measures, I really didn't want to get back into that level of responsibility with a candidate. Plus, I completely misread the dynamics of Angus and his wife, Mary Herman. I assumed that Mary wanted him to run and that he was a reluctant candidate. And I thought he would be a very needful candidate.

I was wrong on both counts. Mary actually didn't want him to run and he turned out to be very inner-directed and grounded. His early efforts on the campaign trail were unrewarding and he had a hard time getting many people, especially those in the press, to take his candidacy seriously.

They had all but held the coronation for Joe Brennan. But King persevered and kept at his quest fueled by inner resources.

I thought Angus could become a good candidate; he was bright, personable, and very likable, a kind of cerebral Ken Curtis. But I wasn't sure he had what it took to be elected. Seeing him at political gatherings with no staff and no supporters, I felt sorry for him. Yet, he went out there on his own and made himself into a first rate campaigner. He shouldered on virtually alone for several months and made me believe he would go the distance.

I also felt much better about his chances once he had a full campaign team in place. His campaign manager, Kay Rand, turned out to be a big asset. Calm under pressure, able to delegate and keep things moving, she became an alter ego for King and someone he trusted implicitly. Although she had no real campaign experience, she was a natural manager and absorbed campaign strategy and tactics like a sponge. She would end up with Sharon Miller, Abby Holman, Rosemary Baldacci, and Nancy Chandler in the first tier of Maine campaign managers. She also acted as a den mother to the sometimes unruly male egos on the King team.

For his media, King ended up with Dan Payne of Payne and Company in Boston. Initially no major national Republican or Democratic media firm would consider helping an Independent and Payne took the leap in part because Mary Herman's brother, Tom, asked him as a personal favor. And, Dan told me, because he wasn't hired by Brennan! Payne brought with him a talented film crew and the Democratic research firm headed by Erwin "Tubby" Harrison of Harrison and Goldberg. Payne and Tom Herman were to come up with a brilliant campaign slogan: "Angus King:

Coming this Fall to a Polling Place Near You." This would set the stage and flag people's memories that King would be around as a choice in November no matter what happened in the meantime.

King also found a young, dedicated professional, Jim Doyle, to do the ground game. Doyle came up with county chairs for every county in Maine and did yeoman service.

Early on, King expected business leaders and like-minded citizens to join his campaign and donate money. He was very disappointed in the way many business leaders already assumed Brennan would win and didn't want to even donate to his campaign. In addition, King discovered that he truly, truly hated asking people for money so as the campaign went on, he asked less and less and wrote more checks of his own. This, I believe, is called in economics the theory of comparative advantage and it worked very well for him.

He also decided to publish a book. Entitled *Making a Difference*, the 132-page paperback established King as a serious thinker about governing as well as a purveyor of folksy wisdom, ending up calling himself a "compassionate pragmatist."[25] Ingrained in the book and fueling the entire run for office was King's vision: Give Maine people self-confidence again in government and in the state.

The book amazingly provided instant credibility. My only contribution to it was to make sure King's picture was on the cover. I doubted that many people would read it; I knew nobody in the press would. Therefore to me it was a piece of advertising and needed his face on the cover. The candidate worried that it wouldn't look like a real book with his face on the cover, but even today you can go in a library and see a very handsome and determined leader of the people.

I don't know how many people actually did read the book. But one person, Joe Brennan, did from cover to cover. According to Brennan staffers, Joe went from refusing to take King seriously as a competitor before he saw the book to being consumed by his candidacy after he saw it. A prominent aide remembers his quoting from the book time after time, attacking it section by section all spring long.[26]

I felt much more relaxed about joining after the basics of his team were in place and carved out a "consultant on consultant" role for myself. I loved the King campaign from beginning to end for it duplicated the best aspects of a ballot measure. There was a great feeling of comradeship fostered by the good working relationships of the principal decision makers. We all felt we were living in William Shakespeare's *Henry V*: "We few, we happy few, we band of brothers; for whoever has shed his blood with me shall be my brother."

Remarkably there was none of the usual jockeying for power. You won the political, tactical, and strategic arguments on the merits or you didn't win. There was no point in "going behind the back" of someone. King could be swayed, but not by office politics. This pattern is exceptional in my experience and neither George Smith, who did his direct mail, nor I, with sixty years of campaign experience between us, had ever seen the harmony duplicated.

In February, March, and April, King met with people in small groups. It was tough going. Virtually nobody gave him a chance and people, while polite, were skeptical. During this period, we did a focus group in Lewiston. That showed that people didn't feel strongly about Brennan one way or the other in that critical swing town, but unless voters were given reasons to vote against him, they would "drift" back to him at the end of the campaign.

King was a *tabula rasa*, "a pleasant face with lots of blanks." He got a fine reception based on his appearance and his personality, but few thought he could win. We saw the tremendous need to go on TV and use that medium to make up for King's lack of a party base. Our game plan called for three campaign segments: April until June 15, June 15 to Labor Day, and Labor Day to Election Day. All would feature their own special TV component. Initially, Angus, never free with a buck, did not want to advertise on TV until October.

In the late spring, however, I wrote a memo entitled "May is the cruelest month," arguing for "an Independent primary" to establish Angus as the alternative to Brennan.[27] This "primary" would run in May and June. Especially after the Democratic and Republican primaries, King would seize center stage as if he had won his own "Independent primary."

The strategy was adopted and King advertised heavily in June, setting up the fall election. As King later stated, "That was considered radical at the time because I wasn't in the primary. Turns out it was probably the best thing I did."[28] This tactic was a major turning point in the campaign because it went against conventional wisdom and set the stage for King's move into second place by the end of the summer. It is now widely imitated as a campaign tactic, most recently (although unsuccessfully) by Dave Flanagan in his run for governor in 2002.

On the Democratic side, Joe Brennan ran a strong primary campaign. Brennan's long career included service in the Maine House (1964–1972) and the Maine Senate (1972–1975) and as Maine attorney general (1974–1977). He lost the first time he ran for governor, in the Democratic primary of 1974, but won the Democratic nomination and the general election in 1978, serving two terms in that office before running for Congress in 1986 where he served until 1990. That year he ran again for governor, losing to Jock McKernan.

In 1994, he won the primary against four other candidates. Brennan crushed Tom Allen 56 percent to 24 percent, while Dick Barringer (9 percent),

Robert Woodbury (8 percent), and Donnell Carroll (3 percent) also ran. Brennan was back and raring to go and he had a new campaign team around him, led by Phil Merrill (campaign manager), Alan Caron (communication's director and chief strategist), and his previous pollster, Massachusetts-based Tom Keily.

But I don't think he realized how messed-up his image had become thanks to the pounding in the press Tom Allen had given him in the primary. Although Brennan won handily, it was primarily with blue collar, Franco American support. Allen really hammered him with upscale yuppies and I thought the Brennan campaign would need to take remedial action before this became a "class" attitude. Surprisingly, they didn't and King was eventually able to build on the doubts first raised by Allen. The King triumph of 1994 owed a small but important debt to Democrat Tom Allen, now Congressman Allen.

The Brennan campaign organization ended up having some interesting dimensions and dynamics. Joe Brennan, both as candidate and governor, always liked to have a number of people around him and even with the new campaign manager and communications director, he continued to reach out to longtime confidants such as Severin Beliveau, Arthur Stilphin, Hal Pachios, Jim Case, Dave Redmond, Barry Hobbins, and Dave Flanagan. Campaign manager Merrill says this group was very reluctant to see King as a threat since he was from out of state, came from public television, and didn't have any political experience.[29] Stilphin was active in the ground game along with Jim Betts and Tom LaPointe.

But also in the mix for 1994 were Brennan's fiancée, Connie LaPointe (whom he would marry after the election), and some young Turks such as Kevin Mattson, Jim Clifford, and Chris Lehane. Lehane, from Kennebunk, Amherst, and Harvard, was to be increasingly active in the campaign especially in the fall, ending up handling a lot of press and other matters. He bridged the gap between the old Brennan loyalists and the new campaign team. Lehane would later serve as one of Al Gore's press secretaries and chief advisers in the 2000 presidential race. Bright, savvy, and with a good grasp of politics, he was a huge asset to the team.

The interplay among these various advisers, old friends, and staffers was to play an important role in the course of the campaign during the critical month of October. We thought even with Dennis Bailey on King's campaign, their ability to manipulate the *Portland Press Herald* would be considerable. They were a formidable group and the *Press Herald* was well known among political insiders as almost always giving Democrat the edge, not just on the editorial page.

King worked hard to pick up Dennis Bailey to help offset this advantage. Regarded as liberal at the time, he was working for Tom Allen and had also worked for Tom Andrews. More importantly, we believed he could spin his friend, the chief Portland political writer, Steve Campbell. Campbell could be a pretty good reporter when he put his mind to it, but he often played favorites such as Tom Andrews. King called Bailey the day of the primary and said, "Hope you guys can pull it off but if not, I've got a place for you."[30]

Bailey was hired to make sure Campbell and others took King seriously. He became a trusted advisor to King and something more than just a press secretary. A University of Maine graduate with a degree in journalism, he'd worked on a variety of Maine papers from the *Maine Times* and *Maine Sportsman* to the *Press Herald, Sun Journal,* and *Biddeford Journal.* More importantly from my point of view, he was a battler, a fighter, someone who played to win. Someone we would want at our side by the time we got to the OK Corral.

Later, during the 2002 election cycle, Bailey would become the only press secretary/communications director in Maine political history known to have worked for at least three different gubernatorial candidates (Wathen, Flanagan, and Baldacci!) in the same year! No ideologue Dennis!

With Dan Payne and Tubby's input concerning media and imaging, the core decision-making group soon became King, Rand, Bailey, and myself as well as George Smith and Angus "Goose" King Jr. Also in the mix whenever we were on TV was Peter Burr, whose analysis and projections of the nightly tracking calls went directly into the process on a weekly basis. Burr's contribution to the campaign was significant.

The Republican field for governor was even more crowded that year. No fewer than eight candidates: Susan Collins, Sumner Lipman, Jasper Wyman, Judith Foss, Paul Young, Mary Adams, Charles Webster, and Pam Cahill vied for the nomination. Collins won with 21.5 percent to Lipman's 19.9 percent. Jasper Wyman got 16 percent, Foss 13 percent, Young 9 percent, Webster 7 percent, and Cahill 6 percent. It had been a long, hard-fought campaign that had exhausted the candidates and their war chests.

King and most of his staff and friends were very disappointed by the outcome of the Republican primary. For its part, the *Portland Press Herald* was gleeful: "Party Choice for Governor's Race Bodes Ill for King," wrote Paul Carrier on June 16, 1994, while Steve Abbot, Collins' campaign manager, said, "The fact that the Republicans nominated Susan certainly strikes a blow at Angus King."[31]

King and many of his supporters had thought and hoped Wyman or Adams or Webster, all conservative and less well known, would win. They thought Collins would be a very strong candidate. Overall, the King camp was despondent over her victory.

But George Smith and I saw the outcome very differently. We thought Collins would be easy to vault over into second place. We were delighted with the postprimary situation. She had been a staffer for Cohen and although bright (a Phi Beta Kappa graduate of St. Lawrence), hardworking, and highly motivated, we were quite convinced she was about to face the extreme demands of a vigorous statewide general election campaign after her bruising primary without a united party behind her and with no campaign funds for summer TV.

We knew our Republicans and we were confident that the Republican losers in the primary were not happy campers and with the exception of Jasper Wyman and perhaps Pam Cahill, not one would lift a finger to help Collins. In particular, the McKernanistas were extremely upset about the loss of their candidate, Judy Foss, and we knew they would be of no help to Collins.

Forty-one at the time of the race, Collins had been a Cohen staffer for a number of years, been deputy treasurer of Massachusetts and director for the New England Small Business Administration, and had served as Maine's Commissioner of Professional and Financial Regulation under McKernan so she had a good deal of government experience.

Collins was untested in a general election, however, and exhausted by her primary contest and her very narrow victory. She soon made several missteps and had several misfortunes not of her making in the early crucial postprimary period. The euphoria of her primary win quickly gave way to very difficult problems.

Additionally, she had spent all her money winning the primary and was now both exhausted and penniless. We figured to make a big move before her campaign coffers filled again. George and I were very confident if King campaigned hard and well during the summer and stayed on television with good commercials by spending lots of his own money, he could move past her by the fall.

We also knew there was no love lost between her supporters and those of Senator Olympia Snowe or former governor Jock McKernan and that whatever lip service the McKernanistas would pay to party unity, they would not be sad to see her lose or do much to prevent it. Also, as matters turned out, various McKernanistas from all levels bonded with the King campaign although it may be going too far to say that Kay Rand took Sharon Miller as her role model. With Jock McKernan as the head of the Republican governor's conference, this was not a positive situation for the Collins campaign.

Collins was going alone on this journey.

Her general election campaign soon and rapidly was stressed. Much of her time in June after the primary was taken up with an ill-advised outreach attempt at a meeting with the Christian Right engineered by Jasper Wyman. Wyman was trying to do the right thing but the Christian Right burned the bridge he was building from them to Collins—and him along with it.

On June 13, the Christian Civic League of Maine, the Maine Right to Life Committee, the Christian Coalition, and Concerned Maine Families turned down invitations to even meet with her.

"I think she has a problem within the Republican Party, especially with conservatives," said Michael Health of the Christian Civic League while Collins somewhat incautiously stated, "Conservative Republicans can't stomach the thought of King, Brennan, or Carter being governor," but Steve Abbott later confirmed that the whole incident and the legal challenge by Mark Finks were "brutal."[32] Even bothering to try to keep the Christian right happy was a huge mistake. They are best ignored by any Republican candidates in the general election.

Mark Finks, another Republican activist and conservative, challenged her residency requirement for even running. Collins, a Maine native who worked in Massachusetts in 1992 and 1993, was eventually proven eligible by the court but in the meantime it was another huge distraction. This was more than a nuisance to the Collins campaign. It took away time and money and focus and having to spend a month explaining that she really was a resident of the state (the suit claimed she did not meet the constitutional residency requirement because she once worked in Massachusetts) was trying, irritating, and draining.

It is difficult not to feel sorry for this proud woman who had won a vigorous primary only to have elements within her party doing all they could to sabotage her general election effort. After losing his suit against her, Finks would run as a write-in candidate for governor! Ralph Coffman was also in the race as an Independent.

As if this were all not enough, just as the Collins campaign was settling down after the cataclysmic events of the summer, her brother Michael was indicted in late September for having more than $1 million worth of marijuana in his possession! The story was front page news in both the BDN and the PPH, the PPH concluding: "His surprised sister says the charge has nothing to do with her campaign," while the BDN headline read, "Susan Collins' brother arrested."[33]

Although Collins was soon shown to be far removed from the entire situation, it was another distraction and still another problem to get behind her. How she kept going is a credit to her inner fortitude. I give her enormous credit for persevering in the face of such adversity.

By the end of this period, Collins was so preoccupied and likely to slip to third place in the fall polling that Phil Merrill, campaign manager for Brennan, was extremely worried and tried to get people to donate to her campaign! In this regard, "We were actually quite helpful," he said, although the Collins people deny that "any help" was actually forthcoming: "It was talked about as I recall, that's all," said her campaign manager, Steve Abbott, and another Collins insider, Tom Daffron, declared, "We never saw a dime."[34]

By Labor Day, the Collins camp had pulled up stakes in Portland and headed back to their base area in Bangor. They now knew this was going to be a three-way race and believed if they had any chance it would be in the northern part of the state.

Thus King had a real chance to be in second place in the September polls. He was to make it a contest between him and Brennan. The King camp advertised during the summer to make sure by mid-September, King was in second place and Collins had slid to third.

The King strategy was working perfectly.

Were there many wedge issues in the summer and fall campaign? Not many. Brennan supported term limits and opposed the banning of late-term abortions. He also supported a constitutional amendment to balance the federal government and opposed the death penalty and a law requiring motorcyclists to wear helmets. King, a motorcyclist, didn't.

Looking back, between Brennan and King, there were not too many issue differences but stylistic ones. The election was really decided more about "atmospherics," style and the size of government. Brennan at heart was a big government man. The size of state government grew during his term. The Brennan team tried to create a new persona for the candidate, one which combined being a tested veteran of state government with that of innovator. They were more successful with the first part than the second. The subsequent irony, of course, would be that in Angus King's eight years as governor, the size of the state budget would rise precipitously.

As the campaign wore on, Phil Merrill as Brennan's campaign manager was joined at strategy sessions by Chris Lehane, press secretary and strategist, as well as Alan Caron, communications director. Brennan, Merrill, and Caron were the internal decision makers with Merrill in charge of execution. Longtime Brennan stalwarts such as Davey Redmond, Dave Flanagan, Arthur Stilphen, and Frank O'Hara were also in the mix, although only from time to time.

Their core strategy was dictated by the Keily numbers: Brennan's upside was 40–45 percent. They had to create and execute a game plan that got him 40 percent of the vote by holding his base and expanding it slightly. The plan only had one flaw: Susan Collins had to get above 25 percent of the vote to make their strategy viable. The analysis of the Longley victory, however, focused the King team like a laser on the rural Republican portion of the equation. That was the part over which the Brennan forces could have no control.

Also, in this campaign, there developed a rather strange positioning: Carter on far left, Brennan on center left, King on center right, Collins pushed to the "right" of the political spectrum but didn't fit. Carter would end up helping King get elected. In fairness to Collins also, much of the Republican money that summer went to Olympia Snowe and her Senate race against Tom Andrews.

By the end of September, Collins could only chide King for sending out a letter saying the choice was between him and Brennan. "Collins scolds King for appeal to Republicans," reported the *Portland Press Herald* on September 25.[35] Citing "political experts," however, the *Portland Press Herald* stated Collins was drifting out of contention: "Brennan vs. King Showdown Foreseen."[36] This type of publicity did not do her struggling candidacy any good.

A September 26 *Portland Press Herald* and Central Maine Newspapers poll didn't help either, for it showed Brennan at 36 percent, King second at 23 percent, Collins a "dismal" third at 12 percent, and Carter at 2 percent. King's own tracking had Brennan at 34 percent, him at 31 percent, Collins a distant third at 16 percent (she would slide to 15 percent by the end of the month), and Carter at 1.5 percent.

For Collins, the race was over.

She may or may not have known that as she then launched a significant negative attack against King, questioning his credentials as a conservative businessman in an ad and stating that King was a lifelong Democrat who worked for Pine Tree Legal Assistance and William Hathaway. Although designed to undercut King's support among Republicans, the Collins ad was supported by the Brennan campaign staff. Phil Merrill, his campaign manager, said her ad "reflects the kind of questions we get every day. People are groping to decipher King."[37]

By early October, the King tracking polling told him to ignore Collins completely and to begin upping the attack on Brennan as "the government as usual candidate." Collins was stuck permanently in third place. In speeches and debate forums, King began to sharpen his attacks on Brennan, citing his propensity to "get up in the morning, take a vitamin, hire a bureaucrat," while Brennan accused King of "lying to the people." But all of this was taking place at meetings and interviews, not on TV where it mattered.

On October 7, the *Portland Press Herald* poll of that date had King gaining on Brennan: 31 percent for Brennan, 26 percent for King, 11 percent for Collins, and 3 percent for Carter.

"King Puts Brennan on the Defensive" was the headline in the *Portland Press Herald* on October 8, 1994. The Brennan campaign had fallen into a well-sprung trap. They were now talking about King's issue. They were arguing with us over the size of government; how much had it grown during Brennan's time in office? The press was dragged into it as well. For example, Mal Leary of the Maine Public Radio did several stories in which he basically supported King's claims on the expansion of the state autocracy during Brennan's term of office.

So in many ways the King campaign was going well. Collins was out of the race, Brennan was on the defensive, and the press was trying to sort out just how much Brennan's stay in office had increased the size of government. But internally, the King campaign knew the tracking signs were ominous. He was stalled.

King's tracking on October 11 had Brennan at 34 percent (which he had held for two months), King at 30 percent, Collins at 18 percent, and Carter at 4 percent with only 14 percent undecided. We were running out of undecideds. We were very concerned: "If we don't redefine Brennan, he will win."[38] In short, we had to go negative. Dan Payne put it succinctly, "Why run as an Independent if you're not going to go 'negative' on the two party candidates?"[39] Payne was increasingly frustrated by King's unwillingness to confront Brennan directly and say negative things about his political record.

Now it is important to understand what we are talking about here. Newspaper editors and others always rail against "mudslinging" and "negative campaigning" without actually defining them. So it is important to define the terms here and state the philosophical position (expressed many times in many different forums and in many different works) the King staff was pushing.

"Mudslinging" is saying something untrue or something personal about a candidate. This is not what we were advocating. "Going negative" is pointing out things about one's opponent that you think—or if your polling is done right you know—people won't like about your opponent.

There is nothing wrong with pointing out where your opponent differs from you on an issue. Otherwise, incumbents (who don't like "negative campaigning") would always be reelected! You simply have to contrast your positions with those of your opponents or the people won't support you over him or her. This is particularly true in a close race where you and your opponent have already gotten all the votes you are going to get on your personalities and being nice people.

Professor Sandy Maisel of Colby College points out that there are also "negative ads" that, while true, diminish faith in both the candidate attacking and the candidate attacked as well as the democratic process itself. This is a valid point, as the tidal wave of negative ads fueled by national Republican and Democratic soft money showed in the elections of 2002.

Yet, campaigns in Maine have always had elements of negativity in them. Certainly the campaigns we have looked at in this book have had more than their share. But in 1948, 1954, 1970, and 1972, the 30-second TV commercial of the negative variety was not in vogue so the intensity of negative campaigning was seldom an issue. By 1994, however, it was a staple on the campaign trail.

King's media man, Dan Payne, knew, for example, that unless we went negative at the end we would lose. All along, King's polling and espe-

cially focus group data strongly endorsed Payne's concepts: the undecided didn't want to go "backward" to Joe but would if "good old Joe"
was the concept in their minds when they voted. Brennan had "bloated"
or "expanded" the state bureaucracy as spending doubled during his
term but how would they know if King's ads didn't tell them? "I was very
frustrated, going negative is how you finish a tight campaign," said
Payne.[40]

One commercial prepared but not shown immediately because of the candidate's reluctance, for example, showed quick picture flashes of all the
Maine governors from first to McKernan, saying state budget took this long
to get this big. Then it showed a picture of Joe Brennan and said, "Joe Brennan doubled that budget in just two terms." That commercial needed to run.

But neither King nor many of his friends—including the columnist Jim
Brunelle (who had appeared with King on the public television show
MaineWatch for a number of years and who to this day strongly and
sternly dislikes negative campaigning)—ever wanted him to use this tactic. Dennis Bailey recalls that "Angus just didn't want to go forward with
anything negative. He fought it all the way. It was very frustrating."[41]

I found this aspect of the campaign very frustrating as well. Here everybody, and especially the candidate, had worked so hard and so long and
King was so close to victory. But to prevail, he had to go negative to
achieve that goal and he wouldn't, time after time refusing to pull the
trigger.

In this regard King was very different from Bill Cohen who never hesi-
tated to pull the trigger in a campaign situation. I couldn't help but com-
pare King's reluctance to go negative with Cohen's keen espousal of the
1978 negative ads on the Indian Land Claims, senatorial pay raise, and
Dickey Lincoln Dam project that tore Senator Bill Hathaway to shreds.
King just didn't have the zest for confrontation and political battle that
were the hallmarks of the Titans of Maine political history: Margaret
Chase Smith, Ed Muskie (who loved to mix it up), Bill Cohen, and George
Mitchell (perhaps the most partisan of the four).

Finally after hearing about "what Brunelle would say" for the fiftieth
time, I remember in a campaign meeting in Portland becoming very agi-
tated and going to an easel and drawing a quick sketch of the Blaine
House with a stick figure of Joe Brennan in front of it. "The road to the
Blaine House," I said, "doesn't go around or under or over Joe Brennan,
it goes through him." Then I added: "And Jim Brunelle if he's in the way."

Finally in order to get the candidate to adopt specific ads, the staff and media consultant finally agreed to call them "contrast ads" instead of "negative
ads." I'm sure Dan Payne still uses this fine phrase invented for the King
campaign. I remain convinced to this day that if King had gone negative earlier, or with more force, he would have won by an even bigger margin.

Certainly, without going "negative" at the end, King would not have won. Brennan may have been a lackluster candidate at this point, but like an old shoe, he was not ready to be thrown away by the voters. The King campaign had to point out the holes in the soles of that shoe. All told, in the final flurry, there were seven or eight commercials, only several of which were negative.

Finally, after weeks of anguish and the sense we were all "dying for a tie," the King camp got a huge break. Brennan not only told King to his face to "stop lying" but his campaign brought out a commercial asking voters if they wouldn't like candidates to take a lie detector test! King was furious. His credibility was at stake. Brennan had touched a raw nerve.

But more importantly from the King staff point of view, the Brennan campaign staff was finally able to get King to do what his own staff had been unable to accomplish: go negative! We were overjoyed when we saw the "lie detector" ad; it was one of the major turning points in the campaign.

We put on our negative spots the next night.

Brennan claimed King's negative ads were ready to go and that King was just waiting for an excuse. He was at least partly correct. The ads were there. And the campaign staff was dying to use them. But King was not. He had agonized over them over and over again, driving his staff half-crazy with his Hamlet-like irresolution. He anguished over them and their use, often calling up like-minded people who didn't like negative ads either. It went against his basic nature. Had the Brennan team not forced his hand, I doubt he would have allowed the closing commercials to be used. And I doubt he would have been governor if he hadn't.

In any case, if Brennan thought King was just waiting for an excuse, why give him and his camp the excuse/opportunity they were looking for? Brennan's decision to go negative was to have profound ramifications for the outcome of the race. It was probably the most important decision that campaign made during the entire race.

Certainly, the King campaign staff took the Brennan lie detector ad as a political godsend, prompting the reluctant candidate to take the action they had wanted for weeks. Now, we were getting the opportunity to use the ads we had wanted all along. We were ecstatic. We were in the hunt. The battle was on.

We were especially pleased when Jim Brunelle's next column headline predictably lamented: "Too-long Campaigns Made Worse by Attack-Ad Onslaught."[42] *The Portland Press Herald* of October 18 reported that "the nasty ads are sharpening the focus of the campaign."

That's when we knew we had won, if not the election, then at least the battle for King's political soul. We knew he couldn't go back now. We didn't want his soul permanently, of course. We only wanted to rent it for a couple of weeks.

Campaign staffs love the action, the smell of gunpowder. Going negative is just part of the game. It's often the most fun the staff gets in any given campaign. Whatever their feelings toward each other today, in 1994 Joe Brennan clearly thought of King as an upstart neophyte and King thought of Brennan as a tired, burned-out politician but neither man wanted to destroy the other. And, to be fair, neither man liked the "negative campaigning." Like many politicians, they wanted to be elected because they were such fine fellows.

For the staffs, however, it was different. For them, there was no tomorrow, the contest was strictly a zero sum game. Negative campaigning was not only fine, it worked. Almost always, campaign staffers would much rather fire away and take their chances than to sit back and hope their candidate can squeak through. Now staffers in both camps were excited and energized. "Attack, attack, attack" became the order of the day on both sides. The Brennan team loved the fact the gloves were off. The Collins team joined in as well, seeing a chance to gain ground by attacking King. Years later, in interviews for the book, staff members from all three campaigns brightened considerably and became much more animated when we discussed this portion of the campaign.

Campaign staffs love excitement and the punching and counterpunching of political action much more than do most candidates. During the whole campaign, starting in the spring, I had constantly used the image of the OK Corral: "Let Joe bring his hired guns and you bring your hired guns and we blaze away and see who's standing when it's over." The staff always loved the analogy, but the candidate thought it somewhat demeaning! Now we were at the OK Corral and would find out who were the Earps and who were the Clantons. We smelled the delicious scent of gunpowder and ran toward it.

The King "contrast" ads worked very efficiently as the daily tracking numbers began to show movement away from Brennan and toward King. Once they started to run, we were convinced we were going to win. But the candidate was still uncomfortable with them and didn't like the criticism he was taking for running them and the campaign staff had to fight very hard to keep them on the air. But without those ads, Angus King would have finished a genteel second.

In addition to his negative TV commercials, in print Brennan had also attacked King for what he termed the SAM "scandal" after it was disclosed that George Smith, the executive director of SAM, had received $7,000 for a direct mailing effort to sportsmen and women!

Brennan was shocked, simply shocked at such behavior coming from an interest group! Whoever heard of an interest group sending out mailings to support the candidate of their choice? Whoever heard of campaigns paying for mailings from interest groups?

Collins, too, attacked the SAM endorsement, her assertions appearing on the front page of the *Bangor Daily News*. In reality, of course, Collins had much more to complain about. She had received an "A" grade from SAM along with King while Brennan had only gotten a "C." George Smith had made the difference when it really mattered and steered the endorsement to his man King. Smith, as much as any other individual, deserves credit for helping put King over the top.

Later, it turned out that the SAM board had voted unanimously (with one abstention) and as James Gorman put it: "I think it's fair to say Joe Brennan was not going to get our endorsement . . . the endorsement would have gone to Collins if the polls showed her to be a stronger competitor."[43]

Another *Portland Press Herald* poll was released on Friday, October 21, 1994. It had Brennan at 38 percent, King at 26 percent, and Collins at 12 percent while Carter was still at 2 percent. The Brennan camp was ecstatic. They trumpeted that King was "fading in the polls." In fact, the latest King tracking poll had Brennan at 34 percent, King at 31.8 percent, Collins at 15.1 percent, and Carter at 2.5 percent with 18.4 percent undecided. We had picked up 2 percent since the ads had started. Now 2 percent may not seem like much in most two-person elections, but believe me, 2 percent is huge when you are at 30 percent and your opponent is at 34 percent in a five-way contest (don't forget, Collins's old nemesis Mark Finks was running as a write-in candidate!).

The *Portland Press Herald* had decided early on that Joe Brennan was to be the next governor and their reporting as well as their editorials moved in that direction. For example, on October 23, Paul Carrier had written a piece indicating that King couldn't govern if elected: "Some believe an independent governor's job would be harder. Some say it would be virtually impossible."[44]

This surely sounded like an echo of Nancy Perry's earlier piece in the same paper, "Independent Could be Governor but not Just any Independent," listing all the reasons King wasn't Longley![45]

Now the Portland papers hit the King candidacy with a double whammy. On October 29, *Portland Press Herald* published a poll putting Brennan at 33 percent, King at 28 percent, and Collins at 15 with Carter still at 2 percent. They followed that up the next day with a strong editorial for Brennan, claiming Brennan should be elected. "Brennan Right Leader at Right Time for State" ran the lead editorial in the *Maine Sunday Telegram*, calling Brennan "the right person at the right time to get Maine going again, and he deserves voters' support."

King rated only a half sentence: "Angus King, Independent, has conducted a year-long "making a difference" campaign drawing on his unusual perspective as a businessman." This was thin gruel for a candidate who was, at that moment, within a percentage point from the front-runner and *Press Herald* favorite! King's polling on October 30 had Brennan at 33.4 percent, King 33.2 percent, Collins 18.1 percent and Carter 4 percent with 11 percent undecided.

Despite the efforts of the state's largest newspaper, King was almost there.

On October 31, there was a four-way debate on Maine public television and on November 1, there was a final debate carried on WCSH in Portland and WLBZ in Bangor/Presque Isle. The candidates sparred about education, the environment, and the budget. Carter called for additional taxes, Collins objected, and King challenged Brennan's math, comparing his budget plans with Richard Nixon's secret plan to end the Vietnam War![46]

In one very interesting occurrence the last week of the campaign, the Brennan staff, now more than a tad worried, released the findings of a "poll" that purported to show Susan Collins gaining and King declining. A long time Democratic operative calls it "a leak job" of dubious origin and dubious methodology ("a few numbers got added here and there") but said Mark Woodward (editor) and Rick Warren (owner) of the *Bangor Daily News* were so desperate for any reason to justify their endorsement of Susan Collins, they seized on it and published the surrealistic results. "Trust me, this was not a Tom Keily poll," said the Democratic operative.[47]

Phil Merrill, campaign manager for Brennan, recalled laughingly years later, "The whole poll was legitimate, but we only peddled a small part of it, the part that showed Collins gaining in northern Maine. The reporter at the BDN we gave it to said: 'I know this is phony as hell but my editors say I have to run with it,'" while another principal Brennan strategist, Chris Lehane noted, "The BDN was desperate for a fragment."[48]

King's tracking in the 2nd CD at the time had Collins at 16 percent, right where she'd been in mid-October. King had moved slightly ahead of Brennan (33.6 percent to 34 percent) while Carter was at 3.7 percent. The King campaign was on the move.

But whatever the merits and origin of the polling fragment and the Brennan camp's concomitant strategy, the *Bangor Daily News* used it to justify supporting Collins, saying a vote for her would not be wasted. On November 5, the paper trumpeted: "She Can Win." The *Bangor Daily News* then endorsed Collins a second time, citing her "rise in the polls"! The BDN editorialized further, "This campaign has turned sour . . . the two men, King and Brennan, have clawed at each other through last week, even as they slipped in the polls."

The net results of all these shenanigans was that Collins did eventually pick up some votes in Maine's 2nd CD on election day (gaining 1 percent), but the exit polling showed she took them from Brennan's support among Democratic blue collar women, not from King! She was to carry the five northern counties of Penobscot, Aroostook, Washington, Hancock, and Piscataquis. Her late surge was an important factor in putting King into the winner's circle. Had she quit the campaign in October, he might not have won! This was a final irony within a host of ironies this election cycle.

Election day was as exciting as only close elections can make it.

Although the actual results weren't tabulated until well into the next morning (AP and Voter News Service declaring King the winner at 3 A.M.) and Brennan did not concede until noon that day, Peter Burr's exit poll projections at 1 P.M. on election day gave the election to King, with "less than 5 percent margin." Burr's conclusions were right on the money but the King staff didn't tell the candidate until 5 P.M. so that he would continue to work the various polling places right up until the end.

One look at his excited and happy staff told him the story when he came into the campaign headquarters. We all were very jubilant and rejoiced at what was happening. Not only had we won, we had won our way. We also got a tremendous kick out of a Federal Express package containing a big check from one of Maine's wanna-be king makers. He had already given money to both Collins and Brennan so the 11th hour "cover your bets" money was more than a little amusing.

When all the votes were counted the next day, King had pulled off a huge upset, only slightly less surprising than that of Longley's previous effort.

The final tally was

King	171,529
Brennan	147,529
Collins	95,954
Carter	27,304
Finks	6,576

Final results were very close in percentage terms: 35.4 percent for King, followed by 33.8 percent for Brennan. Collins got the basic Republican vote, 23.1 percent, while Jonathan Carter got 6.4 percent and write-in candidate Mark Finks 1.3 percent.

The results were fantastic if you were a King supporter, a huge disappointment if you were a Brennan supporter, and devastating if you were for Collins. Carter supporters, however, could take great comfort in the fact that the Green Party had now reached the magic 5 percent threshold for the first time ever.

But as in Mitchell's rise to prominence six years before, the seeds planted by Collins during her first run for office would sprout into victory flowers the next election cycle. She had held her head high in defeat, refused to publicly blame anyone but herself. Among insiders and the public, she got high marks for the way she refused to quit even when the chase became hopeless. She would become a U.S. Senator in 1996, only two years later, in part because she learned her lessons the hard way in 1994 and party because she showed such class in defeat.

In 1996, her opponent was again Joe Brennan and his defeat that year would mark the end of his elected political career that had spanned twenty-five years. During that time, whether winning (five times) or losing (three times) Joe Brennan would be the standard against which all Democratic candidates were measured.

For the politics of Maine, the 1994 election reaffirmed the pattern established twenty years earlier:

The Francos had again delivered, big time. King won three of the Franco towns outright with pluralities: Auburn (48 percent), Lewiston (43 percent), and Brunswick (45 percent) as well as the total Franco American vote overall! Brennan held narrow margins in Biddeford, Saco, Sanford, Waterville, Westbrook, and Winslow but when you totaled up all the Franco votes, King had won statewide.

History had repeated itself.

The seemingly odd alliance of urban Franco American Democrats and small-town Republicans had once again produced an Independent governor. It put the pattern in the history books, this time to stay.

REASONS WHY KING WON

1. He was a good candidate. Self-made in business and self-made in politics, he created himself on the campaign trail. He worked hard, grasped political concepts quickly, and didn't hesitate to go any place and talk with any group at any time. He became a human Rorschach test in which people read into him whatever their best political values. "I disagree with him but I respect him," said many. He faced huge odds and triumphed through force of will.
2. He had an excellent staff. Like Muskie before him, King put together a first-rate team that helped him keep his balance and perspective and provided a much needed killer instinct when one was required. Kay Rand turned out to be in the tradition of fine campaign managers of the modern era and served him very well as chief of staff during his second term and part of his first. She had his trust and confidence and those of the rest of the staff. She seldom made political or personal points at the expense of others.

Dennis Bailey exceeded even King's high expectations for him. He conned the press right and left and got away with it with grace and humor. To this day, he is still able to manipulate many members of the fourth estate. Other staffers such as Jim Doyle played undersung and underreported roles. Brennan, too, had a fine staff with lots of veteran operatives but in the final weeks of October, events got away from them.

3. Inner-directed, King was calm under pressure and intimately involved in campaign decisions but deferred to professionals as required. His TV commercials occupied a lot of his time and his rewriting of them was legendary during the campaign but he eventually went with the commercials that Dan Payne developed. He was quite ill the closing weeks of the campaign but he soldiered on, often with a high fever. Like Longley before him, he achieved what he achieved because of great inner strength and fortitude, against all odds or at least a lot of odds!

4. The campaign was grounded in superb data, whether polling or focus groups. The information about what Maine people wanted and how they wanted it packaged was spot on. In addition to my polling and focus groups, he had the daily tracking of Peter Burr and also the polling of the media man, Dan Payne, done by Harrison. The polling and focus groups provided the overarching themes of the campaign and grounded it in specifics desired by Maine voters. King's vision was supported by the data.

This was also true of the campaign dynamics. I remember doing a focus group in Lewiston that duplicated the exact process of the campaign. The participants were tired of Joe Brennan but still liked him: "He's done a lot of good over the years." They also loved the idea of a fresh new Independent. Many were initially attracted to the idea of the King candidacy but would end up voting for Brennan unless given specific reasons not to. That is exactly how life imitated art in 1994.

5. Not only did King have a lot of polling, he had the most continuous in Maine candidate history. Because of my experience with Maine Yankee and having seen the importance of nightly tracking to measure the effectiveness of television commercials, the King campaign got data for every wave of TV in all three designated market areas (Portland, Bangor, and Presque Isle). The King campaign of 1994 was the best researched and tracked campaign in Maine history. No other campaign comes even close.

In addition to the polling done by Tubby and me, we had the advantage of Peter Burr and Cotton Mountain Enterprises to do the daily tracking. Burr's projections turned out to be extremely accurate. He always knew where he was within a point or two. This meant that his advertising could be tailored to specifics in specific markets and commercials that were not working were taken off the air. The King staff could call Burr at anytime and get the overnight "rushes" to see if anything had changed due to campaign activity. King owes a huge debt of gratitude to Peter Burr.

6. The Brennan campaign also claimed to have excellent polling from Tom Keily: "He was dead on from day one. He put Joe's ceiling at 40 percent. We had the picture right up until the last weekend."[49] But Barry Hobbins, a longtime Democratic strategist and a Brennan insider, put it differently: "The basic polling was fine but the Democrats have never had the daily tracking available to some of the Republicans. The Brennan campaign did not have nightly tracking and that probably cost us the election," or as Chris Lehane put it, "We thought we were safely ahead until the last weekend and the night before the election, everybody predicted Joe would win by one or two percentage points."[50]

7. The media firm of Payne and Company, led by Dan Payne, did a marvelous job in bringing the King campaign to the voters of Maine. Reviewing the commercials for this book, I was struck again by their absolute appropriateness for the task at hand. Payne set a mood and a tone into which the campaign flowed. For example, we knew we had to get rural Republicans whose cues and values are conditioned by small-business leaders.

Payne's "evening in Brunswick" spot positioned King as one of them while his and Tom Herman's slogan, "Angus King: Coming this Fall to a Polling Place Near You," enabled the public to anticipate King's presence at the end of the campaign. It was one of the most important spots of the decade. Payne was to eventually do twenty-two or twenty-three different commercials (although some were variations on the same theme).

Payne's task was not always an easy one. There were many cooks in the media kitchen, not the least of which was the candidate himself. Having been on TV for eight years, King fancied himself something of an expert—and truth be told, he did know a lot about TV. But often, however, he would take a perfectly good Payne idea and worry it to death. He was also slow to see the value of high quality production techniques although he did end up recognizing that they made a difference.

Conversely, however, he would sense a bad Payne idea and make sure it was still-born. So King was a demanding candidate when it came to the media, the most demanding I've ever seen, but ultimately a persuadable one. When the chips were down in late

October, however, he put his faith and future in Dan Payne's hands. Payne did not let him down.

The biggest problem in the media situation was the "rolling focus group" King would conduct with his upscale friends and neighbors. Whenever he didn't like a concept or an idea for an ad, he could summon a small group of like-minded people and they would, of course, agree with him. Then he would come to the campaign meetings and say "people don't like that."

Since the campaign staff and consultants always assumed these people were wrong and they were right, this often made for long meetings. Usually the campaign staff was correct about what had to be done, but getting an aspect by the rolling focus group was often a trial. I know I spent hours and hours on the phone with Payne after some of his better, but tougher, ideas were shot down by this mysterious and shifting "rolling focus group."

8. Some Maine papers saw the potential of King. While the *Portland Press Herald* and *Bangor Daily News* were unrelenting in their criticism of his candidacy and did a very poor job of covering his rise, the *Sun Journal* (Lewiston), the *Kennebec Journal* (Augusta), and the *Central Maine Morning Sentinel* (Waterville) all endorsed him, giving much needed support at the very end. These three papers were not as caught up in the polling frenzy and none of them had made up their minds early enough in the campaign so as to skew their coverage.

In many ways, King's victory was even more impressive when you think that Longley, when he won in 1974, at least had the endorsement of the state's second largest newspaper, the *Bangor Daily News*. But King got no support from the BDN or from the *Portland Press Herald*, the newspaper with the largest circulation in the state. "Thank God for television," he could say with a great deal of credibility.

The *Bangor Daily News* did publish on November 7 a John Hale article called "Independent Gains Notable Endorsements," which underscored the endorsements of King. But the BDN editorialized for Collins not once but twice in the final days of the campaign.

Once again, as they had been with Longley's earlier triumph, the *Portland Press Herald* was surprised: "He (King) also picked up surprising support in some blue-collar industrial communities, such as Lewiston and Waterford, that were considered to be Brennan's base of support."[51]

Having failed utterly to see the King potential—especially in its own editorials—the paper now saw his victory in sharp perspective. In this race, local political reporters picked up the groundswell for King much better than the statewide reporters who seemed to have the mind-set of their editorial writers.

9. Importance of the Green Party. Carter siphoned off votes most of which would have gone to Brennan had Carter not been in the race. Statewide Carter received 6.4 percent. In Brennan's old Senate District he got 15 percent while on Munjoy Hill where Joe lived, he got 17 percent. Joe was from Munjoy Hill, but it was a different Munjoy Hill than he had ever known. While Carter did pull some upscale or "high end" Republicans from King, he pulled many more left-leaning Democrats who found Brennan too conservative.

10. Impact of SAM. There can be little question but that the endorsement of SAM and the activities of George Smith played a key role in the election of King. Smith took King under his wing on outdoor issues, pushed hard for the SAM endorsement, and put King in a commercial paddling a canoe. George Smith gave Angus much needed credibility on outdoor issues. After the election, Smith's survey of SAM members indicated that 65 percent of them supported King, almost twice the percentage he received from the general public.[52]

WHAT IMPACT DID THE ELECTION OF
INDEPENDENTS HAVE ON MAINE POLITICS?

Longley (1974)

1. The success of Longley greatly increased the number of viable Independent candidates for governor. From 1940 until 1974, there were only four Independent or other third party gubernatorial candidates. Of these four, only Neil Bishop, running as an Independent Republican in 1952, earned enough votes (14.4 percent) to qualify as a serious candidate.

   In 1974, James B. Longley won the governorship with 39.2 percent over five other candidates including Stanley Lee (.8 percent), William Hughes (.04 percent), and Leith Hartman (.2 percent). His victory was a huge stimulus to more Independent and third party candidates.

   From 1974 until 2000, for example, there were 10 Independent or third party candidates, four of whom were major players: Herman "Buddy" Frankland in 1978 (17.8 percent), John Menario in 1986 (15.1 percent), Sherry Huber in 1986 (14.9 percent), and Angus King in 1994 (35.4 percent) and 1998 (58.6 percent). Green Party candidates Jonathan Carter in 1994 (6.4 percent) and Pat LaMarche in

1998 (6.8 percent) and Independent Andrew Adam (9.3 percent) also deserve historical notice.

These heightened expectations for Independent and third party candidates also spilled over into the congressional and Senate races of the era, although without any major success. But Longley had demonstrated that someone could be elected to high political office in Maine outside of the existing two party system.

For governor, Senate and Congress, for example, from 1940 to 1974, there were 11 unenrolled or third party candidates. But after Longley, from 1974 until 1998, there were 25 such candidates. This shows a most discernible impact. Even though independent candidates did not win a major office for twenty years, their presence on the ballot added an important dimension to the political process.

2. Longley's election produced something of a name dynasty. Son Jim Longley Jr. ran for Congress in 1994 and despite truly meager credentials won the race for Maine's 1st CD in large part because of his name identification. Later, in 2002, his daughter Susan would run for Congress and start with the highest name recognition and choice ratio, leading the race until the last weekend when fellow liberal Sean Faircloth drew enough votes from her coalition to enable Mike Michaud to triumph.

   Note that the name Longley had a great deal of magic, transcending party affiliation. James B. Longley ran and was elected as an Independent, son Jim Jr. ran and was elected as a Republican, and daughter Susan served in the Maine House and Senate and ran for Congress as a Democrat! In my book, that's star and staying power for a political name.

3. Longley proved that an Independent could govern and thus made future Independent candidates for governor more credible. This topic lies beyond the scope of this book but Longley, although controversial, was a popular governor and could well have been reelected. Despite horrendous battles with Democrats and the press and over 100 vetoes cast, Longley did govern and in the minds of a majority of the people, governed well. Certainly, his tenure as Maine's first Independent governor established that an Independent could run the state more or less effectively for four years.

4. Longley's election established a pattern of how an Independent could win. Looking at his performance, it was possible to see a winning pattern. Thereafter, any Independent candidate who could put together the coalition of urban Franco American voters and small-

town Republicans could have a meaningful chance at a winning candidacy. This was the most important legacy of the Longley campaign; he not only showed it could be done, he showed the only way it has ever been done!

5. But the Longley (and subsequent King) successes also pointed out the limits of Independent attainment. Even with credible candidates, even with the adoption of the strategy linking urban Francos with small-town Republicans, Independent candidates had to rely on both major parties either nominating weak candidates or having those candidates run weak campaigns.

   Of the two party candidates, the collapse of the Republican's campaign is the most important. Both Jim Erwin and Susan Collins ran terrible or star-crossed campaigns and both were in third place by mid-September. The ability of the Independent candidate to "climb over" the Republican candidate and thus be in a position to challenge the Democratic leader was crucial.

   But both Longley and King would have been known for their second place finishes had not Mitchell (1974) and Brennan (1994) run lackluster campaigns. Mitchell's was a true disaster. Given his eventually substantial lead and his enormous resources, his fall from electoral grace is truly amazing and, even 28 years after its occurrence, stunning.

   Brennan ran an only slightly better campaign than had Mitchell. He went to the wrong places, had the wrong messages, seemed oddly out of step and "off key," and finished not with a bang but with a whimper. His decision to go negative with TV ads and thus give King staffers what they desperately wanted was a major blunder.

6. His defeat in 1974 turned George Mitchell into one of the Pine Tree State's best campaigners. If George Mitchell had left the political lists in 1974, he would have been but a negative footnote in Maine's political history. He had the governship in his grasp and he lost it. But the humiliation of losing was compounded by having lost to a man he considered something of a demagogue. Lesser mortals might have given up politics but Mitchell did not and when Ed Muskie resigned his Senate seat in 1981 and Joe Brennan eventually chose him to replace Muskie, Mitchell was ready.

   By the campaign of 1982, George Mitchell was truly prepared for prime time. By dint of will and brains he made himself into a superior candidate and ran one of the most effective campaigns of modern times, winning reelection 61 percent to 39 percent over popular 1st CD Congressman Dave Emery.

King (1994)

1. His victory reiterated the only pattern by which a Maine Independent candidate has been elected. Being a professor is a wonderful opportunity to try out ideas and concepts. For many years after Longley's triumph, I lectured about how I thought he did it, with a combination of small-town Republican votes and urban Democratic votes from the Franco American areas of Maine. And of course, in the King campaign, I tried to get King to reproduce that pattern and lo and behold, it actually worked that way a second time.

    So, in some sense—at least to myself—I proved it could be done and done again in the same way. But my assertions and its second occurrence would never satisfy true academicians so it was left for two of my students to actually prove the proposition. Chris Stearns did a great deal of research on the subject in 2001, and in 2002 Susan Price did a Bowdoin honors project on it. Her senior project, "As Maine Goes . . . Independent: The Impact of Partisan Defections by Urban Franco Americans and Small Town Republicans," won the prize as the best government department thesis of the year. Her data now proves the proposition for all to see and is part of the historical record.[53]

    Price took the results from thirty randomly selected small towns (with populations less than 2,500 or between 2,500 and 6,000 as defined by the U.S. census of 1990) with Republican plurality enrollment or voting patterns in both 1974 and 1994. Her analysis shows that both Longley and King carried them: Longley with 5,143 to 3,585 for Erwin and 3,304 for Mitchell and King with 8,863 to 5,630 for Brennan and 5,304 for Collins.[54]

    Likewise, using the results from eight Franco American cities, she showed Longley with 25,617 while Mitchell only received 23,996 and Erwin 6,210. King did slightly less well in these eight towns, losing them to Brennan 24,291 to 20,669 with Collins a distant third with 9,044. King, however, carried the total Franco American population statewide.[55]

    Urban Francos and small town Republicans: they are an unlikely but important set of building blocks for an Independent plurality.

2. King established a model for candidates who must go that route. King proved there was only the Longley model to follow. This does not mean no other model could ever work, but the fact that it has been the only model over twenty years to work suggests there is a lot to it, both conceptually and operationally.

3. His victory confirmed the centrality of grassroots organization in general election statewide outcomes. The ground game remains an

important tactical asset in a campaign. King bought what he needed and that wasn't very much but he did have the fun of having workers come up from Boston one Saturday and blitz Joe Brennan's old state senate district and the nearby town of Westbrook. By nightfall they were back in Boston.

4. 1994 continued to show the vitality and centrality of negative campaign ads for challengers. Although we called them "contrast ads," they were negative ads, showing how the financial reservoirs had run dry during Joe Brennan's terms as governor and how under his administration, the size of government increased consistently. They worked. Just as they always work when you have a credible candidate; good and true ads tell a story and provide a meaningful contrast between one candidate and another.

5. Further erosion of the power of political parties continued. Both major political parties lost credibility with the success of the two Independents. More and more voters became "Independent" or unenrolled and the parties played less and less an important role in determining the outcome. For the Republican Party, the losses were quite devastating but somewhat expected. For the Democratic Party, they were devastating and quite unexpected.

6. With two Independent governors elected (compared to no Independent congresspeople or senators), Maine became something of a national example for third party and Independent candidacies. Maine was the first to have an Independent governor. Alaska, Connecticut, and Minnesota would follow.

   But interestingly enough, no viable "Independent" party was formed in Maine as a result of their triumphs. Only the Green Party managed to achieve viability during the period in question.

7. King's tactics changed the dynamics of later Independent runs. Previous conventional wisdom had been that candidates should save their money for late TV efforts, but for Independents, that tactic would almost always doom them to third place. To be considered viable, an Independent had to be in second place by the middle of September.

   The only way to achieve that was to advertise during June and the summer months. In King's case the "Independent Primary" he ran in June set the model. In 2002, for example, David Flanagan, the Independent candidate, copied this approach using his own money to advertise on TV in the spring and early summer. His lackluster performance and early departure from the race should not detract from the importance of the model he tried to follow.

8. Susan Collins was prepared to run for the U.S. Senate in 1996. Like George Mitchell's unexpected defeat in 1974, Collins's loss to both

King and Brennan in 1994 made her a much better candidate in the Senate race of 1996. As Steve Abbott, her skillful campaign manager, put it, "We wouldn't have won in 1996 if we didn't have 1994. That toughened us up a lot and we learned a great deal."[56]

Usually in Maine politics, you only get one initial loss and you are out of the game. Mitchell, Collins, and Tom Allen (who lost the Democratic primary to Joe Brennan in 1994 but then came back to win the 1st CD in 1996) are the exceptions that prove the rule.

A lesser person or lesser candidate might have thrown in the towel in August 1994. Susan Collins bravely slogged on, facing each discouraging day with determination and effort. She didn't give up. She didn't blame her staff or her circumstances. She soldiered on with her head held high. When the 1996 opportunity to run for the Senate seat vacated by Bill Cohen presented itself, she was ready, jumped into the race, and never looked back. Without the soul-testing crucible of 1994, she might not have become a U.S. Senator.

8

The Case for Campaigns

Before I wrote this book, I had the firm belief that campaigns make a difference in elections. By that, I mean that the campaign as campaign is a vital, often independent, variable in the process of elections. The more research I did on the elections that shaped Maine political history, the more I became convinced this hypothesis was correct.

The years 1948, 1954, 1970, 1972, 1974, 1980, and 1994 all turned out to be elections in which the campaign dynamics proved to be most efficacious. So much contemporary observation has previously focused on the candidates themselves, accenting their strength and wisdom and leadership qualities (or if they failed, their lack thereof). But in examining the elections themselves, it is very clear that the totality of the campaign effort in each is the independent variable that turned these key elections one way or another.

This in no way downplays the contributions of the principal political actors themselves. Obviously Margaret Chase Smith, Ed Muskie, Ken Curtis, Bill Cohen, James B. Longley, Skip Thurlow, and Angus King were absolutely central to their own success. Not only were they to prove strong candidates or leaders in their own right; they did, in fact, put together the campaign teams and campaigns that elected them or won their causes.

But they would not have been elected without their respective campaigns and, as was stated in various chapters, it was the campaign manager, or media expert, or pollster, or press secretary, or some combination, who provided the strategic insights that enabled the candidate to be successful.

It was the total campaign effort, not simply the candidate, that carried the day.

Margaret Chase Smith had drive and determination and political savvy to spare, but facing two extremely popular political figures in 1948, she needed a campaign that would help her to carry the day. It is difficult to see the magnitude of her victory without crediting Bill Lewis and his strategic overview and tactical mastery. In that election cycle, of necessity, she even broke her own rules about accepting campaign donations. He was the reason she did so.

The year 1954 provides an even clearer example. Ed Muskie made his own revolution, but it would not have succeeded in 1954 without the major contributions of Frank Coffin and Don Nicoll. He would have made the Democratic Party viable, he would have breathed new life into its somewhat moribund state, but he would not have gone over the top without the campaign dynamics outlined in the previous chapter. In particular, the campaign's handling of the new medium of television as well as its skillful use of Republican Neil Bishop stand out as independent variables in Muskie's rise to power.

The reelection of Ken Curtis in 1970 is another example of the interplay between candidate, campaign, and outcome. Curtis started that campaign year almost as far back as James B. Longley in 1974 and Angus King in 1994. The totality of his campaign brought him back from total and irrevocable disaster to stunning upset. He was 28 points back when he started and he won by less than 800 votes. There is ample credit to go around for him and his campaign manager, Neil Rolde.

Bill Cohen was not preordained to beat either Abbott Greene or Elmer Violette in 1972 either. Had he run different campaigns, he might well have lost to Greene and would most likely have lost to Violette. From Bob Monks to Mike Harkins, Joe Sewall and his Bowdoin contingent, Bill Cohen's total campaign effort was essential to him emerging victorious in both primary and general election.

In 1974, James B. Longley had no business beating Mitchell or Erwin. No doubt without his staff, the strength of his personality would have bled through and he would have made a credible showing on his own. But without Jim McGregor and Jack Havey, he would not have prevailed no matter how vibrant his charisma. Longley won because of who he was *and* because his talented campaign team made the difference in a close race. He would have finished second or third without them.

By the same token, Angus King was up against a still-popular former governor, a political figure who was to win a smashing victory in his 1994 primary. Joe Brennan had a top-notch campaign team and they had a most viable strategy when the campaign began. The King campaign had to be at the top of its game to beat Brennan who began with a huge lead in the polls. With another team supporting him, King most likely would not have gone over the top. He was a cerebral and intelligent candidate who would have finished a genteel second or even third had he not had a campaign team that forced him to adopt the strategy he did. King's debt to Peter Burr, Dan Payne, Dennis Bailey, Kay Rand, and others is considerable.

Also, with hindsight—and the research in this book—it is now possible to see how the antinuclear forces in 1980 ran a campaign that enabled those who wanted to save the plant to carry out their strategic plan. There was no *a priori* reason why the plant—no matter how much money was spent—should have ipso facto prevailed. The Maine Yankee effort, led by Skip Thurlow, simply was better across the board and utilized the talent available to it far better than did the more exclusionary hierarchical constellation on the other side.

Chuck Winner, John Menario, Mike Healey, Bob Turner, Bob Leason, Annette Stevens, Peter Thompson, Pat Lydon, and others made the idea of saving Maine Yankee into reality.

Campaigns made the difference in all the races we studied in this work. They were the independent variable.

There is also another way to see the importance of the campaign dialectic at work. We all give credit to the winners, and I hope, by now, will pay more attention to the overall contributions of the campaign staff and the strategic thinkers who provide the overarching themes for successful campaigns.

But there is an additional aspect that needs to be stressed as we conclude our examination of the key races of the last fifty years.

Successful campaigns require unsuccessful campaigns by opponents. Margaret Chase Smith, Ed Muskie, Ken Curtis, Bill Cohen, James B. Longley, and Angus King lead successful campaigns. Whether each was a "better" candidate than their opponent, whether each "deserved" to win, or whether each fielded a superior campaign effort, all were aided by the type and quality of campaign waged by their opponent.

This yin and yang aspect is often overlooked. Margaret Chase Smith won in 1948 in part because the sitting governor and his campaign staff made some very bad judgments as to strategy and how to handle a woman candidate in a hotly contested race. Burton Cross absolutely gave Ed Muskie the opportunity to win in 1954. His campaign—or more accurately, his anti-campaign—provided the situation, the objective reality into which the Muskie revolution fitted so perfectly.

Likewise, even the most ardent Curtis admirer would be forced to admit that had Jim Erwin and his campaign team not allowed, even encouraged Curtis to climb out of a 28 point deficit, the political outcome of 1970 would have been very different. Erwin would have easily defeated Curtis had he had a campaign team that (a) saw the new power of the 30-second TV commercial and (b) were able to convince/force him to adopt its use.

Elmer Violette in 1972 gave Bill Cohen the closest race he would every have. Violette started out with many advantages, not the least of which was the experience of already having run a statewide campaign in 1966. But he and his campaign made a series of scheduling, strategic, and issue framing mistakes that enabled Cohen to ride the accomplishment of his walk into Congress.

Even after Cohen changed the "terms of trade" with his districtwide walk, Violette's campaign had the opportunity to alter their general election strategy to meet this changed circumstance. The Violette campaign did not rise to the occasion. Cohen's victory depended—at least in part—on the failure of the Violette campaign to compensate for the new realities of a Republican whose campaign knew how to use TV to maximum effect.

So, too, it was with the tremendous upset victory of James B. Longley in 1974. Longley was unusually dynamic and charismatic. His campaign strategy and implementation by Jim McGregor and Jack Havey were brilliant. But all would have come to naught if Jim Erwin and George Mitchell had not run the two worst campaigns of major political candidates in this half century. Erwin had learned nothing from his narrow loss in 1970 and George Mitchell threw away every advantage—including a large and late lead—he possessed.

Without both Republican and Democratic candidates running very poor campaigns (both strategically and tactically), Longley would have been a footnote, not a major story in the history of Maine.

Also, the improbable victory of Angus King ended up relying not just on his own character and force of will and the quality of his campaign. To succeed, he needed a Susan Collins whose (then) inept campaign was buffeted by terrible difficulties early on and who never really recovered from these initial setbacks. He also needed a Joe Brennan campaign that was top heavy with campaign strategists and plagued with erroneous tactics. When all was said and done, Joe Brennan had no one to blame for his defeat except himself; he made the decisions and listened to the advice of the campaign staff he assembled. There was a lot of talent in the Brennan campaign headquarters.

Even Maine Yankee, with its stupendous advantage in campaign staff, their experience and campaign funds, succeeded in part because the antinuclear campaign was run in the fashion it was and because it threw away its biggest advantage when it allowed the No side to dominate the debate by focusing on economic, not health and safety, issues. The No side needed the Yes side to underutilize their advantages and overneutralize their weaknesses in order to win that race 60 percent to 40 percent.

Polling, media, scheduling, field work, opposition research, staffing, and organization—all played a role in both the successful and unsuccessful campaigns.

It was the candidates *and* their campaigns that prevailed or lost. It was the ballot measure proponents and opponents who made the difference.

This was true in the key elections of 1948, 1954, 1970, 1972, 1974, 1980, and 1994.

It continues to be true in most other major elections in Maine as well. That is why, despite ideology and personality, economic changes and demographic shifts, politics in the Pine Tree State remains "This Splendid Game." Its outcomes are not preordained nor completely controlled by individual candidates.

Candidates and causes come and go, but "This Splendid Game" has a life of its own.

Notes

CHAPTER 1: "THIS SPLENDID GAME"

1. For a sensational and provocative account of this phenomenon, see Jean Hay Bright, *A Tale of Dirty Tricks So Bizarre: Susan Collins v. Public Record* (Dixmont, Maine: BrightBerry Press, 2002).

CHAPTER 2: "THE 1940s"

1. The life and career of Margaret Chase Smith has been covered in considerable detail by a number of authors, including four recent publications: Alberta Gould, *First Lady of the Senate* (Mt. Desert, Maine: Windswept House, 1995), Patricia Wallace, *Politics of Conscience* (Westport, Conn.: Praeger, 1995), Patricia Schmidt, *Margaret Chase Smith: Beyond Convention* (Orono: University of Maine Press, 1996), and Janann Sherman, *No Place for a Woman* (New Brunswick, N.J.: Rutgers University Press, 2000). Readers interested in delving into her personal as well as her political life would be well served to read all four since they each provide different perspectives on what was a truly remarkable person and political career.

Two earlier works more laudatory and endearing are Frank Graham, *Margaret Chase Smith: Woman of Courage* (New York: John Day, 1964) and Alice Fleming, *The Senator from Maine: Margaret Chase Smith* (New York: Thomas Crowell, 1969).

2. Mert Henry, long time Republican activist and strong supporter of MCS, has long maintained that if only the Republican state committee had voted, it is unlikely Margaret ever would have been elected to anything!

3. Sherman, op. cit., p. 79.

4. While most candidates insist they campaign hard, I believe that the four hardest working, hour-by-hour, day-by-day campaigners in the modern history of Maine politics are Smith, Bill Cohen, Dave Emery, and John Baldacci. The number of their 16–18-hour days of constant campaigning are unmatched in Maine political activity since World War II. According to Paul Mills, other candidates who are perceived as being tireless include Jim Oliver and Ken Curtis.

5. Sherman, p. 83.

6. Sherman, p. 81.

7. Of course, the downside to this personality trait—and one that was exacerbated by her long-time relationship with William "Bill" Lewis—was her later political disposition, which often bordered on paranoia. Her autobiography, *Declaration of Conscience*, is replete with examples of Smith/Lewis pettiness and vindictiveness toward anyone who was less than 1,000 percent dedicated to her cause. George Dixon and Don Hansen, political writers for the *Portland Press Herald*, and others called those who fell into her disfavor receivers of the "Order of the Wilted Rose."

8. Sherman, p. 85.

9. Margaret Chase Smith, *Declaration of Conscience* (Garden City, N.Y.: Doubleday, 1972), p. 105.

10. Ibid., p. 109.

11. Ibid., p. 111.

12. Dan O. Gordon, "The Lady from Maine," *Parade* (June 6, 1948).

13. Schmidt, p. 191.

14. Ibid.

15. Ibid., p. 190

16. Fleming, p. 129.

CHAPTER 3: "THE 1950s"

1. For details of this watershed race, see John Donovan, *Maine Elects a Democrat* (New York: McGraw Hill, 1960).

2. An interesting and quite flattering account of Muskie's career up until he lost his presidential bid in 1972 can be found in David Nevin, *Muskie of Maine* (New York: Random House, 1972). Surprisingly enough, Nevin's work is one of only two book-length treatments of Muskie's life. Given the quality and depth of the Muskie archives at Bates College, Lewiston, Maine, and the importance of Muskie's career to both the history of Maine and the United States, this seems truly remarkable.

3. Edmund S. Muskie Archives, series: Governor, box 1, folder 1.

4. Theo Lippman and Donald Hansen, *Muskie* (New York: W.W. Norton, 1971), pp. 65–66.

5. Nevin, p. 66.

6. Donovan, pp. 3–4. Nicoll had been active behind the scenes pushing various Democrats, including Coffin, to get more engaged in the electoral process because he sensed "there was dry rot" in the Republican Party (Don Nicoll, interview with the author, January 16, 2002).

7. Ibid.

8. Nevin, p. 97.

9. Ibid., p. 98.

10. "1954 Platform of the Democratic Party of Maine," Muskie Archives, Series: Political Files, MSC. 1954, GV2–1.

11. Ibid.

12. *Portland Press Herald*, April 8, 1954.

13. "Muskie Candidate for Governor on Democratic Slate," *Lewiston Daily Sun*, April 8, 1954, and "Muskie Decides to Run as Governor Candidate," *Portland Press Herald*, April 9, 1954.

14. "Governor Says Muskie Not Strongest Possible Opponent," *Portland Press Herald*, April 21, 1954.

15. *DownEast* (June 1996), p. 37.

16. Democratic National Committee memorandum, May 4, 1954, Muskie Archives, Series: Governor, box 1, p. 1.

17. *Kennebec Journal*, August 6, 1954.

18. "Muskie Says GOP Makes Quoddy Biennial Football," *Bangor Daily News*, August 11, 1954.

19. Undoubtedly Muskie worked very hard but it must be said that the schedules listed in the Muskie Archives (for example, Muskie for Governor Campaign Material GV1–3) seem relatively modest by the standards of contemporary Margaret Chase Smith and later Bill Cohen, Dave Emery, or John Baldacci. Don Nicoll cautions that comparisons between the 1950s and 1960s campaigns and those of later decades can be misleading due to changed road conditions, however.

20. *Portland Press Herald*, September 1, 1954.

21. Muskie Archives, Muskie for Governor: Speaking Engagements, GV2–5, 1954.

22. *Portland Evening Express*, August 3, 1954.

23. "Political Observers Predict Nip and Tuck Battle for Governor," *Portland Press Herald*, August 21, 1954.

24. "Cross Sees 45,000 Vote Win Margin," *Portland Press Herald*, September 1, 1954.

25. The primary exception to the underestimation of Bishop's role in the Muskie success is Lippman and Hansen, op. cit., pp. 70–71. After this chapter was written but before it went to press, I also discovered that Douglas Hodgkin, former professor of political science at Bates College, had done an extensive analysis of the Bishop phenomenon and proved the importance of his contribution in "The Democratic Landslide: Maine Elections, 1948–1960," unpublished master's thesis, Duke University, 1963. See especially pp. 34–46.

26. "Democrat Victory in Fall 'Might' Be Good, Says Bishop," *Bangor Daily News*, May 1, 1954.

27. *Portland Press Herald*, August 26, 1954.

28. "Bishop Throws Support to Demo Ed Muskie," *Waterville Sentinel*, August 26, 1954.

29. "Bishop Speaks for Muskie in Election Fight," *Bangor Daily News*, September 6, 1954.

30. *Bangor Daily News*, September 7, 1954.

31. "Paid Political Advertisement," *The Ellsworth American*, September 8, 1954.

32. Don Nicoll, interview with the author, January 9, 2002.

33. Muskie Archives, Muskie for Governor: Speaking Engagements, GV2–5, 1954.

34. Hodgkin, op. cit, p. 44.

35. See also another famous UPI campaign picture of Muskie holding a shotgun and two dead cock pheasants, "Each Bagged With a Single Shot," in Lippman and Hansen, op. cit, p. 134.

36. Letter from Maine guide, Muskie Archives, GV2–5.

37. "Go! Go! Go!," *The Donkey Serenade* (Bath), January 1954, p. 1.

38. "Vote September 13," *Muskie for Governor flyer*, p. 1.

39. See his "Breakthrough Elections: Elements of Large and Durable Minority Party Gains in Selected States Since 1944," unpublished PhD thesis, Duke University, 1966.

CHAPTER 4: "THE 1960s"

1. See Kenneth T. Palmer, G. Thomas Taylor, and Marcus A. LiBrizzi, *Maine Politics and Government* (Lincoln: University of Nebraska Press, 1992) for an overview and in-depth analysis of the various dimensions of change in Maine during this period.

2. For a laudatory but interesting account of Curtis and his political and gubernatorial activities, see Kermit Lipez, *Kenneth Curtis of Maine: Profile of a Governor* (Brunswick, Maine: Harpswell Press, 1975). Lipez, who was Curtis's press aide during the 1970 election, gives a fond and supportive account of the governor's tenure and beliefs. His perspective on the 1970 election is both useful and illustrative of the problems of describing the various efficacies within a political campaign.

3. Lipez, op. cit., p. 67.

4. Ken Curtis, interview with the author, February 26, 2002.

5. Ibid.

6. Donald C. Hansen, *Maine Sunday Telegram*, February 1, 1970.

7. Ken Curtis, interview with the author, February 26, 2002.

8. "Curtis Fights for Political Life in Erwin Challenge," *Portland Evening Express*, November 4, 1970, p. 1.

9. *Portland Press Herald*, January 25, 1970.

10. Lipez, op. cit., p. 79.

11. Severin, Beliveau, interview with the author, February 28, 2002. Gordon Smith, a young Republican working for Ron Speers for Congress, was one of those who helped Truman get on the ballot and like so many other Republicans, was very disappointed when many of the signatures turned out to be invalid (Gordon Smith, interview with the author, March 3, 2002).

12. Jim Erwin, interview with James Bass, November 14, 1999.

13. Jim Brunelle, *Portland Press Herald*, February 17, 1970.

14. Ibid.

15. Lipez, op. cit., p. 73.

16. See C. P. Potholm, *An Insider's Guide to Maine Politics* (Lanham, Md.: Madison Books, 1998) and *"Just Do It": Political Participation in the 1990s* (Lanham, Md.: University Press of America, 1993).

17. Ken Curtis, interview with the author, February 25, 2002.

18. "Erwin's Credibility is Central Issue," *Portland Press Herald*, November 1, 1970.

19. Lipez, op. cit., p. 83.

20. Don Hansen, "Curtis' Future takes Distinct Turn for the Better," *Maine Sunday Telegram*, September 20, 1970.

21. *Maine Times*, October 16, 1970.

22. Jim Brunelle, "ETV Cheers Curtis Team," *Portland Press Herald*, October 3, 1970.

23. Lipez, op. cit., p. 85.

24. Don Hansen, "Communications Consultants New Campaign Aides?" *Maine Sunday Telegram*, October 4, 1970.

25. Ibid., p. 89.

26. Jim Brunelle, "Curtis-Erwin Radio Debate Continues Budget Battle," *Portland Press Herald*, October 31, 1970.

27. Jim Erwin, interview with the author, February 23, 2002.

28. *Maine Sunday Telegram*, November 1, 1970.

29. Jim Erwin, interview with James Bass, November 14, 1999.

30. Jim Erwin, interview with the author, February 23, 2002.

31. Ibid.

32. Jim Brunelle, "Erwin? He's the Guy Trying to Beat Curtis," *Portland Press Herald*, October 11, 1970, and "ETV Cheers Curtis Team," *Portland Press Herald*, October 3, 1970.

33. Severin Beliveau, interview with the author, February 28, 2002. Thirty-two years later, Beliveau was still a very important political operative, this time (along with Senator George Mitchell, Larry Benoit, and others) skillfully making sure that the sitting governor, Angus King, did not endorse the Republican candidate for governor, Peter Cianchette. By staying neutral, King in effect elected John Baldacci. With Cianchette holding 90 percent of the Republicans and Baldacci 90 percent of the Democrats, in the 2002 race, the balance of power lay with the Independents.

34. "He came to the third floor of the State House," said Harrison Richardson, Republican majority leader in the House, "and strutted around like a caricature of General Douglas MacArthur. He had a very imperious style. But to be fair, he was a straight guy, not a huckster. We watched his fall with amused neglect." (Harrison "Harry" Richardson, interview with the author, February 25, 2002. Erwin was later to narrowly defeat Richardson in the 1974 Republican primary for governor).

35. Robert "Bob" Fuller, interview with the author, March 11, 2002. Still, the fact that Democrats, including the state party chair, Severin Beliveau, referred to them as "our friends" certainly does little to dispel Erwin's basic assumptions. (Severin Beliveau interview with the author, February 28, 2002).

36. Gordon Smith, interview with the author, March 3, 2002, and Robert "Bob" Fuller, interview with the author, March 11, 2002.

37. Stan Tupper, interview with the author, February 28, 2002.

38. Neil Rolde, interview with the author, March 10, 2002.

39. I am indebted, as always, to the Bowdoin students over the years who brought various episodes such as this to my attention. In this case, it was James Bass in 1999.

40. George Mitchell, "In Politics There Are Two Maines," *Maine Sunday Telegram*, January 10, 1971, p. 10.

41. Ibid.

CHAPTER 5: "THE 1970s"

1. Bill Cohen, comment to the author, January 28, 1972, upon his return from the meeting.

2. Christian P. Potholm, *"Just Do It!" Political Participation in the 1980s* (Lanham, Md.: University Press of America, 1993).

3. *Portland Press Herald*, June 15, 1972.

4. Hilary Rosenberg, *A Traitor to his Class: Robert Monks and the Battle to Change Corporate America* (New York: John Wiley and Sons, 1999), p. 46. Obviously, Rosenberg's analysis and that of this chapter presages his somewhat erratic later political activity, supporting Michael Dukakis, Ralph Nader, and Chellie Pingree and, in 2002, declaring himself as favoring Democratic control of Congress!

5. *Portland Press Herald*, February 24, 1972.

6. Dave Swearingen, "Violette Bothered by Fights With People, " *Portland Press Herald*, June 12, 1972.

7. C. P. Potholm, "General Strategy: The Walk," campaign memo (1972).

8. *Bangor Daily News*, July 20, 1972.

9. John C. Day, "Candidate Cohen Begins His Walk Across Maine," *Portland Press Herald*, July 21, 1972.

10. Kent Ward, "Cohen, GOP Get Boot Out of Walk" *Bangor Daily News*, July 22, 1972.

11. Neil Rolde, interview with the author, May 28, 2002.

12. *Portland Press Herald*, July 20, 1972.

13. Neil Rolde, interview with the author, May 28, 2002.

14. Ibid.

15. Barry Hobbins, "Elmer Violette: A Public Servant for All the Right Reasons," *Sun Journal*, June 25, 2000.

16. Neil Rolde, interview with the author, May 28, 2002.

17. Ibid.

18. *Bangor Daily News*, August 4, 1972.

19. *Bangor Daily News*, August 10, 1972.

20. See, for example, *Bangor Daily News*, August 26–27, 1972.

21. *Bangor Daily News*, August 22, 1972.

22. Decision Research Corporation, Maine 2nd Congressional District Voter Study, October 1972.

23. "National Health Insurance is Backed by Bill Cohen," *Bangor Daily News*, October 4, 1972.

24. "Cohen–Violette Debate Aired Over Public TV," *Bangor Daily News*, October 11, 1972.

25. Cohen for Congress, campaign flyer, October 1972.

26. *Bangor Daily News*, August 22, 1972.

27. *Bangor Daily News*, October 28–29, 1972.

28. Barry Hobbins, interview with the author, March 19, 2002.

29. Neil Rolde, interview with the author, May 28, 2002.

30. *Bangor Daily News*, October 30, 1972.

31. Barry Hobbins, interview with the author, March 19, 2002.

32. *Portland Press Herald*, October 29, 1972.

33. *Bangor Daily News*, November 4–5, 1972.

34. *Portland Press Herald*, November 10, 1972.

35. Barry Hobbins, interview with the author, March 19, 2002.

36. Bernard Asbell, *The Senate Nobody Knows* (Garden City, N.Y.: Doubleday, 1978).

37. Christian P. Potholm, "1976: Go or No Go," Cohen campaign memorandum, p. 4.

38. Market Opinion Research, June 1975, "Current Voting Intentions."

39. Asbell, op. cit., p. 5.

40. Ibid., p. 45.

41. Ibid., p. 59.

42. Ibid., p. 56.

43. Ibid., pp. 279–80.

44. Tom Daffron, interview with the author, March 20, 2002.

45. Asbell, op. cit., p. 312.

46. We did have the results of the Muskie poll but not from the hand of Shep Lee as Charlie Micoleau thought (Asbell, op. cit., p. 387). Like "Deep Throat," the contact's identity is safe.

47. Market Opinion Research, "Current Voting Intentions," December 1975.

48. C. P. Potholm, "1976: Go or No Go," campaign memorandum, p. 22.

49. Asbell, op. cit, p. 389.

50. This campaign provides one of the finest examples I have ever seen of political irony. In the 1978 race, you had two candidates. One candidate was a decorated, wounded, air force veteran who had fought in World War II (Hathaway). He was an authentic hero. The other had lasted a single week in Bowdoin ROTC (Cohen). Yet the polling that year showed Cohen defeating Hathaway 2–1 among Maine veterans. Why? Cohen opposed turning the Panama Canal over to Panama while Hathaway favored it. I've never forgotten the political lesson of "What have you done for me lately?"

CHAPTER 6: "THE 1980s"

1. John Rensenbrink, *Against All Odds: The Green Transformation of American Politics* (Raymond, Maine: Leopold Press, 1999), p. 126.

2. John Rensenbrink, *The Greens and the Politics of Transformation* (San Pedro, Calif.: R. and E. Miles, 1992), p.8.

3. *New York Times*, August 21, 1980.

4. *Newsweek*, September 22, 1980.

5. *Time Magazine*, October 6, 1980.

6. *The Times Record*, May 22, 1973.

7. Ibid.

8. C. P. Potholm, "Thinking about the Thinkable," *The Times Record*, 1980.

9. *Newsweek*, September 22, 1980.

10. C. P. Potholm, *An Insider's Guide to Maine Politics* (Lanham, Md.: Madison Books, 1998).

11. John Rensenbrink, interview with the author, June 4, 2002, and John Rensenbrink, interview with the author, June 14, 2002.

12. A poll done by Cambridge Reports, who did work for the nuclear industry all over the United States, on August 9 showed the number at 46 percent against the shutdown, 28 percent in favor with 26 percent undecided.

13. Bernie Monegain, "Dean to Review Nuclear Commercial Tapes," *The Times Record*, July 7, 1980.

14. Ibid.

15. Pam Strayer, "Dean Drops Bid for Ad Disclaimer," *The Times Record*, July 10, 1980. The Maine Arts Festival was held at Bowdoin that summer from August 1–3, and I had the pleasure of sniffing out a potter who was passing out antinuclear shutdown material from his booth and was thus able to point out to the Dean that both sides were using Bowdoin space for their own purposes! He seemed relieved.

16. *Portland Press Herald*, July 14, 1980.

17. *Lewiston Evening Journal*, August 14, 1980. Asked about the contents of the poll twenty years later, Joseph Steinberger could not recall any polling Common Cause did at the time. (Joseph Steinberger, interview with the author, July 1, 2002).

18. Ibid.

19. Ibid.

20. *Barron's*, September 22, 1980.

21. *Maine Sunday Telegram*, August 3, 1980.

22. "Don't Send a Message," *Portland Press Herald*, July 13, 1980.

23. Ray Shaddis, interview with the author, June 24, 2002.

24. John Rensenbrink, interview with the author, June 14, 2002. He also indicated: "We weren't that well coordinated."

25. Ray Shaddis said, "That's pretty cheap insurance." *Washington Post*, September 9, 1980.

26. John Menario, interview with the author, July 3, 2002.

27. *Portland Press Herald*, August 22, 2002.

28. John Newell, "Nuclear Power is Neither Cheap Nor Necessary," *Maine Sunday Telegram*, September 14, 1980.

29. *Bangor Daily News*, August 29, 1980, and *Bangor Daily News*, September 15, 1980.

30. *Portland Press Herald*, September 23, 1980.

31. See for example, "Maine to Vote on Shutting Down of a Nuclear Plant," *New York Times*, August 21, 1980, and "Maine to Decide Whether It Remains in the Nuclear Era," *Washington Post*, September 9, 1980. The *Post* claimed it would "galvanize" the antinuclear movement. *Newsweek*, on September 22, 1980 said, "Pro- and anti-nuclear forces around the country are watching the fight closely—well aware of the old adage that as Maine goes, so goes the nation." *Barron's* titled its lead editorial "Damn Maine Yankee? The Fate of the U.S. Nuclear Power May Be Settled Tomorrow," *Barron's*, September 22, 1980.

32. On a personal note, I was ecstatic. After the celebration at CMP headquarters election night, I left to go on Maine's first moose hunt with permitee Professor Richard "Dick" Morgan who had been the one who convinced Professor Hughes to be in the commercial that had carried the day.

On September 25, we bagged an 1,100-pound moose, shooting it through the heart in the middle of a beaver bog five miles from camp. For years we said we had "bagged a Shaddis and a moose" the same week. Not many can make such a claim!

In writing this chapter, I debated whether or not to put in this anecdote. But I ultimately decided to include it because it does capture what for me is the essence of a consultant's driving motivation. I seldom fight for a cause. I rarely get energized about a concept. But I always want to beat my opposite number. To be my most effective, I have to personalize the struggle, to make it a one-on-one contest, a zero sum game between (temporary) adversaries. I love the irony that your opponent in this election cycle is likely to be in your coalition the next. Unlike party politics, ballot measure efforts have constantly changing sides and players.

The money is nice and the comradeship is always rewarding, but for me, ultimately, the shootout at the OK Corral is always what keeps the competitive juices flowing.

For example, I played to beat Abbot Greene in 1972 (Cohen for Congress), I played to beat John Cole in 1983 (Moose Hunt), I played to beat Bob Reny in 1990 (Sunday Sales), I played to beat Bruce Reeves in 1981 (Elected PUC), I played to beat Brownie Carson and Alan Caron in 1997 (Widening the Maine Turnpike), I played to beat Mike Heath in 1995 (Gay Rights I), I played to beat Alan Caron and especially Phil Merrill in 1994 (King for Governor), I played to beat Brownie Carson and Jonathan Carter in 2000 (Forestry Referendum), and I played to beat Phil Merrill that same year in a different referendum (Physician Assisted Suicide). It is the battle qua battle that I love, what Richard Nixon once called being "in the arena."

I hope the reader will not misunderstand. I would call most of the above individuals my friends and on other occasions we have been on the same side fighting for the same cause or candidate but when we are on opposite sides, they personalize the struggle and provide my basic motivation.

33. By then, John Menario had run for governor as an Independent in 1986 and switched his position on nuclear power to favoring the shutdown of Maine Yankee. Ironically, at the time, the plant had gotten 58 percent of the vote or better three times. Menario cited the technological disasters of Chernobyl and the space shuttle Challenger as influencing his decision. He would get 15 percent along with 15 percent for Sherry Huber, another Independent, 30 percent for Jim Tierney, the Democrat, and 40 percent for Jock McKernan, the Republican.

34. See Doug Hodgkin, "Closing Maine Yankee: Self-Interest and Symbolic Voting," paper prepared for delivery at the Annual Meeting of the Northeastern Political Science Association, November 1983.

35. *Portland Press Herald*, August 16, 1980.

36. *Bangor Daily News*, September 20–21, 1980.

37. This is a slightly different version than the original one found in C. P. Potholm, *"Just Do It!" Political Participation in the 1990s* (Lanham, Md.: University Press of America, 1993), pp. 138–39.

CHAPTER 7: "THE 1990s"

1. For a hilarious, hostile, and yet insightful account of Longley by Governor Curtis's last press secretary, see Willis Johnson, *Year of the Longley* (Stonington, Maine: Penobscot Bay Press, 1978). For a more in-depth and sympathetic—yet oddly satisfying—look at Longley, see Susan W. Longley, "James B. Longley: A Governor and His Independent Political Style," unpublished master's thesis, University of Maine Department of History, fall 1992. Other academic analyses of note concerning Longley include: Douglas I. Hodgkin, "Voting for the Independent Wealthy Businessperson: Perot and Gubernatorial Candidates in Alaska, Maine and Utah," paper prepared for delivery at the New England Political Science Association meeting, April 23, 1994, and Howard Reiter, "Who Voted for Longley? Maine Elects an Independent Governor," *Polity* 10 (fall 1977), pp. 65–85.

2. *Portland Press Herald*, July 19, 1974.

3. *Portland Press Herald*, July 25, 1974.

4. Jim McGregor, interview with the author, June 17, 2002.

5. *Portland Press Herald*, October 21, 1974, and "Longley Notes Many Lawyers in Government," *Bangor Daily News*, September 11, 1974. Interestingly enough, Susan Longley quotes her father giving much credit after the election to the coverage he received: "We should never forget that one of the reasons I am probably Governor is that we have had, almost without exception, a fair press that gave an Independent candidate fair coverage," Longley, op. cit, p. 22.

6. "George Mitchell: Democrat for Governor," newspaper ad.

7. *Portland Press Herald*, August 21, 1974.

8. *Portland Press Herald*, September 10, 1974.

9. *Portland Press Herald*, September 15, 1974.

10. *Portland Press Herald*, October 29, 1974.

11. *Portland Press Herald*, September 17, 1974.

12. V. Paul Reynolds, "Erwin Takes off Gloves," *Bangor Daily News*, October 23, 1974. The *Portland Press Herald*, apparently pleased with some action in the race, covered Erwin's attacks prominently: "Last Round Finds Jim Out Slugging at George," Donald Hansen, *Portland Press Herald*, October 24, 1974.

13. Kent Ward, "'Smear' says Mitchell," *Bangor Daily News*, October 24, 1974.

14. Jim Erwin newspaper ad.

15. "Muskie Blasts Erwin's Mitchell–Vahlsing Tie," *Portland Press Herald*, October 26, 1974.

16. J. A. Farrell, "Integrity for Sale? George Mitchell's Post-Senate Career: from Northern Ireland to Big Tobacco," *Boston Globe Magazine*, March 3, 2002, pp. 13–end.

17. Johnson, op. cit., p. 38–39.

18. Governor Jock McKernan, interview with the author, June 17, 2002.

19. Johnson, op. cit., p. 39.

20. Jim McGregor, interview with the author, June 17, 2002.

21. Jack Havey, interview with the author, May 31, 2002.

22. Jim McGregor, interview with the author June 17, 2002.

23. Jack Havey, interview with the author, June 18, 2002. I have not seen this figure quoted elsewhere.

24. John S. Day, "Three-Way Race Developing," *Bangor Daily News*, October 28, 1974.

25. Angus King, *Making a Difference* (privately printed, 1994).

26. Alan Caron, interview with the author, June 13, 2002.

27. C. P. Potholm, "The Cruelest Month," campaign memo, May 9, 1994.

28. Angus King, interview with Bonnie Washuk in the *Sun Journal*, April 6, 2002.

29. Phil Merrill, interview with the author, June 15, 2002. This was also the view of the Collins camp. They didn't realize King would spend over a million dollars of his own money and initially thought he was "just a talk show host" (Tom Daffron, interview with the author, June 19, 2002).

30. Dennis Bailey, interview with the author, June 10, 2002.

31. Paul Carrier, *Portland Press Herald*, June 16, 1994. But contrary to the spin the Collins and Brennan camp successfully fed Carrier, the more astute Brennan advisers were worried, perceiving Collins as a "very weak candidate" (Chris Lehane, interview with the author, September 6, 2002).

32. "Far-Right of GOP is challenge for Collins," *Portland Press Herald*, June 24, 1994, and Steve Abbott, interview with the author, June 21, 2002.

33. *Portland Press Herald*, September 29, 1994, and *Bangor Daily News*, September 29, 1994.

34. Phil Merrill, interview with the author, June 15, 2002, and Tom Daffron, interview with the author, June 19, 2002, and August 14, 2002, and Steve Abbot, interview with the author, June 21, 2002.

35. *Portland Press Herald*, September 25, 1994.

36. *Portland Press Herald*, September 18, 1994.

37. *Portland Press Herald*, October 5, 1994.

38. C. P. Potholm, Week of October 11, 1994, Tracking Update, p. 1.

39. Dan Payne, interview with the author, July 2, 2001.

40. Dan Payne, interview with the author, July 2, 2001.

41. Dennis Bailey, interview with the author, June 10, 2002.

42. Jim Brunelle, *Portland Press Herald*, October 27, 1994.

43. *Portland Press Herald*, October 14, 1994. The *Bangor Daily News*, October 14, 1994, also carried spirited rejoinders from George Smith and James "Jim" Gorman, president of SAM.

44. Paul Carrier, "Experts Disagree on Independent in the Blaine House," *Portland Press Herald*, October 23, 1994. In fairness to Carrier, there may well have been no connection between the editorial board's support for Brennan and the working reporters' sense of who was going to win. They both may have reflected simple conventional wisdom at the time. But at the time, the King campaign had no doubt that the paper was for Brennan no matter what. We have never seen evidence to the contrary.

45. Nancy Perry, *Portland Press Herald*, June 26, 2002. Al Diamond also joined in the deriding of King, stating that October "may be the month when Angus learns there's more to being governor than oiling up the old sales pitch" in his "Angus Thinks He's King of the Whole World," *Bangor Daily News*, October 8, 1994.

46. A. J. Higgins, "Gubernatorial Hopefuls Share Stage for Debate," *Bangor Daily News*, November 1, 1994, and Peter Jackson for the Associated Press, "TV

Debate Ends with Appeals to Voters," *Portland Press Herald*, November 2, 1994. See also John Hale, "Gubernatorial Hopefuls Debate Education Issues," *Bangor Daily News*, October 29, 1994.

47. Unnamed Democratic operative in an interview with the author, June 12, 2002, on condition of anonymity.

48. Phil Merrill, interview with the author, June 15, 2002, and Chris Lehane, interview with the author, September 6, 2002.

49. Alan Caron, interview with the author, June 13, 2002.

50. Barry Hobbins, interview with the author, July 12, 2002. Contrary to popular opinion, Joe Brennan had more than enough money to hire a good tracking poll operation. In the end, he was to spend $1,370,044 to King's $1,743,105 and Collins's $585,309. Finks would spend $27,655 and Ralph Coffman $1,393. That same year, Snowe would outspend Andrews $2,041,034 to $1,482,060 (Maine Commission on Governmental Ethics and Election Practices, *Biennial Report, 1994–1995*). The Lehane quote is from Chris Lehane, interview with the author, September 6, 2002.

51. *Portland Press Herald*, November 10, 1994.

52. George Smith, e-mail to the author, August 16, 2002.

53. Susan Price, "As Maine Goes . . . Independent," an honors paper for the Department of Government and Legal Studies, Bowdoin College, 2002. For another view of the sea changes in Maine politics, see L. Sandy Maisel and Elizabeth Ivry, "If You Don't Like Our Politics, Wait a Minute: Party Politics in Maine at the Century's End," in Jerome M. Mileur, ed., *Parties and Politics in the New England States* (Amherst, Mass.: Polity Publications, 1997), pp. 15–35.

54. Price, op cit., pp. 44–46.

55. Ibid., pp. 41–42.

56. Steve Abbott, interview with the author, June 21, 2002.

Index

Photo: Courtesy of Paul Franco.

About the Author

Christian P. Potholm is Professor of Government at Bowdoin College. He is the author of a dozen books including *An Insider's Guide to Maine Politics* (Madison Books, 1998) and *The Delights of Democracy: The Triumph of American Politics* (Cooper Square Press, 2002).

A participant in Maine politics for over 30 years, Dr. Potholm brings fresh insights and extensive research to this very important history of politics in Maine since World War II.